D1599326

OXFORD HISTORICAL MONOGRAPHS

Editors

BARBARA HARVEY   A. D. MACINTYRE
R. W. SOUTHERN   A. F. THOMPSON
H. R. TREVOR-ROPER

THE APOCALYPTIC
TRADITION IN
REFORMATION BRITAIN
1530-1645

by
KATHARINE R. FIRTH

OXFORD UNIVERSITY PRESS
1979

Oxford University Press, Walton Street, Oxford OX2 6DP

OXFORD LONDON GLASGOW
NEW YORK TORONTO MELBOURNE WELLINGTON
KUALA LUMPUR SINGAPORE JAKARTA HONG KONG TOKYO
DELHI BOMBAY CALCUTTA MADRAS KARACHI
IBADAN NAIROBI DAR ES SALAAM CAPE TOWN

British Library Cataloguing in Publication Data

Firth, Katharine R
    The book of times. — (Oxford historical monographs).
    1. Bible — Prophecies   2. Bible — Criticism.
    interpretation, etc. — History — 16th century
    3. Bible — Criticism, interpretation, etc. — History —
    17th century
    I. Title   II. Series
    220.1'5   BS647.2   78-40263

    ISBN 0-19-821868-0

*Set by Hopes Services, Wantage,
and printed in Great Britain by
Cox & Wyman Limited,
London, Fakenham and Reading*

PREFACE

This is the revised version of a doctoral thesis submitted to the Board of the Faculty of Modern History of Oxford University in 1971. Many are the debts I owe from those years of research from 1967 to 1971, but none is greater than that I owe to my supervisor, Professor Hugh Trevor-Roper, for his interest and encouragement, for his guidance and criticism. I wish to express my thanks also to Dr. Christopher Hill and Dr. Marjorie Reeves both of whom examined the original version and offered suggestions for its improvement. Dr. Paul Christianson and Dr. Richard Bauckham have not only read and criticized the text, but also allowed me to draw upon their own works in advance of publication. At a later stage, Dr. G. E. Duffield offered useful suggestions for the further improvement of the text.

The project would never have begun without the material support granted me for the year 1967-8 by the Rotary Clubs of District 779 in the United States through their programme of Fellowships for International Understanding. Support came also from the Principal and Fellows of St. Hugh's College with the award in 1968 of the Dame Catherine Fulford Senior Scholarship. And finally I wish to thank my husband Robert for his help throughout.

History, like prophecy, is liable to many interpretations. In each generation new questions are asked and new answers found. In recent years a few historians have responded with new interest to the apocalyptic language used by both religious and political leaders in the sixteenth and seventeenth centuries. Their labours have made the task of illustrating the importance of apocalyptic thought much easier. Although my study has led me to some different conclusions from his, Dr. William Haller's work on John Foxe first suggested the topic to me. Since I began work, several other contributions have been made and my debts to them are recorded, I hope adequately, in the notes.

Abbreviations have been kept to a minimum, and are used only in notes following closely upon a full citation. Some

titles of well-known reference works have been abbreviated
without explanation in the notes. These include:

D.N.B. — *Dictionary of National Biography*

S.T.C. — Short Title Catalogue (Pollard and Redgrave)

S.T.C. (Wing) — Short Title Catalogue (Wing)

for which full details can be found in the Bibliography.

In quotations and references i's and j's, and u's and v's
have been modernized and abbreviated forms expanded, but
otherwise the spelling and punctuation remain unchanged.

Shrivenham   K.R.F.
May 1978

CONTENTS

LIST OF ILLUSTRATIONS

I

INTRODUCTION AND THE EARLY YEARS

For centuries certain texts of Scripture were held to depict in the disguised language of prophecy the future of the Christian faith, the Church, and the Roman Empire. The apocalyptic tradition in historiography is as old as the history of the biblical texts, but, in each age of awakened interest, the story is told differently and the prophets' words are interpreted and shaped to a current estimation of the past, present, and future. By revealing something of the shape of the tradition in early Protestant Britain, it is hoped that this study will illustrate one aspect of the intellectual history of the period. In recent years historians of Puritanism and of millenarian movements have explored the effects of apocalyptic belief upon the political and social history of Britain.[1] More needs to be done in this field, but first the beliefs themselves must be seen in the context from which they emerged. Without a more precise and disciplined understanding of apocalyptic studies in the sixteenth and early seventeenth centuries, errors can be—and indeed have been—made.

Interest in the relation between prophecy and history was neither peculiar to the Reformation nor generated in the sixteenth century exclusively by the Reformation debate, nor was the formation of the tradition among English Protestants a wholly Puritan or even British affair. Interest in prophecy was current throughout Europe, among Catholics as well as Protestants and among Renaissance thinkers as often as reformers.[2] Nevertheless, a Protestant version distinguished

---

[1] Most have concentrated on the seventeenth century. Some of the most recent published contributions are: William M. Lamont, *Godly Rule: Politics and Religion 1603–60* (Oxford, 1969); C. Hill, *Antichrist in Seventeenth-century England* (Oxford, 1971) and *The World Turned Upside Down* (London, 1972); B. S. Capp, *The fifth monarchy men* (London, 1972).

[2] This study would have been much more difficult without the perspective and latitude of Marjorie Reeves's *The Influence of Prophecy in the Later Middle Ages* (Oxford, 1969). The importance of prophecy to the way sixteenth- and seventeenth-century Englishmen looked at the world has also been recognized in K. V. Thomas's *Religion and the Decline of Magic* (London, 1971).

itself in both substance and method, and enjoyed in Britain a consensus and respectability denied it on the continent.

Not every age has viewed the obscure prophecies of the Book of Revelation as a hidden history unfolding its pattern in world events. Indeed, even though this view was important in the Protestant tradition, the Reformation also remembered past interpretations that had believed the prophecies depicted an allegory acted out on an eternal plane illustrating a completed and changeless revelation of truth. The Fathers of the early Church debated the issues and implications, and their arguments provided generations of later writers with authorities for their own divergent views.[3] By the sixteenth century there were many alternatives from which to choose. In England reverence for Wyclif and his writings introduced a powerful expression of the allegorical tradition, while abroad the influence of two twelfth-century writers who had advanced an historical interpretation was still strong. One of these, Otto of Freising, represented views common to the late Middle Ages among those who supported the traditional balance between spiritual and temporal powers. The other, Joachim of Fiore, represented in the scope of his influence the impetus for reform and also the dangers of millenarianism. A closer look at some details of the types of interpretation advanced by Otto, by Joachim, and by Wyclif will help illustrate this intellectual inheritance of the Reformation.

Otto of Freising, the pupil of Hugh of St. Victor, undertook the task of writing a history of the two cities described by St. Augustine.[4] But whereas Augustine had insisted on the transcendent nature of the city of God, Otto equated this city with the Roman Church and so wrote a history of the Church and the Empire as the cities of God and of Man. In doing this he called upon the prophecies of Daniel and of the Apocalypse to support and make systematic several theories about the course of history. Most famous is his idea of the

---

[3] R. H. Charles, *Studies in the Apocalypse* (Edinburgh, 1913), Introduction.

[4] Otto of Freising, *The Two Cities*, trans. Charles Mierow, ed. Evans and Knapp (New York, 1928). The last book is devoted almost entirely to a commentary on the Apocalypse. John M. Headly, *Luther's View of Church History* (New Haven and London, 1963), sees the influence of Otto in Luther's treatment of history.

translation of power and faith from east to west, demonstrated historically by the succession of the four monarchies and the history of the early Church. This construction in turn supported the political theory of the interdependence of the two swords, the spiritual and the temporal, in maintaining a united Christendom. In this pattern of thought the prophecies of Daniel spoke of the Empire and the Revelation spoke of the Church, each revealing the spiritual meaning behind the events foretold. The *translatio imperii* had by the birth of Christ settled the temporal power in Rome, where it would last until the end of time. A *translatio religionis* from the Jews to the Christians had succeeded, after many difficulties depicted in John's Revelation and illustrated historically in the history of the early Church as told by Eusebius, in establishing the Church of Rome. In this story the role of the Emperor Constantine united both streams of prophecy and set the stage for an indeterminate millennium of the saints' rule with Christ until his second coming.

The Revelation of St. John depicted the history of the Church through three basic stages: the time from Christ to Constantine; the millennium of Satan's bondage; and the final forty-two months of the world's history during which the final plagues and trials prepared the Church for the second coming to judgement. Because in the language of prophecy a period of 'a thousand years' could be read as a period of indeterminate length, Otto, and many others before and after him, argued for the continuation of the Roman Church until the end of time. During the second stage the function of the prophecies was to warn Christians of the trials to come and to promise them the final translation of the Church to a heavenly state following the judgement. Thus although the structure of the prophecies was historical, the relevance for the twelfth century and for an indefinite future remained spiritual in nature.

Despite this indefinite suspension of literal expectation, Otto did establish a pattern which implied that the collapse of the Holy Roman Empire or of the Roman Church would be a precipitate sign of the final years of the world. Knowing this, many Protestants were to be both troubled and elated by the events of the sixteenth century. One way in which they might choose to see history placed their own time in the age of the release of Satan from his bondage and the resulting trials of the last days, and thus reintroduced a literal relevance for New Testament prophecy.

Otto's synthesis of known and accepted universal history, political theory, and commentary on scriptural prophecy did not excite a flurry of interest and innovation; it expressed rather the culmination of a number of interrelated modes of thought in the later Middle Ages. His influence was neither as great nor as direct as that of Joachim of Fiore, who was an innovator of great importance for later centuries. Joachim and Otto both lived in the twelfth century, and in many respects they explored the same belief in history as the reflection of a divine pattern.

In contrast to Otto, Joachim[5] maintained a consistently literal expectation of the fulfilment of prophecy throughout the history of the Church. Hidden under the figure of the seven seals of the Apocalypse lay a succession of periods in the Church's history from Christ through Constantine and beyond to the end of New Testament times. The whole of universal history fell into three great stages, each dominated by a person of the Trinity. The present age of the Son would be followed by an equally historical age of the Spirit. Seen in the prophecies of the Apocalypse, the dawn of the age of the Spirit followed upon the pouring-out of the seven vials. By counting the generations of men one could calculate the position of the present in the grand scheme. Although Joachim maintained that the future remained unknowable in any detail, Christians did have scriptural assurance of an approaching time of peace and the perfection of the spirit here on earth before the cataclysm of the final judgement.

The history of the influence of Joachim's thought on later centuries is no more easy to summarize than the complexities of his thought itself. He had numerous imitators; some remained true to the spirit of his work, and others wrenched new and strange meanings from his writings. There was in the sixteenth century something of a revival of his works, both

[5] On Joachim see M. Reeves, op. cit., for his thought and influence. For his place in monastic history and politics see Gordon Leff, *Heresy in the Later Middle Ages* (Manchester, 1967).

the genuine ones and those wrongly ascribed to him. Renaissance ideas of restoration and reformation in both Catholic and Protestant circles owed some of their hope to the expectation stemming from Joachim.[6] Although this was counterbalanced by a mistrust of the cruder interpretations of the age of the spirit, which in the past had led to the scandals of the New Evangel (a third testament to follow the other two) and to a number of disruptive popular movements,[7] the attraction of a future not entirely given over to plagues and destruction inevitably remained.

The mainstream reformers of the sixteenth century were particularly anxious to avoid the charge of engendering rebellion and denied emphatically that they were inspired by any form of new revelation. Although the Reformation resisted a Trinitarian representation of history, Joachim contributed to the Protestant background both the assertion that the Book of Revelation expressed a continuous history of the Church and the hope of a further improvement to that Church within human history.

The Protestant apocalyptic tradition was formed in the first instance from three sources: the Book of Daniel which prophesied the fate of the Empire, the Book of Revelation which traced the history of the Church, and the Prophecy of Elias which encompassed and limited the duration of the world. Of these only the prophecy of Elias originated outside the received Christian canon.[8] It divided the history of the world into three great periods: the age before the law, the age under the law, and the age of the Messiah. To each age was allocated 2,000 years. The scheme was known to be analagous to St. Paul's teaching, and the origin of the actual prophecy in the Jewish Talmud did not detract from its authority in Protestant eyes. The prophecy itself, and its important

[6] Reeves, op. cit., pp. 493–504.

[7] See Leff, op. cit., and Norman Cohn, *The Pursuit of the Millennium* (London, 1957).

[8] The prophecy originated in a third-century Midrash. This was rewritten several times. The version we now have was composed in the tenth century and printed in 1598 from a copy dated 1186. Isadore Singer, ed., *The Jewish Encyclopedia* (London, 1906). Although the complete prophecy reappeared as part of North Italian interest in the late sixteenth century, I have not seen a reference to the Midrash in British material. References were without exception to the version in the Talmud.

mention of the number of years in each age, entered the Protestant tradition through the translation of the Babylonian Talmud made by John Reuchlin and published in Vienna between 1520 and 1523. Reuchlin's great-grand-nephew and one-time pupil Philip Melanchthon, in association with several others, included the prophecy in a Protestant chronicle known as *Carion's Chronicle* (1532),[9] the first to show the influence of the apocalyptic thought. In addition to these three major prophetic texts, Protestants were to make use also of other scriptural passages that augmented themes in the major prophecies.[10]

Thus, the major elements that were to form the Protestant apocalyptic tradition in historiography had each a pre-Reformation history. They rested not, as the reformers would be anxious to assert, upon the vain imaginations of new visionaries, but rather on the biblical texts and upon a Talmudical teaching with ample Christian parallels.

In opposition to the historical interpretation of prophecy in New Testament times, there remained a strong tradition of regarding the prophecies, and the Revelation in particular, as a moral allegory of the inevitable tensions between the demands of the flesh and the spirit. This approach to the prophecies was particularly strong in England, where early English Protestants turned to John Wyclif for guidance. Wyclif's views had been influenced by the commentaries on Scripture made by Nicholas of Lyra in the fourteenth century. Nicholas of Lyra and his followers[11] believed that the prophecies were less a synopsis of the stages of history than an allegorical representation of the continual sufferings of the true Church in a world where the conflicting natures of Christ and Antichrist led men to follow either the principles of Christian life or the teachings of worldly wisdom. The prophecies illustrated this struggle in order to warn the damned of their final end and to comfort the elect. This view was often presented

[9] See below, pp. 15–22.
[10] Most commonly the Book of Ezekiel, the Epistles of John, the Epistles to the Thessalonians, and later the Song of Solomon.
[11] The influence of Nicholas's commentaries on the Wyclif Bible has been noted by Sven L. Fristedt, *The Wyclif Bible* (Stockholm, 1953), and Nicholas's opinions were used in an Oxford debate in the fourteenth century to counter those of Joachim (Reeves, op. cit., pp. 315–17).

both in commentaries on the Revelation and in separate works on the life of Antichrist.

By the dawn of the Reformation the figure of Antichrist had become a very complex one.[12] In the Epistles of John (1, 2: 18, 22; 2, 2: 7) many antichrists are foretold, as preachers of false doctrine to come in the last days; and in the second Epistle to the Thessalonians (2: 3) a warning is given of false preachers, a man of sin, and a great apostasy. At an early stage in the history of the interpretation of the Apocalypse, a single figure of Antichrist was compared with the two beasts, and became a symbol for the chief agent of Satan in the world. In one early interpretation Nero was understood to be the Antichrist of whose spiritual presence one could be assured wherever the persecution of the saints took place. In Lollard eyes the Apocalypse was a revelation of the character of Antichrist, whose picture, painted with the colours of cruelty, immorality, and false doctrine, was a timeless vision of all that opposed Christ or was raised in his place. In one of his two tracts against the papacy Wyclif concluded such a comparison with the words 'it seemeth that the Pope is Antichrist heere in erth, for he is agens crist bothe in lif and in lore'.[13]

At this point a distinction must be drawn between two ways of interpreting the revelation of Antichrist in either the papacy or the Roman Church. If in identifying the pope with Antichrist the author meant to indicate the characteristics of corruption outlined above, then we are not necessarily dealing with a historical interpretation of the prophecies. If, however, the identification is taken further, and asserts that the revelation of such corruption at one time rather than at another is particularly significant, or that by its recognition and defeat a new era in history has begun, then we are dealing with the first signs of the apocalyptic tradition in Protestant historiography. Since both or either of these meanings could be implied, the early reformers had trouble in making themselves clear. The distinction could be made by speaking of a 'Great Antichrist' or of 'the Antichrist of the prophecies'

[12] On the Antichrist legend generally see Richard Bauckham, *Tudor Apocalypse*, Courtenay Library of Reformation Classics (8), (Appleford, 1978) pp. 91-112.

[13] Wyclif, 'De Papa' (1379), in *Wyclif, Select English Writings*, ed. Herbert E. Winn (Oxford, 1929), pp. 66-74.

to indicate the special and ultimate manifestation. Some used these phrases; others did not. In dealing with the English material it is particularly important not to jump to the conclusion that every use of the words 'Antichrist' or 'Antichristian' involves us immediately in apocalyptic thought in any eschatological sense.

I have suggested that some aspects of the Renaissance encouraged the revival of prophetic traditions.[14] This was particularly true in the south of Europe where interest in the more exotic and esoteric literature of antiquity vied with received religious texts. To the north, Christian humanists devoted themselves more closely to the literature of the Church, to biblical texts and patristic commentary. When Erasmus turned his attention to the text of the Revelation he unearthed certain truths which, had they been accepted, would have hindered the foundation of the tradition. It was essential to the formation of the tradition that the Book of Revelation be received as a divinely inspired prophecy of authority and authenticity. The book was widely supposed to have been written by John the Evangelist, but Erasmus set about demonstrating that this, if not impossible, was so improbable as to cast doubt upon its position in the canon. In his Greek New Testament of 1516, he put forward a formidable case based upon a linguistic analysis of the text; and from his deep knowledge of patristic controversies he quoted admissions by Jerome and Chrysostom to support his doubts. Significantly, he did not regard the question as one of supreme importance, for he noted in any case 'that ancient theologians quote passages from this book rather for illustrations and ornament than for support of a serious proposition'.[15] As long as this practice continued it seemed unlikely, he thought, that serious errors would arise. He was severely criticized for casting doubt on the authority of the Church to decide the canon of Scripture and in 1526 was censured by the theological faculty of Paris for his position.[16] Eventually

[14] See Reeves, op. cit., Part IV, chapter IV.
[15] Trans. and quoted from the Greek New Testament by B. F. Westcott, *A General Survey of the Canon of the New Testament*, 7th ed. (London, 1896), pp. 480-1.
[16] Ibid.

in 1546, the Council of Trent adopted the final Catholic position for the period by including the Revelation in the canon as a work of John the Evangelist.[17]

Erasmus's indifference to the Revelation was at first shared by leading Protestants. Luther denounced the book in 1522, saying that Jerome, who had praised it so highly (Jerome had overcome his initial doubts), might have found other places in Scripture more worthy of his praise, and that for himself he found nothing either apostolic or prophetic in the book. His spirit, he said, could not find its way into the Apocalypse.[18] Zwingli took no notice of it at all, saying it was not a book of the Bible. Oecolampadius and Calvin later admitted it as Scripture but with the reservation that it should not enjoy the same authority as the gospels.[19] By the opening years of the next decade, however, positions had begun to change. In 1530 Martin Luther revised his opinion. In 1531 Zwingli died, and Heinrich Bullinger, who was to write a volume of sermons on the Revelation which proved exceedingly popular in England,[20] took his place. In 1532 Melanchthon was to take an important hand in the publication of the first Protestant work of history in the apocalyptic tradition.

The first signs of interest among Protestants in the apocalyptic prophecies appeared in the Lutheran Reformation, and in the radical groups that in the 1520s first threatened to divide it. The radical reformation is not at this period an easily defined movement, nor can it be identified with one specific group of people. G. H. Williams has been able to bring some order to this chaos by forming categories of belief into which scattered groups can be fitted.[21] However, at the time of the Reformation itself, the mainstream reformers mistrusted the motives of the radicals and in dealing with them stressed what they saw as social and political divisiveness, sacramental deviation, and debauchery.[22] Luther

---

[17]Hubert Jedin, *A History of the Council of Trent* (London, 1957), vol. ii, pp. 71-2.

[18]*D. Martin Luthers Werke* (Weimar, 1931), vol. vii: 'Deutsche Bibel 1522-1546', p. 404, 'mein geist kan sich inn das buch nich schicken'.

[19]Westcott, op. cit. pp. 495-6.

[20][Heinrich Bullinger, *A hundred sermons upon the Apocalyps of Jesu Christ*, first published in Latin in Basle (1557), later in English (1561), see below, p. 80.]

[21]G. H. Williams, *The Radical Reformation*, (London, 1962).

[22]John S. Oyer, *Lutheran Reformers against Anabaptists* (The Hague, 1964).

condemned anabaptists for irrationality and for disrespect of Scripture. Scripture and not dreams was the path the Spirit chose to enter the soul. Melanchthon described the anapabtist rebels of 1536 as revolutionary, seditious, and blasphemous. Chiliasm was renounced in the Augsburg Confession of 1530 and later in the Second Helvetic Confession of 1566. Men erred in believing that the millennium could be forced either by the slaughter of the ungodly or by the withdrawal of the elect into a separate community.[23] To many the term 'ana-baptist' was one that could be used to describe any person who preached social or civil disruption. Although preachers of insurrection who sprang up between 1520 and 1536 served only to harden the mainstream Reformation against millen-arianism, those whose works had inspired the revolts but who had not themselves been party to actual rebellion contributed to the formation of the Protestant historical interpretation of the prophecies. An example is Melchior Hofmann: his work on the Apocalypse undoubtedly inspired the leaders of the Münster revolt of 1536, but his name appeared a few years later in John Bale's survey of worthy authors on the prophe-cies of Scripture.[24]

It would be wrong to place great emphasis upon the con-tribution of the radical millenarians to the formation of the Protestant tradition. Both mainstream and radical reformers made use of the materials provided by a wider intellectual movement to revive a historical interpretation of the New Testament prophecies. Luther rejected the revolutionary path to reformation, but he was nevertheless troubled by the immediate events—the invasion of eastern Europe by the Turks and the discovery of Antichrist in the papacy—that many used to justify a call to arms for the final battle.

During the later 1520s many adversaries troubled Luther. Forced to dissociate himself from the Peasants' Revolt and involved in debates with Erasmus on the one hand and with John Eck on the other, he also saw a danger that the threat of invasion by the Turks might divert the German princes

[23] Arthur C. Cochrane, *Reformed Confessions of the 16th Century* (London, 1966).
[24] John Bale, *The Image of bothe churches* (1550), in *Select Works of Bishop Bale* (Parker Soc., 1849), pp. 256-8.

from giving support to his programme for religious reform. In response he sought not only to construct a consistent theology but also to interpret the present in such a way that the Reformation would appear to be the last hope for the preservation of both Church and Empire. One view of the present which held obvious attractions was offered him in a letter from Myrconius in 1529.[25] Myrconius had discovered fragments of a commentary on the Apocalypse by a late fifteenth-century Franciscan monk, Johann Hilten, which not only identified the Turk with Gog and foretold an invasion of Germany but also prophesied that *c.* 1516 a man would reform the Church and overthrow the papacy. Luther passed the letter on to Melanchthon, who drew the obvious conclusion. For his part, Luther became anxious for further material on the prophecies of Gog in Daniel and the Book of Revelation.[26] In November 1529 he wrote to a friend describing the Turk as Gog and the Pope as Magog, the one the external enemy, the other the internal. His attention focused on Daniel 7, where he identified the little horn among ten with the Turk. The image of the little horn that with base motives became great and dominated the others through trickery has had several interpretations, but always it referred to a power in the world and over the Empire. Luther was following more than Hilten in recognizing the power of the Turk in his interpretation.

In 1530, when he revised his preface to the Apocalypse in his German Bible, he stressed the dignity of prophecy and its necessity to the Church. He expanded his preface to include a synopsis which illustrates his new understanding of the meaning of the prophecies.[27] Although his about-face on the importance of the Revelation was dramatic, much of what he newly understood in the prophecies was derived from past expositors. The pattern he adumbrated allowed historical significance to the prophecies in only two limited periods: the early Church before Constantine and his present age. This understanding resembles more the one associated with Otto

---

[25] *Zeitschrift für Kirchengeschichte*, vol. iii (1879), pp. 305–6, also Melanchthon's references to Hilten in *Corpus Reformatorum* (Halle, 1834 onwards) listed in Reeves, op. cit., p. 234 n., Headly, op. cit., pp. 244–9.

[26] The importance of the Turkish threat in Luther's expectation of the Apocalypse is discussed in Headly, op. cit., pp. 242–6 *et passim*.

[27] 'Deutsche Bibel', *Werke*, vol. vii, pp. 406–20.

of Freising than the one associated with Joachim of Fiore.

Luther connected the history of the early Church with the prophecies through his interpretation of the four angels at the four corners of the earth (Rev. 7) and the first four angels of the seals (Rev. 8). These represented the preachers and doctors of the true faith interspersed with heretics and preachers of false doctrine. Although he did not present them in a regular sequence, Luther developed the idea that an age of truth was succeeded by an age of error, followed by another age of truth, and so on. At one other point he addressed himself to the historical interpretation of prophecy. In Chapter 21 the release of Satan stirs up Gog and Magog to do battle with the saints. Here his recent preoccupation with the Turk and the prophecies of Daniel and Ezckiel again emerged in the identification of Gog with the Turkish invasion. At this point he identified Magog with Satan, not with the pope. Although he later returned to his practice of comparing the papacy with the hidden enemy figured in Magog, his reserve in this instance may be explained as an attempt to keep the figure of Antichrist exclusively for application to the papacy.[28] In the next few years many of the German expositors contrived to see the papacy in both guises.

Except in the two instances described above, Luther's exposition of the prophecies resisted the historical tradition and maintained the view that the text portrayed a moral allegory which revealed the nature of an Antichrist, of whom he would go so far as to say no better example existed in history than the papacy. Two years before rewriting his preface Luther had seen to it that a commentary[29] on the Revelation by a disciple of Wyclif was published at Wittenberg, and he seems to have borrowed his view of Antichrist from the Wyclifite tradition. While this interpretation bore the greatest weight in his preface to the Revelation, his identification of Gog with the Turk and his interpretation of Daniel enabled him to place the Reformation in the final years of history.

At the same time as these questions exercised him, he became aware of the use and importance of historical argument for the Protestant cause. In his debates with John Eck in

[28] John M. Headly argues this pp. 246-7.

[29] *Commentarius in Apocalypsin*, written in 1390 and attributed to Purvey in Bale's *Catalogus*.

1519 Luther had been forced to seek justification for his attack on the papacy in the past actions of popes instead of arguing solely from Scripture and tradition. This experience was not lost on him. In 1535, in a preface to Robert Barnes's *Vitae Romanorum Pontificum*, Luther expressed his delight in the discovery that history and prophecy agreed:

Though I was not at first historically well informed, I attacked the papacy on the basis of Holy Scripture. Now I rejoice heartily to see that others have attacked it from another source, that is, from history. I feel I have triumphed in my point of view as I note how clearly history agrees with Scripture. What I have learned and taught from Paul and Daniel, namely, that the Pope is Antichrist, that history proclaims, pointing to and indicating the very man himself.[30]

Like many of his contemporaries[31] Luther was troubled by the impossibility of certain knowledge. In seeking for knowledge of justification his doubts had led him to trust only Scripture. For Luther and his followers the authority of history, like that of any other human knowledge, rested upon its agreement with the spirit of Scripture. The spirit that guided the theologian also guided the historian. Not only did history agree with the moral teaching of Scripture, it also illustrated the truth of prophecy.

The singularity with which prophecy had apparently dignified the age of the Reformation gave a new meaning to sacred history. From about 1530 in Germany there began to appear chronicles of world and biblical history which, although intended to be short guides to the memorable dates and events of the past, were more of an expression of a new way of approaching sacred history. In 1531, Sebastian Franck published his *Chronica Zeytbuch und Geschychtbibel*. Franck, who has been described as a leading speculative spiritualist by Dr. Williams,[32] believed that history revealed an innate reason in man which he called the *logos*. Both the sacred history of the Bible and the profane history of later ages revealed the *logos* equally, and could with equal profit

[30] (Basle, 1535), A 5, trans. N. S. Tjernagel, *Henry VIII and the Lutherans*, p. 148.

[31] See R. H. Popkin, *The History of Scepticism from Erasmus to Descartes* (Assen, 1960).

[32] On Franck see G. H. Williams, *The Radical Reformation* (London, 1962) and his introduction to *Spiritual and Anabaptist Writers*, Library of Christian Classics, vol. xxv (London, 1957).

be studied. Despite theological reservations, Lutherans found his approach very exciting, and his book was eagerly read. It was soon followed in 1532 by a distinctly Lutheran version of a world chronicle known as *Carion's Chronicle.*

Taken together these books represent a departure from an established view of the special nature of sacred history. A certain idea of religious truth was under attack, and Erasmus, quick to see the implications, could not hide his dismay.[33] Sacred history had held its singular place by virtue of its power to display timeless examples of human actions and events and their inevitable results. Scriptural events were figures or types, the study of which gave men insight when dealing with the less perfect examples offered by profane history. In 1531 in his commentary on Psalm 33, he wrote that while the study of history was not in error, it was not much use in getting at the truth of Scripture. Although Erasmus numbered humanist historians among his many friends, and himself wrote biographies of several of the Church fathers, his motive was always a desire to praise great men and to present them as worthy examples for emulation. He did not bother much with what we would call historical context. The industry of his friends in the realms of civil history did not particularly interest him. Twice he persuaded Froben to print Polydore Vergil's *De Inventoribus Rerum*, but never a word for his *Historia Anglica.*[34]

Nor was prophecy important in his search for historical truth. The figures contained in Scripture were not in any way predictions of future events, but only signs of a repeating spiritual content in similar human experiences. They were a source for illustrating moral lessons. The dreary flux of human affairs, the trend of which he perceived went from bad to worse, was relieved directly only by the special intervention of God at critical moments. These interventions usually took the form of the gift of some great man whose life would serve as an example and reminder to his age of that body of eternal truth in Scripture. For those who shared Erasmus's sense of the nature of sacred history, Franck's

---

[33] Peter G. Bietenholz, *History and Biography in the Work of Erasmus of Rotterdam* (Geneva, 1966), p. 16.

[34] Ibid. *et passim.*

chronology seemed to lose sight entirely of its eternal and figurative quality and to demean it to the level of the bare recording of simple historical facts.[35]

A strong belief in the use of history, whether sacred or profane, as a source for a set of moral examples was common to most of the reformers. The spirit Franck found revealed in both forms of history was a profoundly religious one. However, it led him too far from the written word of Scripture for more strictly Lutheran tastes. Through the discovery of the fulfilment of biblical prophecy in later ages, something was done to restore the spiritual authority of history while at the same time directing attention towards the changes that had occurred in Christendom since the time of Christ.

In 1532 Melanchthon, with the help of Camerarius and Corvenius, extensively revised a rough draft of a chronicle by John Carion. Carion was known as a mathematician and student of astronomy and astrology. He intended his chronicle to be a guide to the memorable dates in both biblical and world history and sought in it to argue for the use of astronomy as the means to determine correct dates. For the inclusion of material praising and applying the Prophecy of Elias and those of Daniel we probably have Melanchthon to thank. As mentioned above, he may well have learned of Elias' prophecy from his relative and teacher John Reuchlin and used the prophecy here for the first time in a historical context. Apparently this prophecy was not known to Luther before the publication of *Carion's Chronicle*.[36]

Like Franck's *Chronica* the new chronicle did not distinguish a special importance for biblical history. It did, however, separate sacred from profane history on the ground that the subject matter was different. Sacred history dealt with God's works and the establishment of his kingdom, while profane or pagan history dealt only with human politics. Both types came together into a single chronological sequence through the gift of prophecy to the Church, whereby prophecy not only dealt with the revelation of God's

---

[35] In his commentary on Psalm 33, Erasmus described history as 'rerum gestarum nudam commemorationem' and as 'rerum gestarum simplicem historiam'.

[36] Headly (op. cit., pp. 110-11) traces Luther's reaction to the Prophecy of Elias.

moral judgement on the events of history, but also predicted the general course of political events.

> Neither is yt to be omitted that God hath given us al maner of prophe-
> cyes of exterior kingdomes to stablish our mindes, that of the accom-
> plishment of their chaunce, we myght have wytnesse, that our word is
> come of God, and that none other faith save ours is true. Item that we
> shuld be warned whan Christ must come, and whan the ende of the
> worlde is to be loked for. Item for so muche as we knowe that all
> thynges spoken of in the prophetes are come to passe, that we may
> beleve, that those shall happen also, the which holye scripture sayeth
> shall befal.[37]

In this way prophecy bridged the gap between the spiritual vision and the temporal progression of events. Three reasons for this interpretation of prophecy were given: to affirm the faith, to indicate the time of the second coming; and to foretell certain events, some already history and others yet to come. Although prophecy was the essential element that gave certainty to historical statements it could not alone provide the material of history:

> Moreover to understande prophecyes arighte it is greatlye necessary
> to knowe the order of kingdomes, the nombre of the yeares, and many
> other thynges, whych in readynge of Heathen hystoryes do offer them
> selves: the knowledge whereof is chiefelye necessarye for Chrysten
> men, that they may the better understande the prophecies, and have
> better judgment of them.[38]

The study of history, like all valid human endeavour, had to return to the fount of Scripture to ensure its truth. The interpretation of prophecy was to be the point of departure in the search for truth in history. Early in the chronicle the Prophecy of Elias was introduced, to give the limits and structure of the history to follow. In the English edition the prophecy appeared as follows:

The Sayenge of Helias house.
The worlde shall stande syxe thousand yeres and after shall it falle.
Two thousande yeares wythout the Lawe.
Two thousande yeares in the lawe.
Two thousande yeares the tyme of Christ.

---

[37] All quotations are taken from the English edition of *Carion's Chronicle: The Thre Bokes of cronicles &c gathered wyth great diligence of the beste authours*; whereunto is added an appendix by John Funcke (London, 1550); this quotation, Introduction 'The use of readyng hystoryes', vi^r.
[38] Ibid.

And yf these yeares be not accomplyshed oure sinnes shall be the cause, whyche are greate and many.[39]

This version is a christianization of the Talmud. The sixteenth-century author took the final sentence to limit the age of Christ to less than the full 2,000 years. Melanchthon and Luther both believed the end was not far off and likely to come before 1600.[40] However, in the Talmud the final sentence refers to the age of the law, which because of the sins of Israel had been prolonged, thus delaying the coming of the Messiah. The Prophecy of Elias was mentioned again near the middle of the chronicle and at the close it was repeated in full. The author felt compelled to mention it for a third time. 'Truely', he said, 'I muste before the ende of this wryting put the reader agayne in remembraunce of the sayeng of Elias. . . .'[41]

The second prophecy of great importance was found in the Book of Daniel. There under two visions were portrayed the four monarchies. The vision of the idol and the vision of the four beasts stood for the four empires from Babylon to Rome. Whereas Elias in general terms set the limits of world history and described the development of law and faith, Daniel was concerned with the specific and visible monarchies in world history. For from the time of Daniel was 'the propre and very age of the worlde, in the which the moost myghtye kyngdomes and monarchies have succeeded ech other by a certayn order'.[42]

Melanchthon and his colleagues, like Luther, found a touchstone for the interpretation of prophecy in the current troubles with the Turk. In prophecy they found another kingdom beyond that of Rome.

And there is added that besyde the Romaine empyre there shall ryse an other empyre full of cruelnesse, and suche one that shall make a new

[39] *Carion's Chronicle*, Introduction, vi[v]. Compare this wording with a modern English translation in the tract 'Sanhedrin': 'The world is to exist six thousand years. In the first two thousand there was desolation: two thousand years the Torah flourished; and the next two thousand years in the Messianic era, but through our many iniquities all these years have been lost.' *Babylonian Talmud*, ed. I. Epstein (London, 1935), p. 657.

[40] Peter Fraenkel, *Testimonia Patrum*, Travaux d'Humanisme et Renaissance xlvi (Geneva, 1961), pp. 329–30.

[41] Mentioned fols. lxxxvii[v] and cxcii[r].

[42] Introduction, vii.

lawe agaynst Gods worde: And that is the Mahometish and Turkysh
empyre now a dayes. God wyll have us so truely warned, that as we
knowe the histories of al the worlde, we should consyder that the tyme
of finishyng be not farre of, and that of this wise we should have where-
with to confirme our faith.[43]

The connection between the Turk and the prophecies of
Daniel concerning the last days was corroborated by the identification of the Turk with the descendants of Magog. This
lineage of the Turk passed through the Scythians. Both Ezekiel and St. John were used as witnesses that the Turks were
Gog and Magog.[44]

With this in mind, the interpretation of the rest of the prophecies of Daniel followed Luther's description of the little
horn among ten on the final beast. The Saracens and the
Turks together illustrated this prophecy in the course of
history. *Carion's Chronicle* went further than Luther in making the connection between this kingdom and the Antichrist.

As for ye kingdome [of Saracens and Turks] is ye greatest part of Antichrist, & in the Prophetes are ye most certayne prophecies of it. . . . In
Danyell is he paynted of thys wise: In that terryble beaste whyche is
the figure of the Romyshe empyre, doth growe a horne. . . .[45]

This prophecy was also intended by God to give knowledge
'that it is the laste kyngdome, and that the daye of the laste
judgement is to be loked for'.[46]

In the early years of the formation of the Protestant tradition no term was more widely applied than 'Antichrist'. On
one occasion when he was concentrating on the meaning of
the prophecies of both Daniel and the Revelation, Luther had
avoided connecting the Turk with the Antichrist, but on
others he relaxed his restriction and implied that the Turk
was indeed part of the Antichrist. *Carion's Chronicle* spoke
of the Turk as the greatest part of the Antichrist. This conviction can be explained partly by the imminent invasion and
partly by the concentration of the chronicle on imperial
history, where no greater threat to Christendom could be
imagined than a successor to the Roman Empire. Whatever
Luther's reason for once seeking to reserve Antichrist for
application to the papacy, fear worked against this nicety.

For many years Protestants in the tradition preserved the

[43] Fol. v[v].   [44] Fols. v[r], cxxiii[v].   [45] Fol. cxxii[r-v].   [46] Fol. cxxii[v].

participation of the Turks in the figure of Antichrist, sometimes speaking of 'two Antichrists' and at other times using
Luther's first distinction between an open and a secret nature
of Antichrist. At this early stage the allowing of the visible
hostile empire of the Turks to represent the fulfilment of
prophecy helped to spur the identification of Antichrist in
his entirety with visible human institutions. This step made it
easier to dispense with an allegorical vision of Antichrist and
to connect him with the history and institution of the papacy.

The presence of the Turkish threat to the Empire also
heightened the expectation of the end of the world. In the
1530s, more than for many decades to follow, the immediacy
of the world's end formed a central theme of writings in the
apocalyptic tradition. *Carion's Chronicle*, revised versions of
which were to participate in British expectation in the next
century,[47] laid particular emphasis on this theme. The
Prophecy of Elias was deliberately introduced because it
could be read to suggest a near end, and every other application of prophecy indicated a like conclusion. As in the synopsis of Revelation offered by Luther, only two periods of
church history figured in the argument, the Church at the
time of Christ and his Apostles and the Church of the Reformation. The similarity of circumstance of the two periods,
not the intermediate development of history, pushed the
argument forward. The Apostolic church was a mystical prefiguration of the reformed church, and what had applied then
applied also in the sixteenth century. The state of the world
just before the first coming of Christ was like the present
state of affairs both in the proximity of war and in the proliferation of sects. Just as the Pharisees, Sadducees, and Essenes
divided the Church of the Old Testament in the days of
Christ, so 'Of this wyse nerehand is the church devided in
thre partes also now a daies: for because ye second commyng
of Christe also is harde by.'[48] If the sects of the sixteenth
century did not in all respects resemble those at the time of
Christ, the similarity between the Essenes and anabaptists was
marked and illustrated by a common belief in the community

[47] A revised version by John Sleidan, *De Quatuor Summis Imperiis*, has been
described as 'a text book of English chiliasm'. See below, Chapter III, p.76n.
[48] Fol. lxxiv^v.

of possessions. Such a similarity, it was argued, could not be a chance occurrence, 'For the thinges that happened among the Jewes, are a figure of the Christen religion.'[49]

Thus a theory of prophetic prefiguration united the texts and history of New Testament times with the history of the Reformation. Yet on the whole the force of the argument came from an idea of repeating similarities of character or belief. The Erasmian view was by no means entirely displaced in *Carion's Chronicle*, but it was modified to argue the singularity of the Reformation as the final act of the world. By introducing the Prophecy of Elias in its Christian interpretation, by applying the prophecies of Daniel equally to sacred and to secular history, and by indicating proofs that the end of the world was a matter of decades, Melanchthon and his colleagues brought chronology into the discussion.

At some crucial points the prophetic texts mentioned numbers of days, months, and years. An expositor might interpret such numbers as mystical expressions, and, by breaking them down into sevens (for the universality of the meaning) or into threes (for the Trinity), might arrive at a satisfactory interpretation that contained no chronological significance. Alternatively, he could take the number of days and years literally as expressions of time, though not necessarily as simple expressions. Certain conventions were on the whole obeyed in the interpretation of these numbers, the most common of which was that one prophetic day could, depending upon the context, equal a year or a thousand years. These conventions were based on argument from other parts of Scripture and obeyed an internal logic that could not be disregarded; any expositor who wished to be taken seriously had to support his arithmetical juggling with either quotations from Scripture or precedents from authority.

Although the number-prophecies of the Apocalypse had been taken in either of the two ways mentioned above, those of the Old Testament, particularly those prophesying the coming of the Messiah, were more commonly taken to indicate periods of time. *Carion's Chronicle* took both the Prophecy of Elias and the seventy weeks in Daniel 9: 24-7 as expressions of distinct numbers of years. In accordance with

[49] Fol. lxxv[r].

the traditional method of universal history the chronicle posed and answered the question of the date of Creation, finding it to have been somewhere near 4000 B.C. This agreed with Elias' prophecy and with a Christian tradition which accepted that each day of the Creation might be taken to signify a thousand years, thus giving a total of 6,000 years for the duration of the world. This dating of the Creation remained the norm for the period.[50] The Lutheran historiographers' preference for the literal sense of Scripture, and their unification of sacred and profane history under the aegis of a single chronology in part determined through the interpretation of prophecy, suggested that the prophecies of the New Testament were not different in kind from those of the Old. The reckoning of times hid in Scripture under prophetic language was an important, if recently neglected, duty of the Church. 'And diligently ought Byshops to occupie them in these thynges with doing costs that the understanding of so notable prophecies myght be clerely had in the Churche.'[51]

One of the questions each author had to decide was whether to admit non-scriptural prophecies or visions. Luther showed considerable interest in the prophecies of John Hilten but not in those of Müntzer. *Carion's Chronicle* collected[52] a few prophecies that like Hilten's seemed to apply to the present and support the Reformation. An astronomer had prophesied a great age to come very soon. He had seen a comet which portended such a momentous change. A Latin chronicle one hundred years old had been discovered in Magdeburg which conveniently prophesied that an emperor named Charles would repair the Church and restore the Empire.[53] Another prophecy spoke of a Beast of the West and a Lion of the East who would have dominion over the whole world. Christians would wander in the wilderness for fifteen years and then hear of Antichrist. (Fifteen years had passed since Luther had begun to preach, and Christians were now hearing of Antichrist.) Joachim was quoted as prophesying that

[50] See James William Johnson, 'Chronological Writing: its Concepts and Development', *History and Theory*, vol. ii, pp. 124–45.
[51] *Carion's Chronicle*, fol. xlix.   [52] Fols. clxxxix–cxci.
[53] On the second Charlemagne prophecies see Reeves, op. cit., pp. 320–31.

an emperor would awaken and invade the Turks. To cap it all, another comet had been seen in that very year of 1532. These were presented more as curiosities than as certainties and clearly did not have the same authority as the prophecies of Scripture. However, this collection shows an interest in and a knowledge of the wide variety of late medieval prophetic literature, particularly those prophecies that looked forward to a time of renovation of Empire and Church.

Separately considered and more seriously entertained was the authority of the Sybilline books. *Carion's Chronicle* was undecided. On the subject of the Empire such prophets had often been proved correct, but, since their inspiration was not necessarily the work of the Holy Spirit, one could not be certain of their trustworthiness. On balance the chronicle appeared to accept the books as probable prophecies of the fall of Rome.[54]

Carion's Chronicle made use of the Prophecy of Elias and the Book of Daniel in outlining the course of history. The Apocalypse did not figure as a detailed prophecy of history and was mentioned only in connection with the further illustration of points established in Daniel.[55] The tradition was not fully established in this chronicle, but significant steps were taken towards uniting the materials from which it would develop. Moreover the book conveyed the mood of apocalyptic expectation that encouraged speculation and sent its readers to the Revelation for further proof of the character of the present age.

The chronicle traced the history of empires and ended with the conviction that if the German nation could not defend the Empire and hold it together the resulting turmoils of dissolution would hasten the apocalypse. The prophecies showed that, before another empire could succeed the Roman, Christ would return to judgement.[56] The plea for unity was soon lost, but the construction of belief that placed the present in the last age of the world persisted.

Desire to preserve the Empire was particularly strong among the close followers of Luther in those early years. Elsewhere, however, in Zurich under Zwingli and his successor Bullinger and in Strasburg under the leadership of Martin

[54] *Carion's Chronicle*, fol. xxiv.   [55] Fol. cxciii.   [56] Fol. vii.

Bucer, there grew up a town- or community-oriented programme for reformation that did not look to the institutional
church or empire. Into this picture stepped the first of the
exiled English Protestants.

In England news of Luther stirred the interest and imagination of men already convinced that reformation was necessary. Despite their prohibition Lutheran books managed to
enter England and her universities. The earliest English reformers read Wyclif along with Luther and, when discovered to
be in possession of the illegal Lutheran books, several chose
exile and with it the chance to learn more of reformed theology. These Henrican exiles, and later the Marian exiles,
were the first to come into contact with revived interest in
prophecy.

One of the best known of the early exiles was William Tyndale. After the frustration of his plan to translate the Greek
New Testament into English in England, he left for the continent and settled in Antwerp in order to carry out his project
without the blessing of the English Church. He did not leave
England to become a student of Luther, but once abroad he
recognized an ally in Luther and came under his influence.
The effects of this influence can be seen in the prefaces to his
New Testament first published in 1525. The revision of 1534
differed only a little from the earlier complete version, and
in both the Book of Revelation appeared, but without a preface. Tyndale shared neither the doubts of Erasmus nor in
1534 the new-found enthusiasm of Luther for this book. The
Lutheran reappraisal did, however, leave its mark in Tyndale's
marginal notes to the text of the Revelation. He agreed that
the prophecies depicted in the good angels 'the true bysshops
and preachers' and in the evil angels 'the heretykes and false
preachers'.[57]

The preoccupations of Luther in the late 1520s did not
much affect Tyndale. Neither the threat of Turkish invasion
nor the presence of radicals within a newly formed church
severely troubled him in his work. His major concern was to
translate the Bible into English and, by winning the King to
the Protestant side, to see it safe in England. The fate of the

[57] *The New Testament translated by William Tyndale 1534 with variants of
the edition of 1525*, ed. N. Hardy Wallis (Cambridge, 1938), Rev. vii, p. 539.

Holy Roman Empire paled in significance before this. In all his writings the Turk was presented as a virtuous pagan whose moral life must shame Christians. There was not a hint of the monstrously inhuman cruelty that portended either a mystical or a literal identification with an apocalyptic beast. Whereas Luther's harsh words against the Revelation in his Bible of 1522 were partly occasioned by his recent arguments with radicals given to similar dreams and visions, Tyndale, under no such pressure, simply included the Apocalypse and said nothing.

Tyndale was vulnerable to Lutheran influence on the Apocalypse in two respects: in his demand for the literal sense of all Scripture and in his polemical use of history. In his tract *The Obedience of a Christian Man* (1528) based on a paraphrase of Luther's famous one on the freedom of the Christian, he included a digression from the main argument against the Roman Church discussing the proper method for interpreting Scripture. In the Romish past, he argued, the traditional senses had come to mean only different forms of the allegorical one. The literal sense has 'become nothing at all: for the pope hath taken it clean away' and has 'locked it up with false and counterfeited keys of his traditions'.[58] One could see this in history and in the commentaries of the past. Tyndale was at pains to demonstrate that even the allegories, similitudes, and parables of Scripture could be interpreted literally. His examples came from the parables, which were easy enough. However, when faced with the Revelation of St. John he was forced to admit 'The apocalypse, or revelations of John are allegories whose literal sense is hard to find in many places.'[59] He did not attempt the task, but he maintained that a literal sense must be discernible.

There can be no doubt that Tyndale was extremely fond of using the words 'Antichrist' and 'Antichristian' when referring to the pope and the Roman Church. Difficulty in ascertaining just how literally he intended the description might arise had he not made his position very clear in his *Parable of the Wicked Mammon*. There he separates himself

[58] Tyndale, 'The Obedience of a Christian Man', in *Doctrinal Treatises* (Parker Soc., 1848 onwards), p. 303.
[59] Ibid., p. 305.

from the historical commentators to side with a Wyclifite interpretation:

Mark this above all things; that Antichrist is not an outward thing: that is to say a man that should suddenly appear with wonders as our fathers talked of him. No verily; for Antichrist is a spiritual thing; and is as much to say as against Christ; that is one that preacheth false doctrine contrary to Christ. Antichrist was in the Old Testament . . . he was also in the time of Christ and his apostles . . . Antichrist is now and shall (I doubt not) endure till the world's end.[60]

The quotation is important evidence both of the survival into the Reformation of the Wyclifite view and of Tyndale's refusal to modify that position even to support his interpretation of the past or the present struggle.

Here Tyndale rejected two possible literal interpretations of the prophecies of Antichrist in the last days. He rejected the one that took the whole prophecy literally including the forty-two months given to Antichrist, and which implied that it would all be fulfilled in the last three and a half years of the world. He also rejected an interpretation that assigned any other specific date or period in history before and after which Antichrist would not exist. Like Erasmus, Tyndale clung to the idea that Scripture contained a host of spiritual examples, and that its real meaning was spiritual. At the close of his discussion of the four senses of Scripture he made the cryptic statement 'God is a spirit and all his words are spiritual.'[61]

It is clear that Tyndale referred to the pope as Antichrist, but this did not lead him to expect the climax of world history in the near future. Nor was he in the least interested in prophetic chronology, the Prophecy of Elias, or the theory of the four monarchies. Nevertheless he was well aware of the uses to which Protestants could put history. In his case, however, the argument from history came from sets of examples and not from any theory of progressive revelation or development. He borrowed from Lutheran historiography only two beliefs: that the history of the Church ought primarily to be of doctrine, and that the heroes were the true doctors and the enemies the false doctors—as witnessed, he said, in Christ's words through Paul and in the Apocalypse. But in his own

---

[60] *Doctrinal Treatises* (Parker Soc., 1848), p. 42.
[61] 'The Obedience of a Christian Man', ed. cit., p. 309.

historical writings, Tyndale concentrated not upon the Church and her doctrine but upon the conflict between pope and emperor: between, as he often put it, perfidious prelates and noble princes. In his historically based tract *The Practice of Prelates* (1530), example after example was brought forward to convict Rome of treachery against kings. These examples were taken from both continental and English history. Although the time and place varied, the story was always the same. The examples were marshalled to sustain a theme of Roman treachery and immorality rather than to trace a growth of papal power within the context of historical change. Tyndale's conception of history was as strongly tied to, and as limited by, a theory of moral example as Erasmus's was. Where Tyndale did speak of an event as having importance for further events he echoed Luther's own choice and explanation of key events: the crowning of Charlemagne, the final corruption of the Church under Boniface III in his relations with the Emperor Phocas, and the rise of the temporal power of the pope at the same time as the rise of Muhammad.

In sum, Tyndale typifies the entrenched resistance of the earliest English reformers to the apocalyptic tradition; even his use of argument from history was not enough to involve him. Although willing to accept the material of Lutheran interpretation, most of the important early English reformers were perhaps too much influenced by the Erasmian way of thinking to succumb readily to the historical application of scriptural prophecy. The weakening of English resistance would begin with the simple repetition and translation of Lutheran material. One significant rendition into English of such material was made by John Frith.

John Frith had several brushes with the originators of the Lutheran view. Before joining Tyndale in Antwerp, he had been among those Fellows of Cardinal College discovered by Wolsey to be in possession of books by Wyclif, Huss, Luther, Melanchthon, and Francis Lambert of Avignon. He had been imprisoned in the college fish cellar for some months and was released on condition he leave Oxford.[62] He wisely left the country and for some time stayed with Tyndale in Antwerp.

[62] William Clebsch, *England's Earliest Protestants* (New Haven and London, 1964), p. 80.

There in 1529 he had published a translation of Luther's *De Antichristo* and also Patrick Hamilton's commonplace book on justification by faith, known thereafter as *Patrick's Places.* The translation of Luther's work was published on 12 July. No date is given for *Patrick's Places.* Although no evidence has been found to support it, the suggestion has been made that Frith may have attended the Marburg colloquy between Luther and Zwingli in October of the same year.[63] If so, he may have met Francis Lambert who either had just published or was about to publish his commentary on the Apocalypse.[64] In the preface of that book Lambert commended Patrick Hamilton as a young man of great promise who had recently suffered martyrdom at the hands of Antichrist. (Hamilton's commonplace book was written while he was one of Lambert's students.) It is possible that Frith may have conceived the idea of translating and publishing something by the martyred Hamilton at the suggestion of Lambert. Although Frith's name does not appear on the rolls of the Protestant University in Marburg and there is no evidence that he ever visited Wittenberg,[65] he was more in touch with Lutheran preoccupations with the meaning of the Turk and the imminence of the world's end than any other of the earliest English Protestant theologians.

Under the name of Richard Brightwell, Frith presented his translation of Luther's *De Antichristo*, first written in 1521. Before the translation Frith put an epistle by himself, and after it he put a comparison of the pope with Christ, based on the little tract *Passional Christi und Antichristi* (also 1521), which contained twenty-six woodcuts by Hans Cranach the elder comparing the deeds of Christ with those of the pope, and brief contrasts of Scripture with canon law.[66] The Antithesis reads very like Nicholas of Lyra's *Vita Antichristi* and clearly both the *Passional* and Frith's Antithesis follow the non-apocalyptic interpretation of Antichrist.

The Revelation of Antichrist was in fact a commentary on Daniel 8. Daniel was the first source Luther used in his search for the meaning of Antichrist. In Frith's tract there appeared

---

[63] Clebsch, op. cit., p. 81.

[64] *Exegeseos in Sanctam divi Joanis Apocalypsim* (Marburg, 1528) edition consulted (Basle, 1539).

[65] Clebsch, op. cit., pp.80-1.   [66] Ibid., p. 86

for the first time in English and for an English audience the Lutheran interpretation[67] of the corruption of the Roman Empire into the Church of Rome: 'the tyrannye of the Pope dyd begynne after that the imperye of Rome began to decay | yee of the imperye of Rome and in the imperye it is spronge. And is succedyd and entered | in the stede of the imperye | as it is evydent by all storyes | and this present experience doth also shew it us |.'[68]

Luther's interpretation of Daniel had developed during the 1520s, chiefly under the impetus of the search for the meaning of the Turk. This old Hussite version of the translation of one Roman empire from the emperor to the pope through the papal usurpation of temporal power became more usual in English Protestant historiography during the sixteenth century than did the German interpretation of the four monarchies.

In the prefatory epistle Frith spoke of Antichrist in terms similar to those Tyndale used, stressing the tyranny and false traditions and practices introduced into the Church by the pope, but without commenting on the problems of interpreting the parts of Daniel referred to the four monarchies or expressing any eschatological significance in the revelation of Antichrist at this particular time. Perhaps it was because the tract of Luther did concern itself directly with the interpretation of only one chapter in Daniel that Frith thought the development of the theme of corruption needed further and more explicit stress and so added his epistle and the comparison in order to clarify his intended meaning.

Although *Patrick's Places* became an important summary of the doctrine of justification by faith in British Protestantism, its real significance lay in the lives, and more especially in the deaths, of its author and translator. Frith's major theological interests were in the Eucharist and in the Roman doctrine of purgatory. In 1531 he returned to England in defiance of Sir Thomas More (he had helped Tyndale to prepare his *Answer to More*) and to further the Reformation at home. He was arrested, imprisoned, and executed.

The story of Patrick Hamilton, first hero and martyr of the

---

[67] Itself a revival of the Hussite argument.
[68] *Revelation of Antichrist* (Antwerp, 1529), fol. xiiiᵛ.

Scottish Reformation, reveals nothing that could be called apocalyptic preaching. Hamilton's education at Luther's direction under Francis Lambert may have included some of Lambert's or Luther's ideas on prophecy and the interpretation of Antichrist, but Hamilton returned to Scotland far too early to have learned much of any development of the Antichrist theme beyond the simple expression of anti-papalism. He died in 1528, and while his martyrdom warranted mention in Knox's history of the Reformation similar to Wyclif's in Foxe's *Book of Martyrs*, it does not appear that Hamilton himself was instrumental in advancing Scottish interest in the Apocalypse.

In the years preceding 1530 the English and Scottish exiles, though to some extent exposed to the changes taking place in the Lutheran evaluation of the Book of Revelation and other prophetic sources, did not readily become involved except as translators. Likewise in the early 1530s, which saw the publication for the first time of *Carion's Chronicle* and other works important to the new historiography, the English reformers remained aloof from the tradition. Tyndale's *Practice of Prelates* established a pattern of English argument from history that remained virtually unchanged throughout the decade. In 1535 Robert Barnes made use of the same approach but in a more complete and orderly fashion than Tyndale had. He gathered and arranged examples to prove papal deviation from and alteration of the earlier formulations of canon law, and followed this argument with a collection of the lives of the popes arranged in chronological order. In Barnes's collection there is a first history of the papacy[69] illustrating the popes' affiliation with the ways of Antichrist, but there is no hint that this history fulfilled specific prophecies or that the world was near its end.

The materials for the apocalyptic tradition were being assembled without any commitment to the thematic structure of prophecy fulfilled in a succession of events. While the nature and extent of the Antichrist was still debated, on one thing both the English and the continental Protestants agreed: the *revelation* of Antichrist was a historical event embodied in their own movement for reformation. Even Tyndale was

[69] *Vitae Romanorum Pontificum* (Basle, 1535).

prepared to encourage the idea that to some extent this revelation was a prerequisite for the study of history, though by
this he meant only that antichristian conspiracy could be
held to explain the superstitious errors evident in monkish
histories.[70] Once enlightened by true doctrine, the history of
both Church and State illustrated the essentially antichristian
character of Rome.

By 1540 the apocalyptic tradition on the continent had
evolved two of what were to be its three main constituents.
In *Carion's Chronicle*, the Prophecy of Elias associated prophecy with periodization, tracing the course of history
through three stages. Prophecy was praised for its guidance in
the writing of universal history and chronology, and in the
Book of Daniel for its comprehension of worldly as well as
spiritual changes and for its warning that the fall of the
Empire would hasten the end of the world. Luther, through
his identification of the pope with Antichrist and the Turk
with Gog, was led to see his own time in terms of the fulfilment of prophecy. In addition the position of the Apocalypse in the canon of Scripture was reasserted, and early
doubts and dismissals of it were replaced by interested activity.

Some of the characteristics of English Protestant historiography emerged in Tyndale's use of history and were to
persist after the addition of the apocalyptic tradition. The
relationship between kings and popes came forward as a
major theme, to be treated in terms of divine law versus
prelatical practice. Examples drawn from this subject witnessed to the many instances of the pope's antithesis to
Christ. Corruption in the Church resulted from the gain of
temporal power and wealth. The corrupted church entered
into a conspiracy against the true church, one which had
been hidden and remained hidden partly because of the falsi-
fication and adulteration of histories. Finally Tyndale stressed
the importance of persecution and martyrdom as the signs
of the true church in the world. In this context the English
interest in the Apocalypse grew.

[70] Tyndale's use of conspiracy to explain medieval history was noted by Rainer
Pineas in 'William Tyndale's use of history as a Weapon of Religious Controversy',
Harvard Theological Review, vol. lv, no. 2 (Apr. 1962).

The first original English or Scottish contribution to the development of the apocalyptic tradition was made by a new exile, who fled England after the fall of his patron, Thomas Cromwell. Both before and after John Bale wrote *The Image of bothe churches*, English reformers continued to learn from the continental leaders. In the next chapter, the years from 1540 to 1553 will be shown to contain the English rejection of Tyndale's conception of Antichrist and the growing involvement of England's exiles in a literally historical interpretation of prophecy.

II

FROM EXILE TO EXILE: JOHN BALE AND THE
TWO CHURCHES

As the Reformation spread, its character changed to suit new political environments. Luther had hoped to convert the emperor and preserve the Empire, but this was not to be. As alliances and treaties were made and broken, marriages arranged and the arrangements or the marriages dissolved, religious sentiment, although an issue, could not control the direction of royal policies. Reform by nation as both Luther and Tyndale imagined it had run into difficulty. Meanwhile in the Rhineland in certain cities Protestant leaders were intent upon achieving reform in the local community. In the years following 1540 and the fall of Thomas Cromwell a number of English Protestants left England and once again found themselves working in exile; many of them settled in these Protestant cities. For many the reign of Edward which lay in the future was to be only a brief bright interval between periods of exile.

The apocalyptic tradition had revived in a peculiarly Lutheran background and did not immediately win to itself either the English or the Swiss. In 1536 the millenarian uprising at Münster appalled both Protestants and Catholics. For more than a generation afterwards Münster stood as an example of the dangers of apocalyptic preaching, but interest in the Apocalypse continued. Even upon those who most mistrusted the excesses of Münster, apocalyptic thought had its impact.

When John Calvin accepted his recall to Geneva in 1541, he left Strasburg and the guidance of Martin Bucer to set about his own experiments in reform by community. As a student and a young man Calvin showed great promise. His training had followed humanist principles. He was skilled in philology and trained for two years in Roman law, but his real interest lay in theology. He came to share some of Erasmus's reservations concerning the proper use of the Book of Revelation. The events of Münster particularly horrified

him, and made him a bitter opponent of all radicals. These
two considerations were, however, balanced in his mind by
two others: a belief in the omnipotence of God and his law,
and a belief in God's strict control of history through divine
prescience and predestination. He stood with Luther against
Erasmus's understanding of free will. This balance caused
him to take an officially cautious view of the Apocalypse but
an active part in the tradition as it applied to history.

Throughout his life Calvin assiduously avoided writing any
commentary upon the Book of Revelation, and for this reserve
later generations have praised his good sense. In the place
where one might reasonably expect to find his opinion, in his
Antidote to the acts of the Council of Trent, he does not raise
the subject of this book. Nevertheless he does attack the Catholic canon for its inclusion of a number of 'ecclesiastical books'
on the ground that the primitive Church was not unanimous
in its opinion. Despite the decision of the Council of Carthage,
Calvin brought forward the acknowledgement made by Augustine that even then not all were agreed.[1] These are the arguments used by Erasmus in his criticism of the Book of Revelation,[2] yet Calvin stopped short of applying them to that book.
Thus we may conclude that Calvin had no objection in theory
to the inclusion of the Book of Revelation in the canon, but
that in practice he avoided its use. His references to the
Revelation in every instance I have encountered followed
Erasmus's advice by referring to the book only for illustration.

In order to assess Calvin's involvement in the apocalyptic
tradition it is necessary to look elsewhere than at his citations
from the Book of Revelation. In his case the texts in the
Epistles which referred to the Antichrist and to a Great Apostasy in the last days gave him the opportunity to bring in
some of the ideas and theories that others had linked with
the Apocalypse. In these places his exposition not only uses
many of the Lutheran ideas but also rejects the major rival
interpretations that removed the story of the Antichrist and
the last days from the time of the Reformation.

[1] John Calvin, 'Acts of the Council of Trent with the Antidote', *Calvin's Tracts
and Treatises*, vol. iii, trans. Henry Beveridge, ed. T. F. Torrance (London and
Edinburgh, 1958).
[2] See above, p. 8.

In his commentary on the letters of Paul to the Thessalonians[3] he constructed his exposition so as to support the idea of the Reformation as the final great alteration in the world before its end. To do this he had to explain why Paul had spoken of the end as if it were to come many centuries sooner. Paul had done this, Calvin said, to save men from despair.[4] However, he had given certain signs whereby the future could tell more nearly when the end was to come. The most important pre-condition for the end was a general falling-away of the Church from the true faith. In looking for an apocalypse the early writers had mistaken the pagan Roman Empire for the Antichrist.

The day of Christ, he says, will not come until the world has fallen into apostasy, and the rule of Antichrist has held sway in the Church. The interpretation which some have given that this passage refers to the end of the Roman Empire is too stupid to need lengthy refutation. I am also surprised that so many writers, who are intelligent and good scholars in other respects, have been led into error in such an elementary matter, except that when one has gone astray, others, lacking judgment, followed in droves.[5]

This interpretation rejected by Calvin was held by those who, following the earliest church historians and some of the early commentaries on the Apocalypse, had interpreted the prophecies in the terms of the conflict between the Christian and the pagan Roman Empire. As Calvin sought for his definition of Antichrist, he rejected both this classical interpretation and any that limited Antichrist to a merely spiritual significance. The expression 'man of sin' in Paul's letter occasioned a general inquiry into the meaning of Antichrist and the beasts of the Apocalypse, which the Lutherans considered referred to the same thing. In his interpretation of the great apostasy, Calvin indicated that by 'Antichrist' he meant to indicate the papacy and the Turks.

It was said of Nero that he was taken up from the world and would return again to persecute the Church by his tyranny. This was nothing but an old wife's fable, and yet the minds of the ancients were so bewitched that they believed that Nero would be Antichrist. Paul, however, is not speaking of one individual but of a kingdom that was

---

[3] John Calvin, 'The Epistles of Paul the Apostle to the Romans and to the Thessalonians', trans. Ross Mackenzie, vol. 4 (1960) of *Calvin's Commentaries*, ed. Torrance & Torrance (12 vols., London and Edinburgh, 1959-72).

[4] Ibid., pp. 396-7.   [5] Ibid., pp. 398-9.

seized by Satan for the purpose of setting up a seat of abomination in
the midst of God's temple. This we see accomplished in popery. The
defection has indeed spread more widely, for since Mohammed was an
apostate he turned his followers the Turks from Christ.[6]

An alternative interpretation to the one offered by the
Germans was one that limited the reign of Antichrist to a
mere three and a half years at the very end of human history.
Calvin rejected this also, in favour of the historical revelation
of Antichrist in the papacy: 'The papists have imagined an
antichrist who is to harass the Church for three and a half
years. All the marks by which the Spirit of God has pointed
out antichrist appear clearly in the Pope; but their triennial
antichrist has such hold on the foolish Papists that seeing
they do not see.'[7]

He identified Antichrist not as a single pope but as the succession of popes. In the papacy Antichrist assumed a historical manifestation.[8] Unlike Tyndale, Calvin did not regard
Antichrist as a spiritual thing capable of assuming different
identities in different ages. Even when his text, I John 2,
seemed to suggest an ever-present Antichrist, Calvin replied
that the supposed manifestation of Antichrist in the primitive Church as a profusion of sects was not the Antichrist, because 'properly speaking, antichrist was not yet in existence,
but the mystery of his ungodliness was working secretly'.[9]
This invisible and spiritual influence of Antichrist was replaced by the actual Antichrist of the papacy, which represented the full and final manifestation and was the one of
which Paul had warned.

Calvin wrote a commentary on Daniel[10] and published a
series of sermons on chapters 5-12 of that book.[11] Unlike

[6] Calvin 'Epistles to the Thessalonians', *Calvin's Commentaries*, series cited,
vol. 4 (1960), p. 399.

[7] John Calvin, 'The First Epistle of John', trans. T. H. L. Parker, *Calvin's Commentaries*, series cited, vol. 3 (1961), p. 256.

[8] Calvin, 'Epistles to the Thessalonians', *Calvin's Commentaries*, series cited,
vol. 4. (1960), pp. 403-4.

[9] Calvin, 'The First Epistle of John', *Calvin's Commentaries*, series cited, vol. 3
(1961), p. 257.

[10] *Commentaries on the Book of the Prophet Daniel*, trans. and ed. Thomas
Myers, Calvin Translation Soc. (2 vols., Edinburgh, 1852).

[11] 'Sermons sur les huit derniers chapitres du livre de Daniel', *Calvini Opera*
t. xli-xlii, *Corpus Reformatorum*.

his sermons, his commentary was intentionally scholarly and strictly controlled by his desire to avoid the more obscure passages. His discussion of Daniel's seventy weeks is particularly revealing of the way in which his desire to remain silent warred with the necessity to make all things plain in Scripture.

I therefore am ready to acknowledge all these interpretations to be false, and yet I do not allow the truth of God to fail.

How, therefore, shall we arrive at any certain conclusion? It is not sufficient to refute the ignorance of others, unless we can make the truth apparent, and prove it by clear and satisfactory reasons. I am willing to spare the names of surviving commentators and of those who have lived during our own times, yet I must say what will prove useful to my readers; meanwhile I shall speak cautiously because I am very desirous of being silent upon all points except those which are useful and necessary to be known.[12]

The truth of God must not fail. Scripture and history must agree so that 'whoever will compare all historical testimony with the desire of learning and without any contention, will carefully number the years, he will find it impossible to express them better than by the expression of the angel—seventy weeks'.[13] While Calvin preferred to remain silent on such questions as that of the seventy weeks, when forced he had to admit, 'While we allow much diversity and contradiction united with great obscurity, still we must always return to the same point—some conclusion may be found, which will agree with this prediction of the Prophet.'[14]

Calvin's sermons were less rigorously controlled. There he allowed himself to draw parallels between Daniel's prophecies of Antiochus Epiphanes and Antichrist's persecution of the true Church. These parallels were similitudes, not identifications in a strict sense. He rejected the Lutheran interpretation of the little horn. 'Voila donc quant à ce point de la petite corne, combien qu'aucuns le prennent pour Mahommet, ou bien pour l'Antechrist mais c'est le changement qui est avenue en l'empire romain.'[15] Although Calvin himself may

[12] *Commentaries on the Book of the Prophet Daniel*, ed. cit., vol. ii, pp. 210-11.

[13] Ibid.   [14] Ibid.

[15] 'Sermons sur . . . (le) livre de Daniel', ed. cit., t. xli, cols. 442-3. 'As for this subject of the little horn, however many may take it for Muhammad, or even for the Antichrist, nevertheless it is the change which occurred in the Roman Empire.'

have separated the prophecies of Daniel from those of Antichrist, he placed Antichrist's monarchy (the papacy) in the line of succession after Daniel's four.[16] The delay of the full revelation of Antichrist until the Reformation was explicable only because a new papal empire had been founded upon the ruins of the western empire. The early Church had been mistaken in believing the Roman Empire to be Antichrist. He was to be the Empire's successor and usurper, the tyrant and false prophet of the last times. Here Calvin accepted the historical limitation of Antichrist in a way in which Tyndale had not. Basing his interpretation of the Church's history upon the prophecies in the New Testament letters rather than upon the seals and trumpets of Revelation, Calvin emphasized the prediction of the final apostasy. However, in his interpretation of this prediction he mustered, and to the same effect, the same historical materials used in the apocalyptic tradition. British Calvinists, notably John Knox, often disagreed with Calvin's interpretation of the little horn and did not approach the obscurities of the Apocalypse with the same restraint.

Later generations, reacting against the more fully developed apocalyptic tradition, often cited Calvin in their own defence[17] or praised his restraint,[18] but at the time Calvin's silence proved no barrier to the development of the tradition even among Calvinists. Moreover, Calvin's silence did not prevent elements of the tradition from colouring his commentaries on other parts of Scripture.

Tyndale had expressed the version of Antichrist that agreed with that of most English participants in the Henrican reformation before the second exile. Tyndale's version resisted a historical interpretation of Antichrist, and provided a greater barrier than Calvin to English participation in the

[16] Calvin, 'Epistles to the Thessalonians', *Calvin's Commentaries*, series cited, vol. 4 (1960), p. 403.

[17] Calvin's refusal to write a commentary on Revelation was given in these terms by John Selden to James I as a defence for Selden's own lack of interest in the prophecies. Selden, 'Of the Revelation', *Opera Omnia* (London, 1725), iii, Pt. II, pp. 1402-3.

[18] Joseph Scaliger said of him 'Calvin a tres bien fait de ne rien escrire sur l'Apocalypse' and 'Sapit quod in Apocalypsin non scripsit.' *Scaligerana, ou Bons mots, Rencontres Agréables et Remarques Judicieuses & Sçavantes de J. Scaliger* (Cologne, 1695), pp. 76-7.

tradition. Significantly, the first English contribution was made by a reformer who was more interested in history than in theology. Before Cromwell's fall sent him into Europe, John Bale had shown his historical bent. As a young friar in Cambridge he had written a history of his Order.[19] After his conversion to Protestantism in the mid 1530s he obtained the patronage of Thomas Cromwell and wrote several plays[20] which instructed his audience in reformed theology and pointed out the failings of Rome. The plays, written for the most part in verse, are of little literary merit, but in one way they were highly original. Bale was the first English dramatist to write history plays. These histories were cross-bred with elements of the morality play and illustrated from British history examples of papal treachery against kings. The best play of this kind was largely paraphrased from Tyndale's version of the King John story.[21] The influence of Tyndale on Bale's *King John* was enormous and serves as an illustration of the influence the martyred Tyndale had over the vanguard of the Cromwellian party. Even the mixing of history and morality agreed with Tyndale's use of history.

Bale's interest in history went beyond a desire to make a moral point into an area where the apocalyptic tradition would find him vulnerable. His plays showed a great interest in elaborately constructed historical patterns. In *A Comedy concerning three laws* he used a pattern based on the laws of nature, bondage, and grace. Natural law ruled the conscience, the law of Moses required obedience to rulers, and the law of grace ruled among the faithful. The three laws encompassed seven ages of world history. These were the usual seven: from Adam to Christ in six ages, and the final age from Christ to the end. Infidelity corrupted each of the three laws in turn until at last only a small remnant held to the true faith. Then

---

[19] *Chronica seu fasciculus temporum ordininis Carmelitanae ex variis*, Bodleian Library, MS. Bodl. Selden Sup. 41.

[20] The two plays cited here, *King John* and *The thre laws*, were both written very early. Bale mentions them in a manuscript (Anglorum Heliades) dated 1536, first discovered by J. H. P. Pafford and referred to in Jesse Harris, *John Bale: A Study in the Minor Literature of the Reformation* (Urbana, Ill., 1940). Harris (pp. 67-8) believes *The thre laws* may have been written as early as 1531.

[21] Honor McCusker, *John Bale: Dramatist and Antiquary* (Bryn Mawr, Pa., 1942), pp. 86-96, compares Bale's lines in *King John* with Tyndale's version of the story in 'The Obedience of a Christian Man'.

would come the new heaven of man's renewed faith and the new earth of his understanding of that faith.[22] This construction followed a pattern of seven and three, but the future promise of a new creation was given an entirely spiritual significance. Bale adhered faithfully to his construction, and within this framework his drama developed.

In the late 1530s Bale showed an interest in the Apocalypse which matured during his exile. In 1537 he translated a German play *Pammachius* by Thomas Kirchmeyer, which dealt with the subject of Antichrist.[23] Bale's translation has been lost,[24] but early in his exile he wrote the first part of his commentary on the Apocalypse. This first part of his commentary was heavily documented. He had read by 1541 the commentaries by Joachim, John Wyclif, Francis Lambert, Sebastian Franck, and Sebastian Meyer, to name only a few of the authors cited. He collected together the names of all the authors he could find who had written on the subject, catalogued them by their ecclesiastical order, or by their adherence to Protestantism for the most recent ones, and said he had either seen or read the greater part of the works listed.[25] Bale's commentary on the Apocalypse occupied him on and off from 1541 to 1547. It was written in three parts; the first was completed in 1541, the second was published together with the first in 1545, and the third part was added in 1547.[26]

Bale travelled often during his exile and visited many of the important Protestant cities of the Low Countries, the Rhineland, and Switzerland. The difficulty in tracing his whereabouts for any particular time is compounded by his fondness for pseudonyms and for false if amusing places for the publication of his works. In a tract which declared itself to have been published on 10 December 1543 in

---

[22] John Bale, *A Comedy concerning three laws*, in *The Dramatic Writings of John Bale, Bishop of Ossory*, ed. J. S. Farmer (Early English Drama Soc., 1907).

[23] Bale listed a translation of 'Pammachius' among his works in his *Index Britanniae Scriptorum . . .* , ed. R. L. Poole and Mary Bateson (Oxford, 1902).

[24] Harris, *John Bale: A Study in the Minor Literature of the Reformation*, Bibliography, p. 139.

[25] John Bale, *The Image of bothe churches*, in *Select Works of Bishop Bale*, (Parker Soc., 1849), pp. 255-9; hereinafter *Image*.

[26] Harris, loc. cit.

Zürich[27] by Oliver Jacobson, Bale stated, 'I have written a
large volume called the Image of both churches comprehendynge an whole commentarye upon the revelacyon of Johan,
whych I trust ye schall shortlye have with other thynges
els.'[28] The tract in which these words appeared was Bale's
contribution to a controversy that reached its height in late
1543. Although the place and the printer of this tract might
remain in question, there does not appear to be any reason to
doubt the date. Parts I and II of *The Image of bothe churches*
were not published together until 1545. This book was one
of Bale's most constant efforts during his exile. His interest in
the Apocalypse found its way into many of his other works,
both those that contributed to controversies and those that
dealt with history or the study of history.

The heavy documentation of Part I of *The Image of bothe
churches* was abandoned in Parts II and III because the printers had made such a mess of it in the first part. Part I drew
particularly heavily on commentaries by Francis Lambert
and Sebastian Meyer. Other contemporaries to whom he
often referred were Luther and Oecolampadius. Earlier
writers who received a substantial number of references included three standard medieval commentators, Haymo, Albertus Magnus, and Ambrosius Ansbertus, and special emphasis was placed on works ascribed to John Huss and John
Wyclif.[29] Although some of the works were inaccurately
ascribed,[30] in their preoccupation with the life and attributes
of the Antichrist they all fell within the tradition described
in the first chapter as Wyclifite.

---

[27] Oliver Jacobson does not appear in the record of printers in Zürich for
1543. M. M. Knappen, *Tudor Puritanism* (Chicago and London, 1939), p. 61 n.
Harris, op. cit., pp. 30-1, suggests Bale may have been in Antwerp between 1543
and 1545.

[28] John Bale, *Yet a course at the Romyshe foxe*, a Disclosynge or openynge of
the Manne of synne ('Zürich', 1543), p. 40; hereinafter *Romyshe foxe*.

[29] The number of marginal references to each is as follows: Lambert (38),
Meyer (26), Luther (12), Oecolampadius (11), Haymo (18), Albertus Magnus (15),
Ambrosius Ansbertus (11), Huss (17), Wyclif (20). Richard Bauckham, *Tudor
Apocalypse*, p. 23.

[30] All those attributed to Huss were inaccurately ascribed. The titles cited
were: *De anatomia Antichristi; De Antichristo; Commentarius in Apocalypsim;
De regno, populo, vita et moribus Antichristi; Sermones de Antichristo*. Vaclav
Flajshans, *Literarni Cinnost Mistra Jana Husi*, pp. 154-7, see Bauckham, op. cit.
p. 35, n. 44. Note the concentration on the Antichrist.

Bale's references to Joachim of Fiore are few in number but significant in content. In addition to his accurate reference to Joachim's *Expositio in Apocalypsim* there are references to pseudo-Joachimist works and to derivative authors in the Joachimist tradition.[31] Bale read widely and drew upon both Wyclifite and the Joachimist sources. Although originally, like many of his countrymen, he was drawn into the study of the prophecies in a quest for the identification of Antichrist, Bale's polemical interest was augmented by an equally powerful dedication to the discovery and preservation of the past. The historicist interpretation of the Revelation given by Joachim in his *Expositio* captured Bale's imagination. In Part I of the *Image* he accepted the Joachimist vision of the history of the Church as a progression through seven periods, from the death of Christ to the end of the world, each of which was represented by one of the seven seals of the Apocalypse.[32] This use of the Apocalypse had been missing in Luther's exposition. Its recognition and addition to the English Protestant tradition by John Bale is significant for its future development. The Lollard commentary published by Luther and the commentary by Lambert had each gone some distance in this direction before Bale's *Image*, but it was Bale who in later years gave new emphasis to the sequential implications of the seven seals.

Although this interpretation might be made to support anabaptist revolutionaries, Bale, like Calvin and most mainstream reformers, took exception to the anabaptists because their doctrines showed no respect for divine or civil authority.[33] Like Calvin, Bale reached a compromise position in which the Apocalypse might be interpreted as a revelation

---

[31] They include references to the pseudo-Joachimist *Oraculum Cyrilli cum Expositione*, and *Super Hieremiam Prophetam*, and to several Joachimist-inspired works, the most important of which are those by Richard of St. Victor, the Sybilline Oracles, Arnold of Villa Nova, and Peter John of Olivi (Bauckham, op. cit. p. 25). For the importance of each of the above to the history of Joachimism see M. Reeves, *The Influence of Prophecy*.

[32] Bale, *Image*, p. 312. Bale's own marginal note attributes this idea to the Abbot Joachim: the revival is thus a conscious one.

[33] For Bale on the anabaptists of Münster in verse see *King John*, in *Dramatic Writings of John Bale, Bishop of Ossory*, ed. Farmer, p. 291; in prose see *The Laboryouse Journey & serche of J. Leylande for Englandes Antiquitees . . .* (London, 1549), fols. E viii^r–F i^r.

of the past but when it clearly referred to the future it remained a mystery incapable of certain interpretation.

While Bale hit upon and developed thoughts and methods important for the growth of the apocalyptic tradition, it would be wrong to imagine that he became an apocalypticist in any futuristic sense. His true interest was in the past and he was cautious when his commentary verged on the prophesied future. At such times he preferred to indicate only the general and spiritual significance of the prophecies.

In Part I the seven seals signified seven periods of the church's history. The periods were not given specific dates and followed a chronological order only loosely. They were marked rather by a change of spirit and by the growing power of Antichrist. The first seal was contemporary with the disciples, and Christ should be understood for the rider upon the white horse. The second seal coincided with the first heresies in the Church and the persecution of Christians by the Roman emperors. The red horse signified false teachers, 'blood thirsty doctors' and 'puffed-up prelates'. The third seal was a continuation of these trials but was marked by a greater abundance of martyrs and heresies. The black horse was ridden by Satan. During this period both Muhammad and the pope advanced false doctrines. The fourth seal opened the time of the revelation of hypocrisy. The pale horse signified the hypocrites who were members of the Church of Antichrist. Contrary to this seal and contemporary with it was the revelation of the true Church in the fifth seal which showed the souls under the altar. During the time of the sixth seal the pale horse of hypocrisy was still to be seen. As testimony in support of this Bale cited John Huss, John Wyclif, Francis Lambert, and Sebastian Franck.[34] The sixth seal witnessed the raising up of true spirits to detect the abominations of the past. The earthquake of the sixth seal was identified with an earthquake reported to have shaken parts of England in the year in which Wyclif was condemned. Sebastian Meyer had shown how at the same time in Germany the ferocity of Antichrist had increased. Bale mentioned Germany to give a more universal significance to this same period.[35] The four angels at the four corners of the

---

[34] Bale, *Image*, p. 326.   [35] Ibid., p. 327.

earth held back the wind of God's spirit and therefore signified the hypocrites. But one angel, standing for all true preachers, withstood them. In the time of the sixth seal the remnant of the Jews would be gathered together and converted. The seventh seal would witness the overthrow of Babylon and Antichrist and the binding-up of the dragon for a thousand years.

The binding and loosing again of the dragon became an event of great importance to the Protestant tradition. In Part I Bale had chosen to place the binding in the age of the seventh seal in order to counteract a standard medieval interpretation, advanced by those like Otto of Freising, which combined the millennium of the saints' rule with the bondage of the dragon, and dated both from either the birth of Christ or the reign of Constantine. Then the thousand years was interpreted to mean either eternity or an undisclosed but very great number of years before the second coming to judgement. While commentators might be divided as to whether it was the institution of the Christian Church from the days of Christ and his Apostles or the conversion of the Empire that effectively banished the power of Satan from the Christian world, they agreed that the established powers of Catholic Christendom were the chief instruments for the containment of Satan. Bale of course did not accept this conclusion, and because the association between the Antichrist and Satan was strongly rooted in his mind,[36] he chose to look forward to a future defeat of Antichrist and the binding of the dragon. This he held was to be the work of the Reformation, and while the precise number of years in any future period remained obscure until after the event, it was still possible to assert that the millennium would be a historical period bounded in the seventh seal and that it was not to be taken figuratively to comprehend the entire pageant of church history. Later, as he came more into contact with the continental writers, he reversed his position, returning the bondage to the past for equally persuasive Protestant reasons, but he did not change his insistence on the place of the Reformation in the fulfilment of prophecy.

[36] He often referred to Antichrist as the 'Vicar of Satan' and even more closely as 'the body of Satan'. Like Tyndale he believed that Antichrist was the chief agent and manifestation of Satan in the affairs of the world.

Continuing his discourse on the Apocalyptic scheme of history, Bale paralleled the seven trumpets with the seven seals. The angels of the trumpets stood for all the true preachers throughout the history of the Church. The first trumpet sent out the Apostles; the second those who came immediately after the Apostles. The star that fell with the third trumpet signified the growth of heresies in the early Church. The fourth trumpet sounded in that 'most corrupted and dolorous age of antichrist'. The angel in the midst of heaven signified the particular and special servants of God such as Joachim, Savonarola, and some others. These men showed how 'by prophecies and scriptures have many godly men perceived aforehand, with Paul, the fall of faith, the increase of errors, and that divers should decline from the truth'.[37]

The fourth and fifth of the seals and the trumpets signified respectively the false Church and the true Church. These seals and trumpets coincided with the centuries which had most occupied Tyndale in his comparisons between prince and prelate. At this stage, Bale's exposition began to describe the spiritual and timeless opposition of the two Churches, which functioned like the two cities in Augustine's interpretation. In the time of the fifth trumpet a great star fell and locusts swarmed out of a smoky pit. The fallen star was the true spiritual Church falling into worldliness.[38] During this time papal tyranny over kings increased but remained hidden from view. The swarm of locusts was the whole range of ecclesiastical minions of the papacy, the cardinals, bishops, monks, and friars. This was the woe of the destroyer. In his interpretation of the fourth and fifth seals Bale abandoned for a moment the idea of each seal governing a particular time in favour of a more familiar concept. He spoke of the opposition between spirit and flesh in the history of the Church.[39] The influence of the Wyclifite tradition also helped shape his treatment; Wyclif contrasted Christ and Antichrist in order to illustrate an eternal opposition between spirit and flesh. With the help of Joachim's belief that the seven seals contained a history of the Church in seven times, Bale was able to bring that eternal opposition down to earth in his presentation of two churches, both of whose images or

[37] Bale, *Image*, p. 349.   [38] Ibid., p. 350.   [39] Ibid., p. 350.

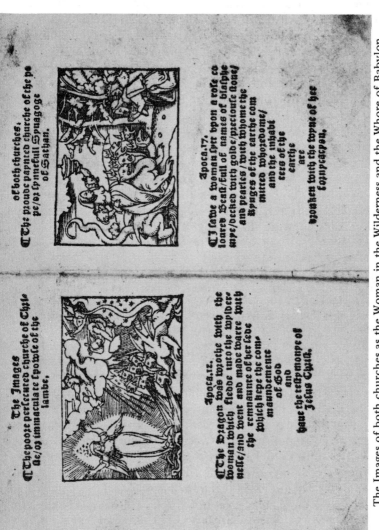

The Images of both churches as the Woman in the Wilderness and the Whore of Babylon from John Bale, *The second part of the image of both churches*, London, 1550?

descriptions were contained in the Apocalypse. The eternal drama of opposition became limited to that period from the institution of Antichrist in the papacy to the Reformation.

The sixth trumpet and seal introduced the then present age of the Reformation. The angel in the cloud holding the little book heralded the sixth age of the Church and the book he held was the Bible. The voices of the seven thunders were not recorded by John, and this Bale interpreted as a warning to those 'which think that they can of their own wit and industry declare such causes, unless God openeth unto them by his word or some evident sign as he hath done in this age most plenteously to many'.[40] He warned that curiosity must follow enlightenment and not precede it, and that enlightenment must follow either from the text or from some evident sign. The sixth age, that is the Reformation, was particularly to be blessed with such signs. The angel with the book betokened the gift of God to his Church of the knowledge of the mysteries of prophecies.

Christ willed all faithful believers to search the scriptures to understand the prophecies, and to perceive the mysteries of them. And, for the performance of his will therein, he hath sent this peculiar angel, beside the common preachers, betokening these singular learned men whom now he hath indued with most high knowledge.[41]

In his commentary Bale used the Apocalypse and the Book of Daniel, but not the prophecy of Elias. He had read *Carion's Chronicle*[42] but did not share the author's interest in or respect for the Talmud, which he later described as 'a book more than ten bibles . . . full of blasphemies and lies, condemning the doctrine of Christ'.[43] Nevertheless by recognizing the correspondence between the time and times and a half a time in Daniel and the three and a half days of the two witnesses (the two testaments) Bale reached a similar conclusion about the duration of the final age.

Not unlike is this oath to the oath in Daniel of time, times, and half a time: wherof, the time from him to Christ, the times were the ages from Christ to the seventh seal-opening, or the seventh trumpet-blowing; the half time from thenceforth, *wherein the days shall be shortened for the chosen's sake.*[44]

In the years between the writing of Parts I and II of *The*

---

[40] Bale, *Image*, p. 372.   [41] Ibid., p. 374.   [42] Cited *Image*, pp. 361, 561.
[43] *Image*, Part II, p. 479.   [44] *Image*, Part I, p. 374 (my italics)

Image of bothe churches, Bale wrote tracts which contributed to the controversies raging between the exiles and the
bishops at home. In these he made good use of the Apocalypse and Daniel to support his denunciation of Rome. In
Yet a course at the Romyshe foxe, subtitled 'A Dysclosynge
or openynge of the Manne of Synne', Bale combined both
sources to advance an interpretation of Satan's bondage different from the one he had suggested in Part I under the
seventh seal.[45] In this later tract he gave the interpretation
that had gained credibility on the continent. In many older
commentaries the thousand years of the dragon's bondage
stretched from the birth of Christ, so that the Protestants
could conclude that the dragon's release corresponded with
the final centuries of papal domination of the Church. Bale
turned to this interpretation.[46] The binding of the dragon
was mentioned in Revelation 20, a chapter which Bale had
not as yet interpreted in his commentary. The subtitle's
reference to the man of sin and the content of *A mysterye of
inyquyte*, written in 1542 and published in 1545 in Geneva,
both suggest that Bale's development seized upon the same
themes that were current among the newer theologians.

Another English exile who became involved in the spread
of the apocalyptic tradition was George Joye. His contribution was less original than Bale's: he chose to translate into
English works originating within the German Lutheran tradition associated with Carion. Bale was not swept along by an
apocalyptic expectancy, and generally refused to hazard
chronological predictions. Joye, however, shared the conviction of several leading Lutherans that the correspondence
between the events preceding the first coming of Christ and
those happening around them was too striking to be dismissed as pure chance. In one of Joye's publications in 1543
he added this comment to his readers.

Now (good reader) thow seest (I thinke) how properlye the tymes
before christes incarnacion | and now this laste time before his coming
to judgement agree to gither and be correspondent for in ether of them |
heretyks & sectesowers did runne and preek before him | miserablye
kutting into peeses and pituously polluting the chirche of God.[47]

---

[45] Above, p. 43. [46] Bale, *Romyshe foxe*, p. 37.
[47] George Joye, *The unite and scisme of the olde chirche* (Antwerp, widow of
C. Ruremond, 1543), fol. ix^r.

The two proofs given, the presence of heresies and of sectaries, were those used in *Carion's Chronicle*.

In 1544 Bale published the first of a series of martyr stories from British history. These he described as histories; his sources were chronicles, and his intention was to present to England the true history of her Christian heroes.[48] He endeavoured to do away with the faults he espied in the humanist historian Polydore Vergil, and others of his day and kind, of praising vice above virtue and of flattery.[49] The subject of Bale's first history was John Oldcastle, who had led a Lollard rebellion against Henry IV. Bale stated he had seen a chronicle printed by Tyndale on the subject of Oldcastle, but that he had found a 'more ample' discussion in Thomas Arundel's process recorded in *Fasciculi Zizaniorum*. To this he said he had added only what he found in other chronicles.[50] This was not strictly true. Although Bale was generally faithful to the content of his sources rather than the order or expression, he allowed his convictions about the validity of the Apocalypse as a guide to history to justify the occasional interpolation.

One such will serve as an example. Bale found occasion to mention that Antichrist began his rise to power in the Roman Church with the wealth and power granted to the prelates by Constantine. He strengthened this very traditional idea by giving it a particular association with one verse in the Apocalypse. Giving as his source Ranulph Higden's *Polychronicon*, the fourth book the twenty-sixth chapter, Bale wrote 'For then cried an angel in the air (as your own chronicles mention): "Woe, woe, woe, this day is venom shed into the church of God".'[51] Beginning with the gift of Constantine, Higden had actually written: 'Proinde et hostis antiquus, facta per Constantinum ecclesiis hac publica largitione, legitur publice in aëre pronuncicesse sic: Hodie infusum est venenum in ecclesia Dei.'[52]

In an edition of the *Polychronicon* prepared for the Rolls

[48] John Bale, *A brief chronicle concerning the examination and death of the blessed Martyr Sir John Oldcastle, the Lord Cobham*, in *Select Works of Bishop Bale*, pp. 5-6.

[49] Ibid., p. 8.   [50] Ibid., p. 7.   [51] Ibid., p. 35.

[52] Ranulph Higden, *Polychronicon Ranulph Higden Monachi Cestrensis*, ed. J. R. Lumby, Rolls Series 41, vol. v (1874), p. 130.

Series, the editor compared the Latin with the translation by
John of Trevisa where it was written: 'therfor it is i-writ that
whann Constantyn hadde i-made that gifte to chirches thanne
the olde enemy cryde openliche in the ayer "this day is
venym i-hilde and i-schad in holy chirche" '.[53] In the text
used by the editor 'the olde enemy' had been erased and
'awngel of hevyn' had been substituted. In another manuscript by an unknown fifteenth-century writer the enemy is
described as 'the enemy to mankynde'.[54] For this reason the
editor quoted the erased version. Even if the version consulted by Bale had been the translation which read 'awngel of
hevyn', the addition of 'Woe, woe, woe,' to the angel's speech
appeared in none of the three. In Revelation 8: 13 the angel
flying in the midst of heaven cried 'Woe, woe, woe,' and in
Bale's commentary this angel at the fourth trumpet signified
those special servants of God who had prophesied the fall
from faith of the Roman Church.

At the close of the chronicle Bale placed a short series of
'Prophecies of Joachim Abbas' taken from Guido of Perpignan's *Summa de haeresibus.*[55] The prophecies asserted that
the latter days would be governed by a 'lawe of Lyberte',
that the Church would become purified and men learned.
The preachers would be more effective in converting the
people than in the days of the Apostles. Further, the Church
of Rome would be destroyed, as the Jewish synagogue had
been in the past, and a spiritual church would succeed. Although this material followed after the main business of the
chronicle, it is clear that Bale considered it appropriate to
place the Lollard martyr in a context that echoed his own
views on the interpretation of the Revelation.

A mysterye of inyquyte repeated the major themes of

[53] Higden, *Polychronicon*, trans. John of Trevisa, Rolls Series 41, vol. v, p. 131.

[54] British Library, MS. Harl. 2261, discussed in Higden, ed. cit. above, n. 53.

[55] Miss Reeves writes 'A note says that the prophecies are drawn from Guido
of Perpignan's *Summa de haeresibus*, written *c.* 1342 and this is, in fact, so. It is
not quite clear if the linking of Joachim's prophecy to the Lollard martyr was
made by a Lollard or by Bale himself. I am inclined to think the former.' *Influence of Prophecy*, p. 475 n. 1. Because elsewhere, principally in the *Image*, Bale
was chary of too much speculation on the nature of the future age, tending rather
to emphasize peace in and among nations than to speak of laws of liberty, I
would agree with Miss Reeves that Bale was here reproducing an association found
in one of his Lollard sources.

The Image of bothe churches Part I, but without the attempt
to tie them to the text of the Apocalypse as part of a consistent interpretation. Its main theme was the slow and secret
advance of Antichrist in the Church. Although the 'great
Antichrist' of the papacy was the central malefactor, the
term Antichrist was also used in the manner acceptable to
Tyndale. This was also true of Part I of his commentary,
where Bale admitted that the pope had not always been Antichrist, nor had the founders of the monastic orders themselves been Antichrist's servants.[56] The mystery of iniquity
had been the gradual corruption of the Church, chiefly
through the agency of wealth and power, culminating in the
great Antichrist of the papacy. The proof that this process
had taken place lay in the moral and doctrinal variance of the
Roman Church from the apostolic Church.

Between 1543 and 1545 Bale completed Part II of his
commentary on the text of the Apocalypse. In Part II the
dominant theme was persecution and martyrdom. The two
witnesses were not, as popularly supposed, Enoch and Elijah,
whose translation, Bale explained, was intended for a witness
to their own age and as a figure of Christ's own ascension.
Instead the two witnesses in the Apocalypse were Moses and
Christ, one representing the law and the Old Testament, the
other the gospel and the New Testament. In the final age the
witnesses became the true preachers of that gospel and also
the martyrs under Antichrist. Bale's long list of martyrs concentrated on the English ones from the time of Lollardy to
his present. To this he added the name of Patrick Hamilton
for Scotland. These martyrs held a special place in the progress of the Apocalypse as the signification of the second woe
under the sixth trumpet.[57] The third and final woe came
under the seventh trumpet and was the battle of Gog and
Magog with the Church.

In the twelfth chapter of the Revelation, Bale interpreted
the woman as the Church and the dragon as the Devil—the
usual interpretation. However, Bale's comment on the heads
and horns of the dragon spun off into another universal pattern of history. Each of the seven heads took the form of a
figure of deceit or idolatry. The first head Bale described as

---

[56] Bale, *Image*, pp. 327-9.   [57] *Image*, pp. 387-99.

that of a serpent because of the temptation of Eve and the Fall. The second he described as that of a calf because of the beginning of idolatry under Nimrod. Then came four heads signifying the four beasts of the four monarchies: the lion for the pride of the Assyrians, the bear for the cruelty of the Persians, the leopard for the fickleness of the Greeks, and the strange beast for the bad laws of the Romans. The seventh head resembled the head of a man and signified the carnal lust of the papacy. The last head was responsible for the subduing of the Roman Empire.[58] The description of the seven heads was not part of the text of Revelation, nor was it explicitly given in Daniel 7 where a similar beast was described. The heads of the four beasts and the monarchies described corresponded to the four beasts of Daniel 7, and the head of a man resembled the little horn among ten in the same chapter. The serpent and the calf were two images of idolatry for the times before Daniel. Bale may have found this in one of the commentaries he read, but having abandoned his detailed system of references, he gave no source. It may have been original, but it is surprising that Bale, whose virtues rarely included quiet humility, did not make more fuss over these images if they were his own.

The same seven heads also symbolized the seven periods or sorts of times in the history of the Church from Christ. The serpent's head depicted the resistance of Judaism to Christ; the calf's head, the persecutors of Christianity; the lion's head, the bold heretics of the early Church; the bear's head, the holy hypocrites and usurpers of empire, those founders of the papacy and Muhammadanism; the leopard's head signified the sects and the locusts; the head of a strange beast, the wicked governors and tyrants responsible for the slaying of the witnesses. The head of the man symbolized worldly policy and falsehood like that found in the Roman Church.[59]

The woman was sent into the wilderness and a battle was waged in heaven, resulting in the binding of Satan in the pit. Bale granted the dragon during his confinement the power to subvert. In Part II, Bale contradicted his interpretation in

[58] *Image*, pp. 387-99. R. Bauckham has traced this interpretation to Francis Lambert. op. cit., p. 36, n. 68.

[59] *Image*, pp. 407-8.

Part I of the binding of Satan, and reiterated his interpretation given in *Yet a course at the Romyshe foxe*. The beast
that arose from the sea symbolized the universal Antichrist.
This beast also had seven heads and ten horns, and reminded
Bale of the beast with ten horns in Daniel. However, the
beast in the Apocalypse had been given power by the dragon
and worked a mystery of iniquity which surpassed the
tyranny of the beast in Daniel's prophecy. The Reformation
had wounded the apocalyptic beast, but because it was not
complete, and because the King of England had entertained
reactionary policies, the wound was healed. The beast that
arose out of the earth signified the false prophets, and his
two horns symbolized the corruption of the two testaments.[60] The number of the beast, 666, had had many interpretations put upon it, but Bale preferred the one he found
put forward by a disciple of Wyclif, in which the substitution
of letters for numbers yielded a Greek word transliterated
as 'arnume' meaning 'I deny'. The number is also described
as the number of man, the number six. This stands for the
six days of Creation, the six ages to the coming of Christ, and
from the Ascension the six ages or seals of the Apocalypse.
Following each of these three sixes comes a sabbath, of creation, of the spirit, and of peace followed, after a shortened
time, by joy. This was said to be the hidden significance of
the forty-two months in that the two numbers involved, six
and seven, multiplied into forty-two.[61] As far as I know, in
the sixteenth century this convoluted Joachimist-sounding
interpretation was not repeated after Bale.

Bale's interpretation of the two beasts and of a universal
Antichrist was greatly influenced by the Wyclifite tradition.
The central figure of the Antichrist held for Bale, as it came
to do for Calvin, both a spiritual and a historical meaning.
Bale referred to the universal Antichrist in opposition to the
Church throughout its history, and hastened to assure his
readers that the Apocalypse was neither an allegory nor a
prophecy restricted to the final three and a half years of
history.

For we must consider that this revelation is in all points no story,

---

[60] *Image*, pp. 420-7.   [61] *Image*, p. 449.

specially here, as many writers have thought it to be, in supposing an antichrist to be born at the latter end of the world. But it is a mystery comprehending in it but one general antichrist for all, which hath reigned in the church since the ascension of Christ.[62]

Tyndale had interpreted Antichrist to allow his existence throughout the entire history of man and the Church, which began with the Creation and continued through the Old Testament times to Christ, and from him to the present. Bale limited the universal Antichrist to the history of the Christian Church from the Ascension, and described the appearance of a final embodiment of Antichrist in the papacy as a result of the historical workings of a mystery of iniquity, just as Calvin explained that Antichrist was not properly in existence before the establishment of the papacy but that his mystery had been at work in the Church long before then.

As a dramatist, Bale had laid great emphasis upon the function of infidelity, which became a leading character in *A Comedy concerning three laws* and took the guise of a monk in *King John*. If during his years in Switzerland he came under the influence of Calvin, Calvin's belief in the final apostasy would only have reinforced an idea he already held. However, this idea and phrase 'the mystery of iniquity', and its function in the subversion and alteration of the papacy into the great Antichrist, presents a more striking similarity. Calvin used the phrase in the first Latin edition of his commentary on Thessalonians, published in Strasburg in 1540. Bale's tract was written in 1542, and published in Geneva in 1545.

George Joye continued to be active. In 1545 he published in Geneva a collection in English of interpretations of Daniel by continental reformers.[63] The interpretation of Daniel's prophecies dealt with the kingdoms of the world, their rise and decline at the will of God, and for this reason Joye described Daniel as 'A Prophecie diligently to bee noted of al Emperoures & kinges, in these last daies'.[64] Michael Wood, the printer for Joye's work on Daniel, also printed in the same year Bale's *A mystery of inyquyte*.

[62] *Image*, p. 442.
[63] George Joye, *The exposicion of Daniel the Prophete* gathered oute of Philip Melanchton, Johan Ecolampadius, Chonrade Pellicane & out of Johan Draconite &c. . . . (Geneva, 1545).
[64] Ibid., title-pages.

During 1546 and 1547 Bale returned to the more historical
and polemical side of his writing, producing in 1546 *The Acts
of Englysh Votaryes*, an exposé of monastic history and practices, rather like Tyndale's *Practice of Prelates* but aimed at
the monastic orders rather than the papal supremacy. Bale
blamed the enforcement of chastity for the moral degeneracy
of monasticism, and pointed out the late introduction of a
celibate priesthood by an antichristian papacy. In July 1546
his name appeared on a list of books prohibited in England;
among his works prohibited was *The Image of bothe
churches*.[65] In November 1546, Bale published the first
examination of Anne Askew, which was followed in 1547
by the second. This was another in the series of martyr
stories, but dealing with a contemporary and drawing parallels between the prosecution of Wyclif, the 'sacred Blandena',
and that of contemporary martyrs.

In Part II of *The Image of bothe churches*, Bale had made
a point of the importance of martyrdom in the history of the
Church, and had hinted at the transformation of the two
cities, represented in the Apocalypse by Jerusalem and Babylon, into two kinds of people and two churches, one dedicated to the spirit and one to the flesh.[66] Part III was intended
to make that distinction more clear by a commentary on
Revelation 20-2. These chapters contained the promise of
the millennium, the two resurrections, the new heaven and
new earth. In Part II, Bale had hesitated to comment on
prophecies as yet unfulfilled. In Part III, he kept closely
within the bounds of figurative exposition for these images,
but he used this further opportunity to define more closely
in historical terms the gradual fall of the Church from purity.
The dragon bound for a thousand years in the pit again presented some problem. Bale was no longer content to explain
the fall of the Church by the invisible workings of a mystery
of iniquity. He suggested that Pope Sylvester II had released
the devil[67] from the pit about the year 1000 through the
agency of the black arts.[68] However, long before this, about

---

[65] John Foxe, *Acts and Monuments*, v, p. 568.   [66] *Image*, p. 411.
[67] The dragon, the devil, and Satan, were names used by Bale to indicate the
dragon in Rev. 12.
[68] *Image*, p. 561.

the year 600, Antichrist, working not universally but among
the wicked, had visibly gained for himself two kingdoms: the
Roman Church through the subversion of the papacy, especially the corruption of Boniface III in his agreement with
the Emperor Phocas, and the Saracens and Turks through the
apostate Muhammad. The universal kingdom of Antichrist
did not long go unchallenged, for soon the first preachers
prefigured in the two witnesses began to preach and suffer
martyrdom.[69]

Bale handled the touchy question of the millennium in
allegorical terms. The millennium in Revelation 20: 11 was
meant to signify eternity.[70] The first resurrection was from
sin to repentance and from ignorance to knowledge. This
resurrection was in the process of fulfilment at the present
time in the work of the Reformation. After this resurrection
came the battle of Gog and Magog with the faithful. Bale
sought an explanation of the genealogy of Gog and Magog
among the opinions of his predecessors. Josephus said that
the Greeks called the Scythians Magog. In Ezekiel, however,
Magog was described as the prince of Mosoch and Tubal,
which some expositors took to mean Spain. Bale preferred
the explanation given by Jerome and Isidorus, who believed
these princedoms signified Italy.[71] Gog represented the hypocrites and Magog the open enemies in the Apocalypse. Taking
the indication of both the text and the history, Bale concurred with the identification of them with the pope and the
Turk.

And all the chief writers specify the Turks of them [Magog and the
Scythians] to have their first original. Now mark this wonderful mystery, and consider therein both the time and story. So shall ye well
perceive the Holy Ghost to mean none other by this Gog and Magog,
but the Romish pope and the Mahomet, with their blasphemous and
wicked generations. Search the chronicles, and ye shall find that their
beginnings were base, and their estate simple, before the thousand years
were finished. But after that they grew up so high by their feigned simplicity and simulated holiness, that they became the two chief monarchs
of the earth, and so in process ruled the universal world.[72]

Further, these two are the horns of the great Antichrist. Bale
also alludes here to the belief that after the weakening of the
fourth monarchy there would arise a fifth universal power

[69] Image, pp. 562-3. [70] Image, p. 567. [71] Image, pp. 570-1. [72] Image, p. 571.

founded on deceit like the one mentioned in Daniel 11, which Bale represented as the seventh head of the dragon, the head like that of a man.

Bale approached the subject of the new heaven and the new earth as cautiously as he had that of the millennium. Without denying that the renovation of the creation would be physical as well as spiritual,[73] he sought to lay his emphasis on the spiritual renovation of God's glory, which had suffered a defilement in heaven because of the angel Lucifer and on earth because of the fall of man. He made little of the question of the saints' rule with Christ on earth, saying, 'Much to and fro hath been among the school-doctors, and is yet to this day, whether the saved multitude shall reign here upon earth with Christ or above in heaven after the judgement day.'[74] Bale suggested that the kingdom might include both heaven and earth, or that after a time on earth the kingdom would be taken up into heaven. In all his considerations of the millennial kingdom, he never thought that more than the first signs of it were contained in the history of the Reformation, nor that it could be predicted in the foreseeable future. These were the high mysteries which, like the mystery of iniquity in the papacy, could not be detected or identified until after the event.[75]

Despite having accepted a progressive historical interpretation of the prophecies, Bale had based his conclusions about the course of history, and most of his identifications of image with event, on moral or doctrinal characteristics and not on their place in the text or on a suggestion of a hidden chronology in the mystic numbers. His understanding of history might be summarized as a belief in the interdependence between Scripture and chronicle. While prophecies had foretold the coming struggle and the natures of the two churches, it was only in the chronicles that evidence of their fulfilment could be seen. Thus the study of the chronicles was of immense importance, and so marvellously did they illustrate Protestant argument that Bale, like Luther, rejoiced at the discovery.

For besides all that is afore expressed, it [the Book of Revelation] containeth the universal troubles, persecutions and crosses, that the

---

[73] *Image*, p. 581.   [74] *Image*, p. 587.   [75] *Image*, p. 588.

church suffered in the primitive spring, what it suffereth in the latter times by the subtle satellites of antichrist, which are the cruel members of Satan. . . . A prophecy is the Apocalypse called, and is much more excellent than all the other prophecies. . . . It is a full clearance to all the chronicles and most notable histories which have been wrote since Christ's ascension, opening the true nature of their ages, times, and seasons. He that hath store of them, and shall diligently search them over, conferring the one with the other, time with time, and age with age, shall perceive most wonderful causes. For in the text are they only proponed in effect, and promised to follow in their seasons, and so ratified with the other scriptures: but in the chronicles thay are evidently seen by all ages fulfilled. Yet is the text a light to the chronicles, and not the chronicles to the text.[76]

In an age dedicated to the purification of the text and rigour of biblical exegesis, Bale's interest in history stands out. Although Scripture and history were equally important parts of the argument, the method and direction of approach were also important. One should view the chronicles in the light of Scripture and not the Scripture in the light of the chronicles, he said. This exhortation on method is a warning not to take the chronicles at their face value, nor to accept the standards and judgements of their writers. They must be accepted in the first place in their own context as a reflection of the progress of prophetic fulfilment. Both the chronicles and their writers must then be judged by the standards and values revealed in Scripture. Despite his insistence on the primacy of Scripture, it is clear where Bale felt the work remained to be done. He was asking as a matter of urgency for a more thorough and critical approach to historical sources. Whenever circumstances permitted him, he would return to his first love, the collection and study of England's antiquities, but that passion would never be distinct from his passion for the reform of religion in the light of Scripture.

Taken as a whole, Bale's *The Image of bothe churches* marked the beginning of original activity in the apocalyptic tradition on the part of the English reformers. Bale's commentary was characterized throughout, but especially in the first part, by a profound knowledge of earlier writers, particularly of the medieval and Wyclifite school. The reintroduction of Joachim's belief in the progressive revelation of history under the seven seals provided him with a starting-point

[76] *Image*, Preface, p. 252.

for his departure from a purely spiritual and essentially timeless interpretation of the prophecies. Bale did not disregard
the spiritual and moral interprctation. From Augustine's two
cities and the eternal opposition of the spirit and the flesh,
he derived an earthly conflict between two sorts of men, the
faithful and the unfaithful, and their two churches, of Christ
and Antichrist.[77] But the history of both these churches was
hidden in the mysteries of the Apocalypse and could be discovered by comparison of prophecy with the history recorded in the chronicles, and that history proceeded under the
figures of the seven seals. In Part II and thereafter, Bale gave
particular meaning to the idea of the Apocalypse as the revelation of the Church's sufferings by concentrating his exposition on particular martyrs, giving lists in most cases. In the
same period he chose martyrs from British history through
whose biographies he intended to support his convictions
with historical materials. By the time he wrote Part III Bale
had begun to define the periods of the seven seals by reference
to dates or single events rather than to 'seven sorts of times'
which in Part I had indicated chronological progression only
vaguely.

Bale's interest in the Apocalypse remained with him when
he returned to England in the summer of 1548. Upon his arrival, he took up residence in London at the home of Marie Fitz-
roy, where John Foxe was also living at the time, and there
began a lifelong friendship with him.[78] Bale's efforts upon his
return were dictated by his desire to give England greater
knowledge of her past. He had found on his travels abroad
that Europe did not respect English scholarship as much as he
thought she should do. In order to rectify this universal
ignorance of British worth, he had begun his catalogue of
British writers, and continued his work on it when he returned
to England. In the course of his journeys up and down England
in search of authors and manuscripts to add to his lists, he
saw many things that kept him on the verge of tears.[79] The

[77] *Image*, Part II, p. 411.
[78] J. F. Mozley, *John Foxe and his Book* (London and New York, 1940), p. 29.
[79] John Bale, *The Laboryouse Journey & serche of J Leylande for Englandes
Antiquitees* . . . (London, 1549), hereinafter *Laboryouse Journey*; The Preface,
Avii.

monasteries had been dissolved and their manuscript trea-
sures sold. Few of them, he lamented, had fallen into careful
hands.

A great nombre of them whych purchased those superstycyouse man-
syons, reserved of those lybrarye bokes, some to serve theyr cakes,
some to scoure theyr candelstykes, & some to rubbe their bootes. Some
they solde to the grossers and sope sellers, & some they sent over see to
ye bokebynders, not in small numbers, but at tymes whole shyppes full,
to the wonderynge of the foren nacyons.[80]

Among his fellow antiquarians Bale admired the efforts of
John Leland. But by then Leland was hopelessly mad. In
1549 Bale wrote a gloss on Leland's *A New Year's Gift* to
King Henry presented in 1536. In this he wrote the words
quoted above and sought to interest his readers in the
recovery and study of what had been lost or disregarded over
the past years. His heartfelt plea was delivered with a sense of
shame both because of the things he had seen and because
'For so lytle. estemynge our true Antiquytees, the proude
Italyanes have alwayes holden us for a Barbarouse nacyon.'[81]
His main theme was the profit from and necessity for the
study of antiquity. In the context of Leland's letter, this subject need not have turned his mind to the prophecies of
Daniel and the Apocalypse. Nevertheless it did so, showing
that Bale's belief in the correspondence between the prophecies and history was not simply a polemical device, or just a
convenience in theology.

By the hystoryes of Antiqyte, are the natures of all ages of the
worlde manyfested from tyme to tyme, & also both the prophecyes of
Daniel and of S. Johans revelacyon more easely of their readers under-
standed. For he that marketh not by the serche of ernest chronycles,
the dysposycyon of tymes, shall never beholde those godly prophecyes
fulfylled in effect. And therfore sayth Leylande here, that thys profyte
amonge other hath ryson of hys studyouse labour. Antichrist and hys
mynysters are lyke to be the better knowne, and their tyrannouse
usurpacyons perceyved how shamefullye they have abused the dygnyte
of Kynges.[82]

For the most part, the chronicles were filled with the fables,
superstitions, and deliberate lies of the monks, but Bale pleaded that they should nevertheless be saved, and in the first
instance even published as they stood.[83] Like Tyndale, Bale

---

[80] Bale, *Laboryouse Journey*, Bi[r].   [81] Ibid., Cv[r].   [82] Ibid., Cv[v]–Cvi[r].
[83] Ibid., Ciii[v].

believed that the corruption of histories was one of the chief
activities of the antichristian Church, whereby Antichrist had
increased error and superstition over the ages, so that in the
sixteenth century they found 'for true hystories most fryvo-
louse fables and lyes, that we might the sonner by the devils
suggestion fall into moste depe errours, and so be lost for
not belevynge the truth'.[84] Besides preserving the original
state of these chronicles as a witness to their own corruption,
Bale desired that the history be rewritten to express the
truth. In his own study of John Oldcastle he made it clear
that for him this was, after the translation of Scripture, the
greatest task that lay before the Reformation.

I would wish some learned Englishmen (as there are now most excellent
fresh wits) to set forth the English Chronicles in their right shape . . .
I cannot think a more necessary thing to be laboured to the honour of
God, beauty of the realm, erudition of the people, and commodity of
other lands, next to the sacred scriptures of the Bible, than that work
would be.[85]

John Leland had laboured long and well, but was now incapable of completing his work. He had not mentioned the
prophecies of Daniel or those of the Apocalypse, but Bale
made up for this oversight by bringing them into his discussion of Leland's letter whenever possible. In one place,
Leland referred to England as an empire, but Bale, being well
enough aware of Daniel's limitation of empire to the pre-
scribed four, sought an explanation of or an apology for
Leland's slip. 'In that he calleth Englande an empire he doth
non otherwyse than did bothe Josephus and Egesippus wyth
other notable historianes.'[86] England was described by one of
these authors as another world beyond the ocean, where presumably the limitation of the four monarchies did not apply.
Except as a revelation of European history, the four monarchies held very little contemporary significance for Bale. Towards the end of his gloss, Bale commended the Apocalypse
chapters 6, 8, 9 as 'a perfighte & sure towchstone, wherby all
ages, doctrines, actes & tytles are from tyme to tyme tryed,
of what estymacyon and value they apere in Gods sighte, to
make us godly wise in receyvyenge them'.[87]

For the next few years Bale concentrated his efforts on the

---

[84] Bale, *Laboryouse Journey*, Diii[r].   [85] Bale, *Oldcastle*, p. 8.
[86] Bale, *Laboryouse Journey*, Dvi[r].   [87] Ibid., Hvii[r].

search for and the cataloguing of the antiquities of Britain. Although, as I have tried to show, this work was connected in his mind with his work on the prophecies of the Revelation, he did not continue to develop his views and only returned to the questions involved when fate once again cast him upon the shores of Europe, an exile from Mary's England. In the meantime that other important figure of the period, George Joye, involved himself more deeply in a stream of the tradition that had as yet found no English exponent or contributor. In 1548 he published in Antwerp his translation of Andreas Osiander's conjectures concerning the end of the world. Osiander's niece was married to the Archbishop of Canterbury, a fact which may have influenced Joye's choice of author for his new translation. None the less the work was in keeping with the interest he had shown in the interpretation of prophecies. In the preface to his earlier venture in this field, his collection of commentaries on Daniel by Protestant authors, he had emphasized Daniel's revelations depicting the wickedness of the Roman Church, but had not connected the Book of Daniel with the Book of Revelation in order to show a historical progression in the prophecies. Osiander's work, however, was an attempt to do this and to find predictive chronological significance in the text of the prophecies. Osiander himself was one of a group of German Protestant astronomers who like Carion combined interest in religion with their interest in science. He corresponded with Copernicus and wrote the preface to Copernicus's *De Revolutionibus Orbium Coelestium* (1542).

Joye's translation of Osiander's conjectures was one of the earliest works published for English readers which used prophecy as a guide to chronology and as a tool for periodization and prediction. It was followed in 1550 by an English translation of *Carion's Chronicle*, also published in London. Thus in effect by 1550, both aspects of the apocalyptic tradition had crossed the Channel to find a home in England, and an original contribution to one of them had been made by an Englishman.

Joye's editing of the expositions of Daniel had prepared him to receive Osiander's further-reaching conclusions about the end of the world. He sometimes interrupted his translation

to comment on the apparent agreement between Osiander's
conclusions and those he himself had drawn in his work on
Daniel.[88] In his preface to the reader, Joye expressed the
approach to the interpretation of prophecy that drew no distinction between methods to be used in interpreting prophecies already fulfilled and those appropriate to understanding
prophecies not yet fulfilled. He commended the book by
Osiander for the comfort and profit of the elect.

And for asmuch as this boke treateth of the signes and conjectures, that
go before the ende of this world, wherof some be paste, some are
present, & some are yet shortely to come, and do tell us certainly the
tyme of the fall of the Antichriste of Rome, and laste ende of thys
myserable synfull worlde, layd in so darke Prophecyes, noumbers of
dayes, tymes & years in Daniell, and in the Apocalipse . . . I have made
thys latyne boke . . . to speake Englysh. . . .[89]

Osiander began his book with an apology for his curiosity,
saying that although the day and hour were rightly kept
secret from the world, the age or year might be learned from
the Scriptures. His was not the idle curiosity of the common
people, but that of the 'wyser and better lerned' men whom
God had given occasion to search out the meaning of his
words. Osiander said that as his conjectures had occurred to
him over the years, he had written them out and sent them
among his friends. These friends were now dispersed throughout Europe, and lest his opinions be stolen he had asked for
their return and had written this book.[90]

Osiander had four principal conjectures to place before his
readers. 'The first conjecture is taken out of Elie the Prophete, which the Jewes recite as out of the mouth of God,
spoken in diverse places of theyr bokes called Thalmude.' He
gave the references in Abodazara and Sanhedrin, and quoted
the prophecy as the saying of the 'house or scole of Elie' in
the usual manner.[91] Although this prophecy was not to be
found in Christian Scripture, it should be believed because it
agreed with Moses in the Psalms and with St. Peter's comparison of 1,000 years with a day in God's sight and the seven
days of Creation. As a subsection to this correspondence of
Elias to the world-week, Osiander referred to conjectures

[88] Andreas Osiander, *The conjectures of the ende of the worlde*, trans. George
Joye (Antwerp, May 1548), Gvii[v].
[89] Ibid., Aii[v].   [90] Ibid., Aiii[v]-Av[r].   [91] Ibid., Av[v].

made by Giovanni Pico della Mirandola in 1486, which he
had based on a search through the Cabbala, a practice which
Osiander did not condemn. Among Pico's ninety conclusions
was one in which the seventh generation of man at the time
of Enoch and Elias, both of whom were translated to heaven
without dying, corresponded to the seventh millennium of
world history, in which men would be immortal. However,
Osiander had reason from the Prophecy of Elias to expect
that the sixth millennium would be shortened and part of its
time added to the seventh. The end and the age of immortality were therefore somewhat nearer than Pico had suggested.[92]

The second conjecture was based on Matthew 24 and Mark
13, which stated that the day and hour of the second coming
were not to be known, but that the days before the Son of
Man were to be like the days before the Flood, 'for in these
wordes, Christe semeth not to compare only the qualyte but
also the quantite of the tyme'. From Adam to the Flood was
1,656 years; so from the second Adam, Christ, to the end of
the world would be the same 1,656 years.[93] Like the second,
the third conjecture devised a way to predict the end. From
the birth of Christ to his passion was thirty-three years, and
Christ as the son of Holy Church signified by his life the
length of the time the Church shall stand. These thirty-three
years were 'great years', which in the language of prophecy
could stand for either of two things. One was what Osiander
called the angel's year or a year of year-days calculated from
the lunar year at 354 days. The other was the great year that
Moses used, indicating the great year as one of Jubilee, coming every fifty years. The former overran Elias' prophecy and
so was discounted; the latter gave thirty-three times fifty or
1,650, within six years of his preceding conjecture. The remaining six years he accounted for in terms of those days
over the age of thirty-three that Christ lived.[94] Further conjectures using those two methods were based on events in the
life of Christ. A year spent in Egypt equalled the years the
early Church suffered persecution under Diocletian. Christ
became lost in the Temple at the age of 12; twelve times

---

[92] Osiander, *The conjectures of the ende of the worlde*, Av-Aviii.
[93] Ibid., Bi-Bii.   [94] Ibid., Bii-Biii.

fifty gave A.D. 600, a time when the Church was confused by a number of heresies and one at which could be seen the rise of the power of both the papacy and the Turks. But Christ was found in the Temple quite quickly, indicating that even in a dark age some found him in the Scriptures. Then at the age of 30 he was baptized and began his preaching. The multiplication gave the date 1500, the dawn of the century of the Reformation.[95] These clever sums could be done in many ways, but the critical dates he discovered were always those that supported the emerging Protestant version of the past. The fourth conjecture,[96] which to Osiander was 'of all the most evident', was based entirely upon an interpretation of Daniel and the Apocalypse. These two prophecies told of the two dominions of Rome over the world. The first revealed in Daniel the rule of the Roman city; the second revealed in the Apocalypse the rule of the Roman court. Osiander sided with those who had maintained that the little horn among ten signified the career of Julius Caesar, but he was aware that another interpretation given by Luther had won the agreement of most Protestants.

I knowe certain men of great name (from whose jugement I dissent not gladly without a cause) to think this lytle horne to have ben that wyked Mahumete and pope, but because this Romane Kingdom wherof Da. here speaketh, was utterly destroid before Mahumete was borne and pope to bere grete rule. And because Mahumete ne pope was never member of the Romane empire, nether the Apoca. in hir x. later hornes maketh mencion of Mahumete, I dout not their sentence (by their favor I speke it) plainly to be refused.[97]

In further support of this argument, Osiander echoed the familiar Christian interpretation of the four monarchies, that at the time of Christ all such monarchies were ended and power given to Christ. This, Osiander maintained, was what should have happened, but Rome wickedly held on to her power until she was eventually overthrown by the translation of empire to Constantinople and then finally destroyed by the barbarian invasions and burnings.[98]

The later domination of Rome revealed in the Apocalypse told of the beast wounded by the death of Caesar, but healed under Augustus, and in the phrase 'was, is not, and will be'

[95] Osiander, *The conjectures of the ende of the worlde*, Bvi.
[96] Ibid., Chapter IIII, Ci[v]. [97] Ibid., Ciii[r]. [98] Ibid., Dv.

looked forward to the usurpation of power by the papacy. Daniel's time and times and half a time, interpreted by the angel's months into angel's days, using the Roman month of 30 days, equalled 1,260 years, which was also the three years and a half given to the beast.[99] In this instance, Osiander was in complete agreement with Protestant leaders against the traditional Catholic belief.

I can not but mervell excedingly & vehemently also howe it shuld happen that men, I wyll not call them lerned, but rude & unlettered, which shuld have but only a crum of humane reason and witte, shuld be brought to beleve, that al these things, which Joan here, & Paul to ye Thessa. have prophecied of this beast might be fynisshed & done within the space of iii of our yearis and an half. . . .[1]

From this point on, Osiander's interpretation offered few surprises. The number of the beast, 666, he interpreted by letter-substitution as 'Lateinos' and says that in Hebrew the sound of the word obtained is 'Rhomah'. Paul's warning about the man of sin indicated that the person would be revealed before the end, and had been in the pope.[2]

Joye became involved in conjecture himself. At the end of his translation, he added a thought of his own based on the closing verses of Daniel 12. The abomination of the beast began in the year 287, in the reign of Diocletian, when heresies abounded. From that date to the year 1577 were 1,290 angel's days, the figure mentioned in Daniel from the beginning to the end of that abomination.[3]

The English edition of *Carion's Chronicle* translated by Walter Lynne carried with it an addition by John Funck of Nuremberg[4] which brought the chronicle up to date. This continuation emphasized a type of material which Carion had used only occasionally, and to which he had not given much weight. At the end of *Carion's Chronicle* the years from 1530 to 1532 were marked by signs in the heavens, comets and the

---

[99] Osiander, *The conjectures of the ende of the worlde*, Ev–Evi[v].

[1] Ibid., Evii.   [2] Ibid., Fiv–Fvi.   [3] Ibid., Gvii–Gviii.

[4] John Funck (1518–66) was the son-in-law of Andreas Osiander and a supporter of his opinions. He was beheaded in Königsberg in 1566 for causing trouble in the state. Besides this addition to Carion, he wrote a chronology from the Creation to the Resurrection (Nuremberg, 1545), a biography of Osiander, commentaries on Daniel in German (Wittenberg, 1565), and a commentary on the Apocalypse (Frankfurt, 1565), now extremely rare. Michaud, *Biographie universelle* (Paris, 1856).

like. Funck carried on from there to 1550, interspersing his
discussion of military and political alliances with many such
signs in the heavens and in visions seen by the townsfolk of
Brunswick in particular and also signs seen near Lübeck and
signs seen in Poland. In these areas splinter groups of radicals
had gained a local devotion amounting to hysteria.[5] The
incidents described included witchcraft[6] and near Lübeck
1,000 persons were reported to have witnessed a vision lasting a whole day and including: lions fighting, a man on horse-
back, a crowned man, a town consumed by fire, half a black
eagle with talons like snakes, a great bloody cross, and other
aerial displays in similar vein.[7] The Münster rebels were condemned for believing that their city was the New Jerusalem
and that all the heathen should be destroyed.[8] Although
Funck once said that not all he reported about these visions
might be absolutely true,[9] he noted that so many visions and
signs must be taken as a warning from heaven.[10] To Funck's
material, Walter Lynne, the printer, added a brief paragraph
on Anne Askew 'gathered out of historiographers' for the
year 1546.[11]

None of these visions occurred in England. This addition
to Carion never wielded as much influence as the original
chronicle came to do. Bale's *The Image of bothe churches*
was of more immediate importance to the course of the apocalyptic tradition in English-speaking Protestantism than
either this addition to Carion or the conjectures of Osiander.
Nevertheless, this material was available in England, and represented an interest and an approach current abroad. Towards
the end of the century, this aspect of the apocalyptic tradi-
-tion was to find its advocate in the Scottish mathematician

---

[5] Both before and after Münster, anabaptism took many forms in its spread
throughout Europe. G. H. Williams, *The Radical Reformation*, outlines many of
these, see esp. chapters 12, 14, 15 in connection with this area and time. Osiander
figured on the fringes of early anabaptism, and Funck died because of his radical-
ism in Prussia at about the time when Williams (p. 46) notes the appearance and
suppression of anabaptism there.

[6] Carion, *The thre bokes of cronicles* . . . whereunto is added an appendix by
John Funcke (London, 1550), fol. cci.

[7] Ibid., fols. cciii–ccvii; similar visions reported by persons living in Whitenhall,
fol. ccl; and in Brunswick, fol. cclxxv.

[8] Carion, op. cit., fol. cviii.   [9] Ibid., fol. ccxliv[v].   [10] Ibid., fol. cclxxvi.
[11] Ibid., fol. cclxx.

John Napier, and so re-enter the apocalyptic tradition in England and Scotland in greater strength.

During the reign of Edward, many exiles returned to England, and many continental Protestants, falling on hard times at home, followed. England became for a short time one of the most important centres of Protestant activity on an international scale. Friendships were made or furthered which would become useful when Mary came to the throne. Having gained the kingdom, the leaders of reform concentrated their efforts on questions of doctrine and practice, liturgy and discipline. Bale obtained a living in Hampshire and then a bishopric in Ireland, which effectively removed him from the company of his colleagues. During the years of seclusion he worked to recover and protect the antiquities of England, collecting in Ossory a library[12] he was later forced to abandon.

Apart from the now uninhibited publication of works written in exile dealing with the Apocalypse and the history of the Church, no important advance was made at this time in the development of the apocalyptic tradition. *The Image of bothe churches* was published twice in London, in 1550 and 1551. *The Acts of Englysh votaryes* was published three times in London, in 1548, 1550, and 1551. Another edition of the chronicle of John Oldcastle appeared in London during this period, possibly in 1548. Bale's gloss on Leland's gift to Henry was published in 1549. To these works by Bale may be added the translation of Osiander's conjectures in 1548 and of *Carion's Chronicle* in 1550.

Protestant interest in the Apocalypse during the 1540s was expressed in either of two ways: one in which the prophecies served as a guide on moral or doctrinal grounds to the character and historical manifestation of Antichrist; the other in which the prophecies assumed a chronological significance ranging through the whole of human history from the beginning in the past to the consummation in the future. Both of these had been potentially present in the German Reformation. Outside Lutheran Germany the former was initially the more successful among the reformers of the Rhineland and among the Henrican exiles. John Bale was first to be attracted

---

[12] Miss McCusker devotes a chapter to his Irish library, reconstructing as many titles as possible from his manuscript lists.

to the tradition by the implications of the discovery of Antichrist and his true character, but he gradually became interested in the full text of the Revelation as the schematic structure for the Church's history. His use of Joachim's central
image of the seven seals is important for the future development of the tradition. This was the first link between its two
branches, uniting a version of the past with a series of images
in the Apocalypse. He also gave new life and meaning to the
two cities, uniting them with the text of the Apocalypse by
seeking in it two parallel histories, of the true and the false
Church.

The development of the branch of the tradition represented for this period by Osiander's conjectures continued to be
a predominantly continental concern, and had no immediate
effect on the development of the tradition in Britain. Osiander
on the continent and Joye among the English exiles represented not the prevailing interpretation but an alternative that
verged on the extreme. The memory of Münster dampened
any enthusiasm for speculative chronology, but the fires of
curiosity were far from extinguished.

John Bale's contribution was the more significant for the
next period. He himself continued during the Marian exile to
exploit the connection between prophecy and history as part
of his tireless campaign to reform religion and history all at
once. As the Church had fallen into error so had the writers
of history. Both had forgotten Scripture. Bale's enthusiasm
for the place of written history in the preservation of faith
reached the heart and mind of his friend John Foxe. When
Foxe undertook his great work, he answered Bale's wish that
some learned Englishman should write the true history of the
Church. Bale's *The Image of bothe churches* identified by
their moral characters and actions the churches of Christ and
Antichrist; Foxe undertook to write the history of both
churches.

III

THE MARIAN EXILES AND FOXE'S
ACTS AND MONUMENTS

For the development of the apocalyptic tradition in Britain no six years were more important than those from 1553 to 1559. The period of the Marian exile, during which some eight hundred persons gathered in a few Protestant cities on the continent, was marked by close association and co-operation between the exiles and scholars from all over the Protestant world. In this period, Matthias Flacius Illyricus and the other centuriators of Magdeburg laboured to produce their immense statement of the new Lutheran historiography, soliciting advice and information from widely scattered students of history, including John Bale. John Philippson, better known as Sleidan, since 1542 professor of history at Strasburg, had finished his commentaries on the times of Charles V and was turning his attention to a revised and improved version of *Carion's Chronicle*. Jean Crespin of Geneva was hard at work on a martyrology, as was John Foxe. During these years, continental Protestantism enjoyed the facilities of many reformed or newly established academies and universities, as well as the goodwill of several influential printers, including Oporinus and Frobenius. Many of the best-educated exiles either took part in the life of the foreign universities or accepted employment at these presses. In the exiled communities themselves great emphasis was placed upon communal study. The study of Scripture and of Hebrew and Greek was an especially important feature of community life. The intellectual activities of the exiles and their relations with continental scholarship would be a subject in itself. The period was productive in many fields, one of which was certainly the study of history.

At first the exiles congregated in Strasburg, where Peter Martyr had many friends, or in Zürich, where Bullinger received them warmly. John Bale was one of the early arrivals in Strasburg, after a series of adventures which he recorded in an autobiographical sketch in which he likened his own sufferings to those of St. Paul.[1] Then in 1554 began the famous troubles in Frankfurt-on-Main. A large group of English exiles arrived in that city where, with the help of Melanchthon, they were granted refuge and the right to hold their own services under certain conditions. These conditions proved less demanding than the disagreements that arose among the exiles themselves. In 1554 Bale moved to Frankfurt. He was suggested by the Strasburg community as a possible candidate for the position of minister, but Knox, not Bale, was elected. In the middle of the troubles Foxe arrived in Frankfurt and sided with Knox against Bale who was then officially aligned with Cox. After a while the more radical party felt called upon to move to cities under the influence of the like-minded Calvin. Knox and Whittingham, who chronicled the troubles in Frankfurt, went to Geneva; Bale and Foxe, attracted by the publishing houses, moved to Basle. There they and some of their friends and their families rented an old convent from the city, and found employment where they could. Bale, Foxe, and Lawrence Humphrey worked together reading proofs from Oporinus's press. Bale kept track of the intellectual output of these exiles 'in collegio nostro'.[2] Towards the end of the exile Foxe wrote a book[3] for use by local university students, in appreciation of the help given him and his fellow-countrymen by the city and university.

Although much of the exiles' important work was done in this community at Basle, Protestant historians from all over Europe contacted each other in the pursuit of information. Jean Crespin read Foxe's *Commentarii*, which was written with the co-operation of Bale[4] and published in 1554, and on the basis of that reading Crespin altered the

---

[1] *The vocacyon of Johan Bale to the bishoprick of Ossorie in Irelande his persecucions in ye same, and finall delyveraunce* 'Imprinted in Rome, before the castel of S. Angell at ye signe of S. Peter in Decembre, Anno D. 1553' (Hugh Singleton, London, 1553?).

[2] Mozley, op. cit., p. 51.

[3] Foxe's *Locorum Communium Tituli*, described Mozley, p. 55.

[4] M. Aston shows that the *Commentarii* drew on Bale's additions to the *Fasciculi Zizaniorum*, 'Lollardy and the Reformation', *History* (1964), p. 167.

second edition of his own martyrology to give first place to Wyclif.[5] Before 1563 Foxe had read works by Crespin,[6] Sleidan,[7] and Flacius Illyricus[8] to which he referred with high praise. Crespin edited Sleidan's works in Geneva in 1556. By then Knox was there and quite possibly came to read Sleidan's *Commentaries*. In the next chapter we shall see how impressed Knox was by Sleidan's history and the influence it had on his own history of the Scottish Reformation. In 1555, the last year of Sleidan's life, Foxe obtained an introduction to Sleidan from Peter Martyr for a proposed visit to Strasburg.[9] In July 1554 Flacius Illyricus wrote to Bale saying he had heard of him through their mutual friend Alexander Alesius who had praised Bale's *Catalogues*. Flacius suggested further correspondence between them to aid in the compilation of the *Magdeburg Centuries*, and mentioned the names of other men in cities throughout Europe who were helping him gather material.[10] Bale was busy about his own publications and may not have been of great use to Flacius,[11] but he did help him with his *Varia Doctorum Piorumque Virorum* and *Catalogus Testium Veritatis*.[12]

Both at home and abroad the accession of Mary had put the reformers on the defensive. The evils of an antichristian conspiracy against the English Church loomed more prominently in their vision. Many of the works by Englishmen that poured from the continental presses were intended for English eyes and can be classed as propaganda.[13] They fell easily into the patterns already set by the Henrican exiles, Tyndale, Frith, Barnes, and Bale. During this period, however, the emphasis began to shift from an appeal to the monarchy to

[5] Mozley, op. cit., p. 119.

[6] Foxe, *Acts and Monuments of John Foxe*, 4th edition, revised and corrected by Josiah Pratt (Rel. Tract Soc., 1877), vol. iv, p. 351; hereinafter *A & M (1583)*.

[7] *A & M (1583)*, vol. ii, p. 706, vol. iv, p. 259.

[8] *A & M (1583)*, vol. ii, p. 778, vol. iv, p. 256.

[9] Mozley, p. 46. It is not known whether Foxe actually went to Strasburg.

[10] British Library, MS. Cotton Titus DX, fol. 180[v], printed in McCusker, p. 70.

[11] McCusker, pp. 62 f. suspects Bale gave little actual help in the writing.

[12] W. T. Davies, 'A Bibliography of John Bale', *Oxford Bibliographical Soc.: Proceedings and Papers*, 5 (1940), p. 227.

[13] C. H. Garrett, *The Marian Exiles* (Cambridge, 1938). This work continues to be the best starting-point for a study of the exiles.

an appeal to the Protestant people.[14] In the wake of events the themes of persecution and exile naturally took on a more prominent role in discussions of the faith, and bodies of militant opinion arose, determined to take all measures to overthrow antichristian tyranny. Gradually the apocalyptic language both increased in use and narrowed in definition, to identify the Antichrist of the prophecies with Rome.

One of the leaders of the propagandists who spoke for the exiles (although he himself was not one) was Nicholas Ridley. His experience illustrates the gradual process of the dawning of an apocalyptic consciousness during the early years of Queen Mary's reign. In a pamphlet entitled *Certain godly, learned, and comfortable conferences between Nicholas Ridley . . . and Hugh Latimer*, published posthumously in 1556 in Zürich but written several years earlier, Ridley gives a good picture of two Protestant leaders steeling themselves for the results of Mary's accession. Ridley spoke of following the laws of God before those of a prince and ended in a militant tone, preparing himself and his readers for the return of spiritual warfare. Dr. Christianson has pointed out that, despite this promising context, Ridley never once mentions Antichrist in the *Conferences*.[15]

However, not long afterwards, when England was once again officially reconciled with Rome and the trials of Protestant clergy were beginning, Ridley, himself destined to trial and execution, did address himself to the disclosing of Antichrist at Rome, going so far as to equate the Antichrist with the beast of Babylon whereon the whore was seated. By Babylon he meant 'the whole trade of the Romish religion . . . which is contrary to the only rule of all true religion, that is, God's word'—an interpretation which stressed the identification on grounds of doctrine and practice. Failing in the winter of

---

[14] Paul Christianson, 'Reformers and Babylon', chap. I. The unpublished revised version of his 'English Protestant Apocalyptic Visions 1536–1642' (Univ. of Minn. Ph.D. thesis, 1971; available through Univ. Microfilms Ltd.). Dr. Christianson concentrates his inquiry upon the development of contrasting appeals to monarchy (the 'imperial tradition') and to the persecuted congregation, thus providing continuous analysis of the political and social import of apocalyptic thought. His work follows on that of Christopher Hill and William Lamont and makes use of material in this and in other studies of apocalyptic thought.

[15] Ibid.

1554-5 to see any hope for the Reformation in England—
Mary was supposed pregnant—Ridley professed himself convinced that the world was nearing its end and in this fact lay
the hope that suffering might not be much longer endured.
He did not propose rebellion but only flight from affliction
and patience under it.[16]

These statements indicate a certain susceptibility to the
apocalyptic tradition. The conviction that the end of the
world was not long to be awaited, expressed with an emphasis that distinguishes it from a mere article of faith, and the
profound sense that the true spiritual meaning of his and his
fellows' sufferings was to be found in seeing them as part of
the struggle against Antichrist, betray the influence of the
tradition on his view of his own times. However, this is still
some way from the conviction that scriptural prophecy revealed the course of history in form and substance as well as
in spirit.

Much of the controversy among the exiles centred on the
question of resistance to tyranny and whether this should be
passive or active. On this question the positive identification
of Antichrist and his church, even his army, had some bear-
ing. So too did the question whether the prophecies of
Scripture and the experiences of the past coincided to give
either a pattern 'or a set of *exempla* whereby the current experience could be judged. Foxe, whose temperament drew
him towards sharing the passivity of the martyrs he chronicled, and Knox, whose inclination was anything but passive,
both turned their minds to the writing of history and to the
prophecies of the Apocalypse and Daniel.

Events at home and the opportunity for study found
abroad both contributed to the formation of the British
apocalyptic tradition during this period and for many years
after the return of the exiles. Although John Foxe's *Acts and
Monuments* did not reach maturity of expression until well
into the Elizabethan period, the first signs of an interest in
the use of the Apocalypse took shape between the 1554
Commentarii and the first edition of the English *Book of
Martyrs* in 1563. Foxe's interest in the Apocalypse may have

[16] Christianson, chap. I, the quotation is from *A Piteous Lamentation* (London, 1566) in Ridley, *Works* (Parker Soc., 1841), p. 53.

arisen in part through his friendship with Bale in the early Edwardian period, but the first signs of it do not appear before the Marian exile. From then onwards, Foxe's interest grew, continuing throughout his life and culminating in a commentary[17] on the Apocalypse, on which he was working when he died in 1586.

Two important traditions in historiography influenced the form of Foxe's history: one the older and well-established tradition for the writing of saints' lives, the other the form of historiography based on the history of dogma and doctrine, which originated in the Lutheran Reformation. At this time there were three major schools of religious historiography on the continent. One stressed the collection of biographies of Protestant martyrs or heroes; a form common to Britain and the continent and particularly attractive to the Christian humanist in the Erasmian tradition because of its reverence for example, and one in which the English and the Swiss were especially active.[18] A second school, arising out of the Lutheran and eastern German Reformation, stressed the continuity of doctrine among the faithful and the abandonment of true doctrine in the Roman Church. The third school, the most important from a modern standpoint, is characterized by the work of John Sleidan in which public records and documents were consulted in the search for a political and a religious history of the Reformation. This too was a legacy of humanism, but showed the influence of the more southern variety which followed after Lorenzo Valla and reached maturity in the Italian city histories. The Marian exiles, especially Foxe and Bale, were in contact with representatives of each of these three schools: Crespin in Geneva collected martyrs' lives; Sleidan in Strasburg, an ex-diplomatic emissary for the Protestant cause to Henry's England and to the Council of Trent and elsewhere in the name of the city of Strasburg, combined politics with his discussion of the development of the Reformation; and Matthias Flacius from the

---

[17] *Eicasmi seu meditationes in sacram Apocalypsin* (London, 1587), published by Foxe's son Samuel with a dedication to Whitgift. A description of this work was made by J. F. Mozley, op. cit., pp. 113–14, but its relation to his history was not discussed.

[18] Eduard Fueter, *Geschichte der neueren Historiographie* (Berlin, 1936).

Istrian peninsula, resident in Magdeburg, traced the fate of
true doctrine through each century of the Church's history.
Each of these representative hisgorians may be said to have
learned something from the others. Crespin, who edited
Sleidan's works after his death, greatly respected and employed Sleidan's methods for gathering material, as did Foxe.
Sleidan borrowed from the eastern German tradition the
belief in the primacy of doctrine, tracing the doctrinal
development of Lutheranism with its political fortunes rather
than writing a biography of Luther and his followers inter-
woven with a biography of Charles V. Sleidan too became
interested in prophecy as it applied to history, especially the
history of the four monarchies.

From the Book of Daniel, Sleidan drew conclusions about
the political situation of Germany fully in keeping with a
most informed and developed belief in the eternal finality of
Daniel's prophecies about the four monarchies. Like Carion,
Sleidan regarded the prophecies of Daniel as a revelation of
the 'succession and alterations' of kingdoms and religions.
This view was expressed not only in his world chronicle[19] but
also in his famous *Commentaries*[20] on which his reputation
rests today. The prophet assured Germany in these latter
times that the 'litle remnant of ye empire, although it be dry
& without juyce' was not to be superseded by any other empire 'for it is not possible to establishe a fifth monarchy'.[21]
From this same prophecy 'it plainly appeareth that ye course
of this world shal take end in this empyre, & none other shall
follow: but that all principalities of the world being abolished,
that perpetuall kingdome shall come, whereof Christ shalbe
the head & conductor'.[22] Sleidan believed that some of
Daniel's words and prophecies pertained only to the Jews,
but in the case of the four monarchies they had universal
significance. He came to the conclusion that 'This truly is
the time that daniel signifieth in ye xii Chap. . . .'[23] The

---

[19] Sleidan, *A briefe Chronicle of the foure principall Empyres* . . . englished
by Stephen Wythers (London, 1536), Biiii[v] (pages not numbered until fol. 10).

[20] Sleidan, *A Famouse Cronicle of oure time, called Sleidanes Commentaries*,
trans. John Daus (London, 1560), Preface Aiiii[r]; hereinafter *Commentaries*.

[21] *A briefe Chronicle* . . . , fol. 103[v].

[22] Ibid., fol. 102[r-v].   [23] Ibid., fol. 104[v].

importance of Daniel's prophecies was pastoral as well as political.

This is the principall cause of his prophecie: to the end that beyng advertised and certified of the calamities & miseries of the last time we shuld not be discouraged, but shuld waite for delivrance by the coming of Christ, who will come shortly after these afflictions, as he saith, & will carie his into a sure and peasible place, wyping al teares from their eies.[24]

Sleidan was particularly impressed by Daniel's 'prediction' of Alexander the Great 'above CC yeres and more before he raigned'. The prophecy painted Alexander 'so effectually, that it seemeth no prophecie, but some historie'.[25] Sleidan was of course nearer the truth than he realized. Not only did he become convinced of the validity of these prophecies for the past, but also he read in the prophecies of Scripture that

There be comming doubtless moste grevous commotions, and wonderful alterations. Which thing also the holy Scripture dothe nether doubtfullye nor darklye Prognosticate, and the present state of thinges doth plainly signify, so that such as will applye theyr minde here unto shall not want matter to wryte of.[26]

The above statement occurred in the *Commentaries*, showing a continuity in Sleidan's beliefs about prophecy in his history of Charles V and in his world chronicle. The use of Daniel was not a mere convenience for ordering world history, although Sleidan like Bale recognized that it made comprehension easier.

Of the three continental historians mentioned, Sleidan was the one whose influence in England was achieved mostly by his own works. The *Commentaries* and *De Quatuor Summis Imperiis* had several editions in England,[27] and in the seventeenth century enjoyed immense popularity among the Puritans.[28] Both Crespin and Flacius enjoyed far greater popularity among their own countrymen than in England. In England, Foxe combined the material and insight of both these men's works in his own *Acts and Monuments*, which

---

[24] *A briefe Chronicle* . . . , fol. 104^{r-v}.   [25] Ibid., fols. 102^v–103^r.

[26] *Commentaries*, Preface, Av^v.

[27] *Commentaries* had three issues in 1560; *De Quatuor Summis Imperiis* was the basis for English editions in 1536, 1584, 1627, 1631, 1635.

[28] Douglas Hamer, ed., *The Works of Sir David Lindsay of the Mount* (Scot. Text Soc., 1934), vol. iii (notes), p. 453 describes it as 'a text book of English chiliasm'.

was especially tailored to the English taste. In Scotland, which had no Foxe although it had a poor man's Sleidan in Knox, the *Magdeburg Centuries* was a far more prominent work.[29]

The 1554 *Commentarii* was almost complete when Foxe arrived on the continent, and was published by him at the first opportunity, probably in order to earn the exile some money.[30] This short work, more an essay on the life and doctrine of Wyclif in relation to the Reformation than the beginnings of an extensive history of martyrdom, contained very few references to the apocalyptic tradition and quoted the Book of Revelation only once as an end-piece. The quotation was from Revelation 7: 14-15 and described a great multitude of the faithful brought in triumph before the throne of the Lamb. This fitting quotation seems to have been chosen more for its descriptive powers than as an indication of place or time in any particular pattern of history. Nevertheless, the quotation did relate the persecuted Church triumphant in Revelation to the persecuted forerunners of the Reformation. Thus Foxe's use of the Apocalypse in 1554 followed more nearly the example of Erasmus and Calvin than that of Bale.

Foxe and Crespin (on whom the *Commentarii* had immediate effect) were both engaged in the same task, and neither at this time appears to have envisaged anything more than a collection of biographies illustrative of pre-sixteenth-century antecedents of Protestant doctrines. However, Crespin's *Actes des Martyrs* was more involved in the apocalyptic tradition than Foxe's *Commentarii*; Crespin traced among the proto-protestant opinions of the late medieval martyrs the opinion that Antichrist was revealed at Rome, and repeated the denunciations of Rome by Huss and Jerome of Prague as prophecies of the Reformation.[31] He included a quotation from the Book of Revelation, 6: 9, in his frontispiece. This quotation referred to the souls under the altar revealed by the opening of the fifth seal. Otherwise the internal organization

[29] Especially purchased abroad by an agent for James VI's library, see below, Chap. IV, p. 132.

[30] Mozley, op. cit., p. 118.

[31] Jean Crespin, *Actes des Martyrs* déduits en sept livres depuis le temps de Wiclef & de Hus, jusques à présent (Geneva, 1565), p. 80.

and the treatment of the material did not follow the patterns that had been discovered in the Apocalypse. The quotation could have been chosen for description alone, and the prophecies were corroborative evidence rather than essential arguments of the history. Foxe's 1559 *Rerum in ecclesia Gestarum* included a long list of prophecies of the Reformation given by Wyclif, Huss, Jerome of Prague, and others.[32]

Foxe moved to Basle after the publication of his *Commentarii* and once again lived in the same house as the irrepressible Bale. In July 1554 Flacius wrote to Bale about the work of the centuriators, and in 1555 Bale was at work on a contribution of his own to the cause of Protestant history of the Church. Bale's *Acta Romanorum Pontificum*[33] was compiled in a hurry and owed and acknowledged a tremendous debt to Robert Barnes's *Vitae Romanorum Pontificum*. Although Bale seems to have compared Barnes's work with some of his sources and to have augmented particularly good examples of corrupt popes, his greatest contribution to the work was his introductions and subdivisions of the material to illustrate the rise of Antichrist in accordance with the prophecies in the Book of Revelation. On the title-page, as it appeared in translation some years later, he described it as a work 'in the which is manyfestlye shewed the beginning of Antichriste and increasing to his fulnesse, and also the wayning of his power againe accordinge to the Prophecye of John in the Apocalips'.[34] The whole was divided into three books. The first covered the popes to Sylvester I, who were represented in the Apocalypse as the stars on the right hand of Christ (Chap. 1). The second contained the popes from Sylvester I to Boniface III whose deeds made way for Antichrist and who were represented in the prophecy by the stars that fell to earth (Chap. 4). The third book represented 'the whole rablement of ye Popes' from Boniface III to Paul IV, who were represented by the stars that fell from heaven in Chapter 9 of the Revelation. The third book was in five parts,

[32] Foxe, *Rerum* . . . (1559), p. 57.

[33] John Bale, *Acta Romanorum Pontificum*, a dispersione discipulorum Christi usque ad tempora Pauli IV (Basle, 1558).

[34] John Bale, *The Pageant of the Popes*, contayninge the lyves of all the Bishops of Rome, from the beginning of them to the year of Grace 1555, trans. with sundrye additions by J(ohn) S(tudley) (London, 1574).

each corresponding to a part of the prophecy. The first covered from Boniface III to the legendary Pope Joan and was the 'Kingdom of the great beast' described in Revelation 11. From the seating of a woman on the papal throne, Bale dated the prophecy in Revelation 11 of 'the Kingdom of the greate harlot' which lasted until the time of Sylvester II. From Sylvester II, the magician, to Innocent IV was the 'Kingdom of the Dragon' of Revelation 20. From Innocent IV to Julius II was the period of the 'Kingdom of locusts' in Revelation 9, which forecast the fall of the papacy. The final period extended from Julius II to Paul IV 'and all the times of their successours unto the judgement of Christ'.[35]

In the above scheme Bale skipped from place to place in the text of the prophecy in his search for suitable images. However, at the end of his introduction to the book he related the whole scheme to one section of the text and followed there the order of the text.

To conclude I have disposed the whole hystorye in such sort that I have compared all the Romaine bishops to the 4. horses in the Revelation of S. John. The godlye and auncient fathers to the white horse: The archbishops and the Patriarkes to the red: The Popes & the Antichristes unto Silvester the seconde to the blacke, and from him to Julius the seconde. . . . I have compared to ye pale horse. I have propounded this mark and methode in my booke, in the which I have chalenged nothing to my self, but my labour in gathering, describing and distributing.[36]

For the first time Bale referred to his use of the Apocalypse as the special 'mark and methòde' of his book. His themes were relentlessly pursued throughout the body of *The Pageant of the Popes*, gaining at times an almost organic reality. The seeds of Antichrist were sown, grew to fullness, and withered, all in due season prophesied. The material Bale gathered combined, as Barnes's had, biographical sketches of the popes with a discussion of the innovations in doctrine or canon law made by each. Barnes had made this the entirety of his proof of the antichristian nature of the papacy. Bale superimposed on this material the argument from prophecy and the structure of the Apocalypse.

Bale's history of the papacy was dedicated to leading

---

[35] Bale, *The Pageant of the Popes*, Dedication, *Cii^v-iii^r-v.
[36] Ibid.

continental reformers—Simond Sulcer, Heinrich Bullinger, John Calvin, and Philip Melanchthon—in recognition of their assistance to the exiled communities. The following year, Foxe dedicated a play to three merchants, thanking them for their assistance to the exiles. In this play, *Christus Triumphans*, allegorical figures like Pseudamnus (False Lamb) and Hierlogus (Preacher) among many others illustrated the fortunes of the gospel through the ages. As in Bale's history of the papacy a series of apocalyptic images identified the different ages. Thus, as early as 1554, Foxe sought to understand and express church history in apocalyptic terms.[37]

In return and at about the same time (1555–6) Heinrich Bullinger gave a series of lectures or sermons on the Apocalypse which were collected and published in Basle in 1557, dedicated to the exiles for the name of Christ in Germany and Switzerland. Bullinger's work was well received among the English exiles and became one of the standard commentaries in Britain, and through its influence upon the notes in the Geneva Bible gained even wider influence there.[38]

Bullinger's sermons dwelt upon the revelation in the Apocalypse of an all-pervading divine providence. The vision portrays the control of God over the affairs of men and through the mediation of the Lamb opens the true meaning of history in the seven seals and trumpets. The knowledge thus offered to the Church is the knowledge of God's love for his elect, his warnings to the damned, and the lessons of patience and hope under affliction in all ages. The elect suffer persecution but in each age are constant in their faith.

This is an old and familiar interpretation. Bullinger's expression of it soon superseded many of his non-Protestant predecessors, and there can be little doubt that his emphasis upon the persecuted as the true elect in each age gave support to the martyrologists of Protestantism. He accepted that the seals and trumpets of the Revelation were a prognostica-

---

[37] Foxe, *Christus Triumphans* et De Christo Triumphante eiusdem autoris Panegyricon (Basle, 1556). Both V. N. Olsen (*John Foxe and the Elizabethan Church*, Berkeley, 1973; discussed by Bauckham) and R. Bauckham deal extensively with the play. Bauckham, op. cit., pp. 75–83.

[38] R. Bauckham, op. cit., pp. 45–9.

tion of history and he freely employed examples from history to illustrate each seal. However, he implied no sequence in his interpretation. Each seal represented an aspect of history running concurrently with each other aspect until the end. The first seal stood for the preachers of the gospel from the days of the Apostles onwards, the fifth for the persecutors of the faithful from the ten persecutions onwards, and so forth. The preservation of faith in God's love and constancy in hope was all that it was needful for a Christian to learn from the Revelation, and Bullinger hoped to discourage further speculation.

These thinges are spoken hitherto of the persecutions of al times, so that in the meane time they have ministred most comfortable consolations to all that suffer persecution to the ende of the worlde: and have likewise cutte of curiouse questions, and sette us save and whole in the will of God, wherein we only restynge, maye knowe that the same is best for us.[39]

Thus, while Bullinger was one of the most widely read and quoted of commentators in England, his contribution was not as dramatic as Bale's or as far-reaching as Foxe's was to become.

The first signs of Foxe's use of apocalyptic material in his historical work appeared in the 1559 *Rerum in ecclesia Gestarum*. Towards the end of the exile a group of scholars in Strasburg under the leadership of Grindal contacted the community at Basle to suggest to Foxe that between them they might the sooner complete a history of the English martyrs. According to this plan, Foxe was to concentrate his efforts on the history of the English martyrs to the end of the reign of Henry VIII, while the Strasburg group would concentrate on the Marian martyrs.[40] Throughout the exile, documents relevant to the Marian martyrs had been smuggled out of England and conveyed to Strasburg, and from there to Foxe in Basle.[41] Foxe was understandably reluctant to put away the work he had already done on the Marian martyrs. Mary died before the planned history was thoroughly worked out between the two groups. When in 1559 Foxe published his

---

[39] Bullinger, *A hundred sermons upon the Apocalyps of Jesu Christe* (London, 1561), p. 203. This translation was prepared by John Daus, a master at Ipswich school. A second edition appeared in 1573.

[40] Mozley, op. cit., pp. 121-2.   [41] Ibid.

Rerum in ecclesia Gestarum, he did not entirely leave out the
Marian martyrs. Upon his return to England, he found himself alone in the field of contenders for the martyrs' historian.
At the first opportunity, Grindal left Strasburg for England
and there became embroiled in the affairs of the Church.
Foxe may have held back some of his material in his 1559
work, but felt entirely free to add to it and publish the whole
in the first English edition of his *Acts and Monuments.* The
Rerum may not be a complete indication of Foxe's development by 1559, but it nevertheless exhibits a new interest in
the collection of prophecies of the Reformation, especially
those of the appearance of Antichrist, an interest developed
to a far greater extent in the 1563 *Acts and Monuments.*

One of the simplest ways to trace the growth of Foxe's
interest in the apocalyptic tradition in Protestant historiography is to compare the titles of the books of 1554, 1559,
and 1563:

1554—*Commentarii rerum in ecclesia gestarum,* maximarumque per
totum Europam Persecutionum, a Wiclevi temporibus ad hanc
usque aetatem descriptio

there appears no sign of influence of the apocalyptic tradition.

1559—*Rerum in ecclesia Gestarum* quae postremis et periculosis his
temporibus evenerunt, maximarumque per Europam persecutionum,
et sanctorum Dei martyrum, caeterarumque rerum si quae insig-
nioris exempla sint, digesti per regna et nationes commentarii . . .

this title describes the present as the latter and most perilous
time, distinct in its persecution of the saints.

1563—*Acts and Monuments* of these latter and perilous days touching
matters of the Churche, wherein are comprehended and described
the great persecutions horrible troubles that have bene wrought and
practised by the Romish Prelates, speciallye in this realme of England and Scotlande, from the yeare of our Lorde a thousand, unto
the time now present.

this title added the date of the year 1000, which we are told in
the text of the book was the year Satan was loosed from the pit.

To be shorte here came in the time that the revelation speaketh of,
whan Sathanan the old serpent, beying tied up for a thousand yere, was
losed for a certain space, of ye which space, here in these bokes . . .
we intend some thing to entreat & speake of. . . .[42]

The latter and perilous times dated from the release of the

---

[42] *Acts and Monuments* of these latter and perilous days etc. (London, 1563),
hereinafter *A & M (1563),* p. 11.

dragon from the pit about the year 1000. Corruption had, however, gained a foothold in the Church before that date. This
Foxe traced in the 1563 edition through a history of the popes,
gathered out of several authors, among whom he listed at the
end his two contemporaries, Barnes and Bale.[43] Foxe like Bale
traced the rapid fall of the Church from the time of Gregory
the Great in about the year 600.[44] The decisive break, however,
did not come until the year 1000. The increase of power and
wealth were the chief agents of Satan, but another was the Turk.

Although the church than, as I said, began something to incline before,
partly by comming in of Mahomet, partly by comming in of wealth and
richesse into the churche of Rome; yet the old age of the Church and
those latter times (which times the Apostles prophecy of to be so
pearylous and daungerous) most of all began at the full M. years and
after, at what time Syluester ii Pope occupied the seat of Rome. An.M[45]

Beside the discussion of Hildebrand a note appeared indicating that 'Here the beast of the Apocalipse appeareth in hys
couloures.'[46] The whole of the first part of the 1563 edition
followed significant points made by Bale in his history of the
papacy.

The second part began[47] with the translation of the substance of the *Rerum in ecclesia Gestarum*, and proceeded
without significant addition to the apocalyptic tradition until
the section on the prophecies of reformation made in the late
Middle Ages.[48] There the prophecies are followed by an additional sermon quoted *in extenso* and dealing with the prophecies of Daniel and John.[49] This sermon Foxe described as
having been given in English in 1388. It began with the
prophecy in Daniel of an abomination lasting 1,290 days.
This was dated from the destruction of Jerusalem (A.D. 70)
1,290 years to the end of the fourteenth century at which
time, the sermon concluded, Antichrist had appeared. Foxe
had begun his work saying that the period of suffering began
about the year 1000 and in later books speaks of the time as
dating from about 1300. This sermon may have suggested to
Foxe his later use of the fourteenth century as the first
century under the tyranny of Antichrist.

[43] *A & M (1563)*, p. 11.   [44] Ibid., p. 6.   [45] Ibid., p. 11.   [46] Ibid., p. 26.
[47] Ibid., p. 85.   [48] Ibid., p. 135; *Rerum . . .* (1559), p. 57.
[49] *A & M (1563)*, pp. 175-82. This is Thomas Wimbledon's St. Paul's Cross
Sermon of 1388, in which he cited the Joachimist *Super Hieremiam.*

The second important contention of this sermon was that the seven seals in the vision of John disclosed the history of the Church from the time of Christ to the end of the world. Four seals had passed before Antichrist's appearance. One covered the time of the Apostles, another the time of the martyrs, another the time of heretics, another the time of the hypocrites. Then between the fourth and fifth seals Antichrist appeared and grew to dominate the Church of the fifth seal, while the true Church suffered quietly. The sixth seal would see the revelation of Antichrist and his defeat. The four angels with the four winds would bring in a reformation and restore the gospel, freeing the consciences of men. There the sermon ended.

Foxe's interest in the Apocalypse grew rather than diminished after his return to England. The *Acts and Monuments* was immediately successful and went through several editions. Foxe used this medium to express his views on topics of more general interest as well as for the publication of further material on martyrs. The bulk of the new material concerned the Marian martyrs, whose persecution Foxe considered one of the most horrible of the Church's sufferings under Antichrist. The new material did not offer greater opportunity to explore the relevance to the Church's history of the different prophecies in the Apocalypse; it only added further proof of an interpretation already made. However, in asides and in a proliferation of prefaces, Foxe expressed his thought on the relationship of prophecy to history. During those years from the return of the exiles to his death, Foxe was the single most important contributor to the establishment of the apocalyptic tradition in English Protestant historiography, but many others used apocalyptic language to describe positions on contemporary issues in religion and international politics.

Dr. Richard Bauckham has distinguished two periods during the reign of Elizabeth in which works on prophecy were published in unusually high numbers. One followed the Northern Rebellion and Pius V's Bull of Excommunication in 1569-70 and was prolonged by reaction to the St. Bartholomew's Day Massacre of 1572, and the other followed the defeat of the Spanish Armada.[50] These spates of activity were distinct in both character and time.

[50] Bauckham, op. cit., p. 140 and Chap. 9 *passim.*

During the early 1570s the bulk of the material published was either in the form of sermons on selected passages of the Revelation, usually demonstrating the identity of the Antichrist with the pope of Rome, or in new editions of familiar works, notably Bale's *The Image of bothe churches* (1570) and Bullinger's *A hundred sermons* (1573). There also appeared two full commentaries of importance, one a translation[51] of Augustine Marlorat's compilation of continental authors with his own observations, which helped to make more readily available the opinions of some continental writers like Sebastian Meyer not previously to be found in English, and the other a commentary by William Fulke published in 1573.[52] Fulke's commentary was based on a series of sermons delivered to the household of the earl of Leicester in 1569.[53] He gave more attention to problems posed by the order of the text and to philological considerations than Bale had done, but did not develop possible historical or chronological implications any further. As in many of the sermons of the time, the emphasis fell on additional reasons, some to be found in current events in Europe and in Britain, for believing the pope to be Antichrist. By this time the idea that the pope was Antichrist had settled firmly into English Protestant thought, though some continued to assert a generalized meaning for the term. Often this assertion was made as a prelude to a rehearsal of the prophesied attributes, each of which was then abundantly illustrated in the papacy, leaving no doubt that the author intended an identification to be made.

What had been propaganda in the days of Mary easily be-

---

[51] By Arthur Golding in 1574, *A Catholike exposition upon the Revelation of Sainct John.*

[52] *In Sacram Divi Joannis Apocalypsin Praelectiones* and also in translation in the same year (1573), trans. George Gifford, *Praelections upon the Sacred and holy Revelation of S. John.*

[53] William Fulke (1538–89) was a Puritan divine educated at St. John's Cambridge. He studied law at Clifford's Inn and turned to mathematics and theology. He attached himself to Thomas Cartwright during the vestiarian controversies. His other works include several essays on astronomical subjects, an almanac, and an attack on the uselessness of some astrology. He also gave sermons in the 1570s proving that Rome was the Babylon of the prophecies. *D.N.B.*; Fulke is the subject of R. Bauckham's Cambridge Ph.D. thesis, and is frequently cited in *Tudor Apocalypse.*

came apology in the days of Elizabeth. The apologist John
Jewel employed a finely ironic blend of caution in identifying the Antichrist with a transparent argument for the apocalyptic tradition in historiography. His attitude, as Dr. Christianson has pointed out, is perhaps best expressed in one of
his sermons.

> I know many men are offended to hear the Pope pointed out for
> antichrist, and think it an uncharitable kind of doctrine, therefore I
> refrain to use any such names, and only will report to you other, by
> what tokens antichrist when he cometh, may be known. . . . 'Who-
> soever calleth himself the universal priest, or desireth so to be called, in
> the pride of his heart is the forerunner of antichrist.' These words were
> written by Gregory more than 900 years since.

To show that the reformers were not the first to identify the
pope with Antichrist, he recited a familiar list of notable
prophets in the apocalyptic tradition, including Bernard of
Clairvaux, Lorenzo Valla, Marsiglio of Padua, Petrarch,
Savonarola, and of course Joachim of Fiore.[54] The furthest
Jewel would allow himself to go in the name of the faith of
the Church of England in his Apology was to write:

> We believe that he the pope does give unto himself . . . a profane, a
> sacreligious, and an Antichristian name; that he is also the King of
> pride; that he is Lucifer, which preferreth himself before his brethren;
> that he has forsaken the faith, and is the forerunner of Antichrist.[55]

A forerunner of Antichrist is not the same thing as the Antichrist himself, and Jewel would here seem to be taking no
sides with respect to the possibility that a future and more
terrible Antichrist might appear nearer the end of time. However, he in no way wished to surrender the historical Antichrist of the papacy. This had become too important a part
of the justification for the break with Rome and for the reconstruction of the traditions of the true Church.

On an even wider front these same years saw the establishment of a group, and finally a society, of antiquaries gathered
around Matthew Parker and dedicated like the apologists to
the reconstruction of the history and traditions of the primitive and the English Church. These men, John Bale among
them, were confident in their use of the words 'Antichrist'

---

[54] Jewel, *Certaine sermons* (1583, S.T.C. 14596), sig. E6ᵛ–7ʳ, Christianson
chap. I; Jewel is also discussed in Bauckham, *passim*.

[55] Jewel, *An Apology of the Church of England*, ed. J. E. Booty (Ithaca,
1963), pp. 75–6. Christianson, chap. I.

and 'antichristian' when discussing Rome and her traditions.[56] In accord with the apocalyptic tradition as Bale expressed it, the antiquaries concentrated upon the persecuted Church from Christ to Constantine and from then to the sixth century with increasing awareness of the workings of the mystery of iniquity. When it came to the Church in England they were anxious as much as possible to remove it from the general pattern of the history of the Roman Antichrist without denying that that pattern was historically true for the rest of Europe. Within the confines of the inquiry the apocalyptic tradition offered little of a specific nature, but may have provided the tacit assumptions that set those limitations.

Thus, although there existed both interest in the revelation of Antichrist and a consensus of the pattern of the past leading to his revelation, not many of Foxe's contemporaries were particularly concerned with refining further the interrelations of history and prophecy. The major work would seem to have been done, the Reformation justified and the enemy identified. The more pressing historical problems concerned the disentanglement of the traditions and rights of the English Church and hierarchy from those imposed by Rome during the days when Antichrist had reigned in England. Indeed, reading the sermons of the 1570s, one is impressed by nothing more original than yet another proof of Antichrist at Rome. Foxe alone among the English commentators stands out as one interested in pursuing the application of prophecy to the organization and presentation of history.

After the edition of 1563 the *Acts and Monuments* went through three more editions during Foxe's lifetime, in 1570, 1576, and 1583. By the 1583 edition Foxe had added a preface in which he considered four questions relating to prophecy and followed it with four further considerations.[57] By this time he had also added an aside in the text entitled 'The Mystical Numbers in the Apocalypse Opened'.[58] When he died in 1586 he was at work on a commentary on the Apocalypse. He preferred to keep his work a family secret

---

[56] For example, Matthew Parker, *De Antiquitate Britannicae Ecclesiae & Privilegiis Ecclesiae Cantuariensis cum Archiepiscopis eiusdem* (London, 1572), Aij[r].
[57] *A & M (1583)*, vol. i, pp. xxvii–xxxvi.   [58] Ibid., p. 290.

until it was published. To a letter written by his wife to their son Samuel at Magdalen College, Oxford, Foxe added a post-script chiding his son for speaking too freely to his old friend Lawrence Humphrey:

Samuell I marvell that you were so unwyse to bable out any thing of ye bok of ye Apocalypse to Doct. Humfrey. Such is my weakness now, and hath been this month I can nether eate, sleape, nor wryte, nor goo up yett to my study, whereby ye boke standeth yett at a stay, in prynting. The Lord knoweth how I shall go forward eyther for fynysh-yng ye bok or dedication therof. Wherof I pray you to make no wordes to any person.[59]

Foxe, Bale, and Humphrey had shared a house at Basle and were fast friends for the rest of their lives, corresponding fre-quently. A draft of a letter of congratulation written by Foxe to Humphrey on the latter's election to the presidency of Magdalen appears to have been preceded by one from Hum-phrey inviting Foxe to a reading in the college of his *Christus Triumphans*. Foxe declined, saying he was far too busy.[60] Humphrey was very active on the Puritan side of the vestiarian controversy, a subject on which Foxe was more cool. How-ever, there is nothing to suggest that Humphrey would not have reacted favourably to Foxe's meditations on the Apoca-lypse, and his admiration for the *Christus Triumphans* rather suggests his general approval. Foxe wished his work to remain secret not only from Dr. Humphrey but also from 'any per-son' until he had finished it. His *Eicasmi* was certainly an extremely significant work in the development of the histori-cal interpretation of the prophecies. Foxe must have been aware of this and also of the uniqueness of his inquiries at this time. Like Bale, he referred to many old commentaries and to those by the early Protestants on the continent. For the Elizabethan period, however, he referred to only one other English writer, William Fulke.

Even in the 1559 *Rerum in ecclesis Gestarum* there were indications of the direction Foxe's interest in the Apocalypse was to take in these later years. There his interest awakens to prophecies of dates and events relevant to the appearance of

---

[59] Agnes Foxe to Samuel Foxe, British Library, MS. Harl. 416, Art. 91, printed *A & M (1583)*, Introduction, p. 54.

[60] Foxe to Humphrey late 1561, printed Mozley, op. cit., p. 66; Mozley notes the invitation and Foxe's reaction, p. 66 n.

Antichrist and the dawn of the Reformation. Like Bullinger he accepted the view that persecution distinguished the true Church during the reign of Antichrist, but he was greatly troubled by its long continuance and was unable to follow Bullinger's advice to have 'cutte of curiose questions'. One consideration that attracted him to prophecy was a need to find an explanation of the function of martyrdom in the divine plan for human history. As an introduction to his section 'The Mystical Numbers in the Apocalypse Opened', Foxe recounted how his questioning of God's mercy had led him to the hidden meaning of the prophecies.

As I was in hand with these histories, and therein considered the exceeding rage of these persecutions, the intolerable torments of the blessed saints . . . I could not without great sorrow and passion of mind behold their sorrowful afflictions, or write of their bloody passions. . . . The further I proceeded in the story and the hotter the persecutions grew, the more my grief with them and for them increased; not only pitying their woful case, but almost reasoning with God, thinking thus like a fool with myself:—Why should God of his goodness suffer his children and servants so vehemently to be cruciated and afflicted? . . . The Israelites in the captivity of Babylon had seventy years limited unto them; and under Pharaoh they were promised a deliverance out; also under the Syrian tyrants threescore and two weeks were abridged unto them. Only in these persecutions I could find no end determined, nor limitation set for their deliverance. Whereupon, much marvelling with myself I searched the Book of Revelation to see whether any thing there might be found; wherein, although I well perceived the beast there described to signify the empire of Rome, which had power to overcome the Saints, yet concerning the time and continuance of persecutions under the beast, I found nothing to satisfy my doubt. For, albeit I read there of forty-two months, of a time, times, and a half time, of one thousand two hundred and threescore days; yet all this by computation coming but to three years and a half, came nothing near the long continuance of these three persecutions which lasted three hundred years. Thus being vexed and turmoiled in spirit about the reckoning of these numbers and years; it so happened upon a Sunday in the morning, I lying in my bed, and musing about these numbers, suddenly it answered to my mind, as with a majesty, thus inwardly saying within me; 'Thou fool, count these months by Sabbaths, as the weeks of Daniel are counted by sabbaths.' The Lord I take to witness, thus it was.[61]

Obviously this incident left a profound impression on Foxe. He was not proficient in mathematics and could not

[61] *A & M (1583)*, vol. i, pp. 289–90.

trust himself to do the simple multiplications necessary to his conjecture. His tale of discovery continued, 'Yet not satisfied herewith, to have the matter more sure, eftsoons I repaired to certain merchants of mine aquaintance.'[62] The merchants checked his arithmetic and found it accurate. The sum he sought was the 300 years of the early persecutions before Constantine. His discovery found nearly this amount by equating each of the forty-two months to seven years, giving a total of 294 years. This was a novel way to prove an old interpretation. The method Foxe used to substantiate this periodization was more similar to the methods of Osiander than to Bale's search among the chronicles for the moral equivalent of the event or image prophesied in the Apocalypse.

Although clumsy in his application of mathematics, Foxe followed his predilection for chronological and numerical interpretation in conjunction with those methods of identification found in Bale. Thus in his adoption of the full Protestant apocalyptic tradition he left Bale far behind. Despite Bale's fascination with the historical content he found in prophecy, his interpretation was still largely spiritual. His reserve when faced with the comparison of prophecy with dates and specific durations of ages was never entirely broken down by his love of the neatly dramatic scheme. We are fortunate in having in Foxe a man who wrote both a history directed by the apocalyptic tradition and a commentary on the historical interpretation of prophetic Scripture. Although written one after the other, the two works are largely interdependent. By the 1583 edition of his *Acts and Monuments*, Foxe had added to the text in prefaces, introductions, and conclusions, titled digressions, and paragraphs of comment, many of his observations on prophecy which he later collected in his *Eicasmi*. In like manner, he illustrated his *Eicasmi* by frequent recourse to his *Acts and Monuments*.

Although many of Foxe's observations on the meaning of prophecies in the Book of Revelation first appeared in the *Acts and Monuments*, they were expressed in a more orderly and systematic way in the *Eicasmi*. Therefore I propose first to summarize his interpretation as it is found in the *Eicasmi*,

[62] *A & M (1583)*, vol. i, pp. 289-90

and secondly to relate that interpretation to the place in his history at which the idea first occurred to him. Both works defined the Apocalypse as a mystical revelation of the history of the Church. In a preface to the *Acts and Monuments*, Foxe wrote a description of the Book of Revelation, 'Which book, as it containeth a prophetical history of the church, so like wise it requireth by histories to be opened.'[63] In the *Eicasmi*, he wrote, 'Hincque Apocalypsis ista, id est, rerum in ecclesia gerendarum Prophetica revelatio . . .',[64] and proceeded to outline the necessity for the Church to give attention to prophecies of such importance. Throughout the *Eicasmi* Foxe inveighed against his predecessors and contemporaries for their disregard of the historical content of the prophecies. Although Foxe admired and used the comments made by Aquinas on the Revelation, he objected to Aquinas's continual dependence on the tropological interpretation.[65] He found his contemporaries more apt in the discovery of the historical meaning. Yet, even among the reformers Foxe noticed a lack of precision, the absence of dates in their interpretations, and a tendency to relate the prophecies 'ad sensum non historicum, sed ad res solum spirituales'.[66] Particularly at fault in this respect were Lambert and Bullinger. Foxe noted that most authors tended to follow Bullinger.[67] In order to improve upon this situation, he proposed a more strictly historical approach and announced that wherever possible he would avoid the allegorical and seek the historical.

In prophetando, non ita propriè luditur allegoriis, aut si in prophetiis usu ita, veniat quandóque, ut per similium collationem, parabolae adhibeantur: at non ideo tamen sensus historicus per allegorismos & tropologias evertendus est, praesertim ubi res ipsa ad historias nos mittit, non ad allegorias.[68]

Foxe's preoccupation with persecution found its way into his over-all interpretation of the Apocalypse. The prophecies, he found, revealed three distinct periods of persecution. The first covered the time before Constantine. He had found the limits and duration of this period by his discovery that the sum of years could be obtained from the interpretation of

---

[63] *A & M (1583)*, 'Four Questions Propounded; the Third Question', vol. i, p. xxx.

[64] *Eicasmi*, p. 3.   [65] Ibid., p. 5.   [66] Ibid., p. 46.   [67] Ibid., p. 45.

[68] Ibid., p. 46.

the forty-two months as sabbaths of years.[69] The second persecution of the faithful was accomplished through the agency of the Saracens and Turks. Because the prophecy spoke of the Saracens and Turks, it was clear that the prophecies were not only valid indications of the history of the church but also 'ad publicam totius universitatis necessariam admonitionem pertinent'.[70] The third period of persecution corresponded with the loosing of Satan and the reign of Antichrist.[71] In the 1563 edition, Foxe had connected the binding of Satan to the thousand years following the birth of Christ; but by 1583 and in his *Eicasmi* he connected the binding of Satan with the cessation of persecution about the time of Constantine, and his loosing-out again with the persecutions of Wyclif and Huss after 1300:

when his severity had been sufficiently declared upon his own house, it pleased him to show mercy again, and to bind up Satan, the old serpent, according to the twentieth chapter of the Revelation, for the space of a thousand years; that is, from this time of Licinius, to the time of John Wyclif and John Huss. [72]

Following the text of Revelation, Foxe dealt first with the seven churches, the seven angels, the seven stars, the seven candlesticks, and the seven spirits. The number seven was common to all the first images. Because seven was a universal number, each of these images was properly interpreted as pertaining to the universal Church.[73] The first section of the text with historical meaning was the history of the seven seals. The number seven in this case showed that the seals covered all the history, either of the world as some expositors held or of the Church as others held.[74] He outlined the opinions of prominent writers on the Apocalypse before giving his own interpretation. He summarized the opinions of Joachim, Bullinger, Lambert, Fulke, and Theodore Bibliander.[75]

---

[69] *Eicasmi*, pp. 5–6.   [70] Ibid., pp. 4–6.   [71] Ibid., p. 5.
[72] *A & M (1583)*, vol. i, p. 292.   [73] *Eicasmi*, p. 14.   [74] Ibid., pp. 41–5.
[75] Theodore Bibliander (Buchmann), born 1504; died of plague in Zürich 1564. A Swiss orientalist, he was offered in 1532 the Chair of Theology at Zürich. When his opinions on predestination proved unsympathetic to Protestant opinion, he was declared emeritus and Peter Martyr took the chair. He is chiefly known for his work on the Koran and on Islam. Many of his works from 1543 to 1560 were published in Basle; a history of Muhammad, 1543, two chronological works, 1551, 1558. Two works published in Basle in 1553 approached the apocalyptic tradition in method or content. *De fatis monarchiae romanae* and *Somnium vaticinium*

Of those represented Bibliander alone equated the seven seals to the whole history from the Creation. He had counted 1,656 years from the Creation to the Flood, an essential number in Osiander's second conjecture.[76]

Foxe's own interpretation identified the four horses of the four first seals with the four world monarchies in Daniel's prophecies,[77] thereby illustrating his belief that the prophecies applied not to the fortunes of the Christian Church alone but to all of world history. At the opening of the fourth seal there appeared four beasts. To Foxe's mind, the appearance of any kind of beast generally meant the beginning of persecution or war. In this case, the four beasts signified the wars waged by the Romans throughout the world.[78]

With the fifth seal[79] the prophecy left the subject of 'politicis imperiis' and began to treat of the affairs of the Church. During the fifth seal, Christ was born. Foxe dates this event in the forty-second year of Augustus and the four-thousandth year of the world. The fifth seal signified not only the persecution under the Roman Empire, but also the later persecutions; it had universal significance. The sixth seal[80] gave Foxe trouble in meeting his avowed method. This seal, he decided, required a tropological interpretation, from which could be gathered the corruption of the Church. The sun signified Christ, the moon the Church, the stars the doctors, and so on. It expressed the divine judgements and retributions.

Whereas Foxe found himself concluding that the seven seals were only a general guide to history, he found the seven trumpets clearly contained seven successive and not simultaneous times.[81] He noted the idea of the world-week and the elaboration into seven millennia. These do not exactly correspond because Foxe believed it likely that the sixth millennium would be shortened out of God's mercy. Nor do the seven seals necessarily exactly correspond with the seven trumpets. All that has been described in the seven seals would happen in six millennia.[82] In effect Foxe expressed the

---

Esdrae dealt with the apostasy of the Roman Church, the conversion of the Jews, and the re-establishment of Jerusalem. These themes are also found in *De restituenda Pace quam turbare studet Antichristus (Michaud)*. Bibliander was frequently referred to in Bullinger's commentary.

[76] See Chap. II, p. 63.   [77] *Eicasmi*, p. 50.   [78] Ibid., p. 53.
[79] Ibid., pp. 54–6.   [80] Ibid., pp. 56–9.   [81] Ibid., p. 73.   [82] Ibid., p. 60.

Protestant interpretation of the Prophecy of Elias, but no reference to that prophecy appeared in either his history or his commentary. He was certainly aware of *Carion's Chronicle*.[83] He dated Christ's birth in the four-thousandth year of the world, and limited the time of history and of the seven seals to 6,000 years. Foxe was not particularly attracted by Jewish literature or history beyond the biblical limits. His only references to the Jews in his history were repetitions of the stories of young Christian boys crucified by certain English Jews on Good Fridays.[84] He does not mention the Talmud, and it may well be that if he had it would have been in the terms Bale had used.

The seven trumpets[85] illustrated God's judgement on the enemies of the Church. The first trumpet contained the judgement of God against the Jews. The second depicted the judgement against the first persecutors of the faith; the third, the judgement against the first heretics; the fourth, the judgement against the corrupters of the Church. The fifth trumpet contained the images of the locusts and scorpions, which authors interpreted differently. Foxe considered especially Joachim and Bullinger.[86] All contemporary doctors, he said, agree that by the locusts are signified the ministers and satellites of Antichrist. This can be illustrated by the history of the Church from Constantine to Gregory I and from Gregory I to Boniface III, and in the ascendancy of the sect of Muhammad from A.D. 623. The text gave the locusts five months. Joachim interpreted this as 150 days or 150 years, that is, five generations. Bullinger took the period to indicate the total duration of affliction. Foxe began his discussion of the second great persecution with these locusts, which symbolized in the first place the barbarian invasions of Rome by Goths, Lombards, and Huns.[87] The scorpions symbolized the heretics and disciples of Antichrist who followed Muhammad. In the end, although drawn to Joachim's exactness, Foxe had to agree with Bullinger that the five months must be interpreted generally to cover a longer period of affliction than 150 years.[88] The sixth trumpet offered fewer problems in

---

[83] *A & M (1583)*, vol. iv, p. 257.   [84] *A & M (1583)*, vol. ii, pp. 188 and 277.
[85] *Eicasmi*, beginning p. 59.   [86] Ibid., pp. 83-91.   [87] Ibid., p. 87.
[88] Ibid., pp. 90-1.

its interpretation as the rise of the Turks, who in the end controlled nearly one-third of the Christian world.[89]

Several of the prophecies in the Apocalypse related to the rise of the Turk. These prophecies Foxe collected and discussed in his history in the section dealing with the history of both Saracens and Turks. His consideration of the Turks and prophecy began in 1556, at which time he wrote, 'it shall not be unprofitable but rather necessary, and to our great comfort to consider and examine the Scriptures, with what prophecies the Holy Spirit of the Lord had premonished and forewarned us before, of these heavy persecutions to come upon his people by this horrible Antichrist'.[90] He first perused the Old Testament and found a correlation between the prophecies of Daniel of the vile person (interpreted to signify Antiochus Epiphanes) and the suffering of Europe threatened by the Turks. The correlation, Foxe observed, was not only a similarity of circumstances but also a similarity of times. Antiochus had raged 191 years before the passion of Christ, and from the time when Bajazet had moved his capital to Adrianople and from there threatened Europe in 1375 to the present year of 1566 was 191 years. Therefore it was possible that Daniel's prophecy of Antiochus 'may well represent and prefigure' the Turk.[91] Like Calvin and Osiander, Foxe limited the prophecies of Daniel to the time before Christ and allowed only a figural significance for Daniel's images to carry over into the Christian era.

After his consideration of Daniel, Foxe turned to the New Testament prophecies. There he found that 'among all the prophecies both of the Old Testament and of the New, there is none that painteth out the Antichristian Kingdom of the Turks better than doth the Revelation of St. John . . .'.[92] In three separate places the text referred to the Turks. First in the description of the sixth trumpet, 'By loosing the angels who had rule of the great river Euphrates is signified the letting out of the east Kings, that is, the Turks, out of Scythia, Tartary, Persia, and Arabia, by whom the third part of Christendom shall be destroyed, as we see it this day hath

[89] *Eicasmi*, pp. 91–9.   [90] *A & M (1583)*, vol. iv, p. 93.
[91] Ibid., p. 97. The capital was in fact moved in 1365 by Murad.
[92] Ibid., p. 102.

come to pass.'[93] Also in Revelation 16 the sixth vial, poured out on the Euphrates and drying it, letting in the Kings of the East, referred to the Saracens and twelve Ottoman Turks.[94] The gathering of Gog and Magog also represented the Turks, 'whereby it is understood that toward the last consumation of the world, great force shall be seen, and a mighty army of the enemies shall be collected and gathered against the people and saints of the highest, and then cometh the consummation, with '"factum est" &c.'[95] These interpretations were repeated in the *Eicasmi*.

A fourth reference to the Turks found in prophecy appearing earlier in the *Acts and Monuments* was denied in this section and in the *Eicasmi*. At one time, presumably before 1566, Foxe interpreted the number of the Beast, 666, to refer to the year when the Muhammadans effectively began to seek power:

> Near about this time in the year of our Lord 666, the detestable sect of Mahomet began to take strength and place. Although Polychronicon, differing a little in years, accounteth the beginning of this sect somewhat before, but the most diligent searchers of them which write now, refer it to this year, which well agreeth with the number of that beast signified in the Apocalypse χξϛ that is 666.[96]

Foxe knew that Muhammad had died in 623, but for the purposes of matters of interpretation—in this case the search for a convenient date to be understood as a turning-point—the better interpretation followed the Apocalypse. The alternative date suggested by Higden's *Polychronicon*, that of the death of Muhammad, could not prevail in the face of a specific and inspired prophecy in the Apocalypse. The proof of this interpretation demanded that not only the number but also the Beast whose number it was should correspond with the Muhammadans. In 1566 Foxe found that this correspondence broke down for reasons evident both in history and in the order of the text of the Book of Revelation. The interpretation he was here denying had been propounded long before by Nicolaus of Lyra and Paulus Burgensis, those two expositors so important in the development of the Wyclifite interpretation of the Apocalypse.

[93] *A & M (1583)*, vol. iv, p. 102 and *Eicasmi*, p. 95.
[94] *A & M (1583)*, vol. iv, p. 102 and *Eicasmi*, p. 386.
[95] *A & M (1583)*, vol. iv, p. 103. [96] Ibid., vol. i, p. 354.

Which interpretation of theirs, although in some points it may seem to have some appearance of probability . . . yet as touching the proper and natural meaning of the apostle in that place, speaking of the false lamb, &c if we consider well all the circumstances of that beast, and mark the consequence of the text both of that which goeth before and followeth after, we must needs grant, that Nicholas de Lyra with his fellows, and with all such-like of the pope's school that follow that school, be deceived, and that the description and interpretation of that false horned lamb must necessarily be applied only to the bishop of Rome, and none other.[97]

Foxe had six reasons[98] for identifying this beast, the second beast rising out of the land in Revelation 13, with the papacy. The description began with the beast's two horns like those of a lamb, whereby Foxe understood a resemblance to the Lamb or Christ. The beast could not therefore signify the Turk, but only the pope, Christ's vicar on earth. This beast spoke like a dragon, that is, behaved contrary to his looks. To prove the pope in this description, Foxe called to mind his actions against kings and emperors, especially his dealings with King John, with Henry IV, and with Frederick Barbarossa.

Because the second beast was described as having the power of the first, some connection must be found between the pope, or alternatively the Turk, and an earlier beast. The first persecutors of the Church had been the Roman emperors, so a connection must be established between the Empire of Rome and the Church of Rome, or the Turk. The connection could be made on spiritual grounds: the same fury and the same cruelty; and on historical grounds: the documented process of the usurpation of the Roman imperial power. Both Turk and pope fitted the first description, but only the pope fitted the second. Further, the description of the first beast in Revelation 17 fitted only the city of Rome.

The first of these beasts described here in the Apocalypse, having seven heads and ten horns, must needs signify the city of Rome, which may easily be proved by two demonstrations. First, by the exposition of the same Apocalypse xvii, where is declared and described the said beast to stand on seven hills, and to contain ten Kings, having the whole power of the dragon given; and also the same city to be named 'The whore of Babylon . . .'; all which prophecies joined together, can agree in no wise but only to the heathen empire of Rome. . . .[99]

[97] *A & M (1583)*, vol. iv, p. 103.   [98] Ibid., pp. 103–6.   [99] Ibid., p. 104.

The fourth reason interpreted the wound that healed to be the re-establishment of the dignity of Rome by the pope, and certainly not by the Turk. Fifthly, the beast forced others to worship him, that is, to maintain Rome. The sixth argument reversed his earlier interpretation of the number 666. Although many alternative interpretations had been proposed, Foxe preferred Irenaeus's rendering of the number into λατεινος.[1] In the *Eicasmi*, Foxe elaborated on this point, and provided a table to illustrate the proof. Such tables were common in commentaries on the Apocalypse, especially in the popularized versions. Foxe's table may be taken as an example:[2]

270		*MEDITATIONES*				
Hebraicè.		*Latinè.*	*Grecè.*			*Anglicè.*
ר	200	RO	P	100		A
מ	40	M	O	70		MAN
ע	70	A	M A	40		OF
נ	50	N	N	50		R
ה	6	V	Y	400		O
ש	300	S	S	6		ME.
		SVMMA	6 6 6.			

The interpretation of the two beasts as the pagan Roman Empire followed by the Roman pope was repeated in the *Eicasmi*.[3] Calvin and Osiander had both arrived at the same conclusion concerning the fate of imperial power after the destruction of Rome by the barbarian invasions.[4] For these men, the reassertion of the western empire had been a creature of the papacy. The temporal powers were either tricked by the pope's disguise as a lamb or defeated by the power of the first beast inherited by the second. The traditional

---

[1] *A & M (1583)*, vol. iv, p. 106.   [2] *Eicasmi*, p. 270.   [3] Ibid., pp. 212–70.
[4] For Calvin see above, p. 36 *et seq.*; for Osiander, p. 64 *et seq.*

interpretation of the *translatio imperii*, from Rome to Constantinople, to Charlemagne and the Franks, and from him to the Germans under Conrad, was most insisted on by the Germans. Sleidan's argument for the uniting and strengthening of Germany in the name of Empire was based on Daniel's prophecies, but his call came rather late in the day. Although Foxe repeated the *translatio* in the traditional German fashion under his discussion of Charlemagne, he made a point of mentioning from whose hands Charlemagne had received the crown.[5] This was not a detail usually stressed by apologists for the secular power. In the Apocalypse, Foxe found an explanation for the gradual usurpation of temporal power by the papacy and a condemnation of that power as a false and antichristian power held from Satan and not from God.

Essential to the whole configuration of prophecies was the identification of the papacy with Antichrist. Foxe recited proofs of this assertion both under his discussion of why the Turk was not the only Antichrist, in the *Acts and Monuments*,[6] and in the section following his discussion of the two beasts in the *Eicasmi*.[7] In the latter Foxe illustrated the similarity between the pagan Roman emperors and the popes: between the first beast and the second. These comparisons emphasized the extent of the secular behaviour of the popes. He also compared the pope to the Turk, illustrating the prevalence of idolatry in the beliefs of both. Although proofs by comparison of moral characteristics and behaviour were not the only ones offered by him, they were an important part of his argument. When dealing with this type of proof, Foxe described as Antichrist both the Turk and the pope; but when by Antichrist he meant to indicate the second beast of the Apocalypse, or the whore of Babylon, then he meant only the papacy.[8] This double use of the term 'Antichrist' shows the extent to which the spiritual meaning, as it had been defined by Tyndale, remained part of the English expression of the apocalyptic tradition.

[5] *A & M (1583)*, vol. i, p. 375.   [6] Ibid., vol. iv, pp. 103–6.
[7] *Eicasmi*, pp. 223–70.
[8] Ibid., pp. 110–15 (110 is misnumbered 100), discusses the final identification of Antichrist. 'Posito enim hoc uno axiomate, Romanum pontificem esse Antichristum ruunt, ilico rudera Antichristianae ecclesiae universa' (p. 111).

When Foxe began to treat the period from 1300, after the release of the dragon from the pit, Antichrist signified the papacy; the locusts and scorpions, and Gog and Magog, the Turk. In a section of the *Eicasmi* devoted to disproving traditional beliefs about the origin and nature of Antichrist, each proof established the appearance of Antichrist in Rome alone.[9] The Protestant position was not yet much troubled by Jesuits, but murmurings of protest were being heard in England in the 1580s. However, it seems to have taken some twenty years before an English author[10] attempted to meet the challenge first presented by Bellarmine.[11] When the attack came,[12] it would be upon the issue of this identification. Foxe presented this section of his proofs of Antichrist in the style of a controversy: issue to be confuted; major and minor premises; conclusion. This was followed by comments on the wilful inability of Jesuits and papists to see reason.[13]

The issues under discussion were the Protestant belief that Antichrist was not a single person to come in the final three-and-one-half years of history, and Protestant objections to traditional descriptions of him as a circumcised member of the tribe of Dan. Beyond all that had already been said by Protestants to disprove the singular and literal interpretation of Antichrist and the forty-two months, Foxe noted the improbability that God would allow so long a persecution as he evidently had without giving full warning.[14] This argument had in his own case proved the most convincing, and he gave it emphasis in proportion. The restriction of Antichrist to a circumcised tribesman of Dan, Foxe correctly traced not to the Apocalypse or to any specific place in Scripture but to a commentary on Jeremiah by Jerome, where Foxe said the text actually indicated that Antichrist should come from those dwelling near Dan. In any case, neither conditions had any clear scriptural basis, only a basis in tradition. Foxe

[9] *Eicasmi*, pp. 223-70.
[10] Thomas Brightman, 'Against Bellarmine touching Antichrist', in *A Revelation of the Revelation* (Amsterdam, 1615), pp. 622-770.
[11] Bellarmine's *Controversies* were published in three volumes, in 1581, 1582, and 1593. In 1589 he wrote an attack on Flacius Illyricus.
[12] The rise of Jesuit interest will be treated in a later chapter.
[13] *Eicasmi*, pp. 286-7.   [14] Ibid., pp. 110-15.

concluded that, had these details been so crucially important, the Holy Spirit would have disclosed them to John.[15]

The first Roman Catholic answer to the new Protestant historiography to be written in England was Nicholas Harpsfield's *Dialogi Sex* (1566).[16] Actually written by Harpsfield in the Tower of London, the work was smuggled out of England to a press in Antwerp and there published under the name of Alan Cope to protect the author from reprisal. Cope, who was the publisher, left a sufficient number of clues to the author's true identity. Harpsfield, the younger brother of Bonner's chaplain, was as staunch a papist as one could hope to find. He left England when Edward came to the throne because he disapproved of the changes being made, returned to England under Mary, and became an archdeacon of Canterbury. He assisted Bonner in the trials of some of the Marian martyrs.[17] Foxe was notoriously unsympathetic to the role of Bonner and Harpsfield in the Marian persecution. It was Foxe's treatment of the Marian martyrs that provoked Harpsfield to write; his objection had nothing to do with the use Foxe made of the Apocalypse. Nevertheless, Harpsfield singled out the leaders of Protestant historiography and attacked the two major works arising out of the Marian period, Foxe's *Acts and Monuments* and the *Magdeburg Centuries*. Moreover, he identified in a list at the beginning of his book those writers whose works he found particularly obnoxious. In all he numbered twenty-eight of them, including each of the centuriators, Andreas Osiander, John Bale, John Crespin, John Foxe, and John Sleidan.[18]

The six dialogues dealt with prominent themes in the Protestant version of history: the first defended papal primacy against the assaults of the centuriators, the second defended monasticism, the third defended the invocation of saints, the fourth and fifth defended the use of images, and the sixth attacked Foxe's 'pseudo-martyres'. Harpsfield objected to Foxe's confusion of heretics with martyrs, and defended the legal process of the courts during the reign of Mary. His

[15] *Eicasmi*, p. 113.

[16] Nicolas Harpsfield, *Dialogi Sex* contra Summi Pontificatus, Monasticae vitae, Sanctorum, Sacrarum Imaginum Oppugnatores, et Pseudomartyres.

[17] *D.N.B.*   [18] *Dialogi Sex*, fol. A8r.

two-page attack on the Protestant identification of Antichrist asserted that if anyone were Antichrist it was just those here-tics whom Foxe defended.[19] He briefly outlined the Catholic position that Antichrist would not appear until after the preaching of Enoch and Elias had converted the entire world.

Foxe's narrative reached a decisive break with his approach to the fourteenth century. He had indicated that the binding-up of Satan had occurred about the time of Constantine, and that his release a thousand years later corresponded with the opening years of the fourteenth century. In fact Foxe broke his narrative between the fourth and fifth books of his history at the year 1360. The opening pages of the fifth book[20] discoursed on his interpretation of the meaning of the Apoca-lyptic prophecies for the time from the release of Satan. He acknowledged that he had 'a little overpassed the stint of time in the Scripture appointed for the loosing out of him again. For so it is written by St. John, that "after a thousand years, Satan, the old dragon, shall be let loose for a season" &c.'[21] He did not require accuracy in numerical prophecies; a difference of sixty years does not seem to have invalidated an interpretation when other conditions were satisfied. The early fourteenth century fits the prophecies of Satan's release in two important respects. Not only was this the beginning of the persecutions of Christian preachers such as Wyclif and Huss, but this time also corresponded with the move of the Turkish capital and the strengthening of the Ottoman Empire. Thus, as predicted in the Apocalypse, after the release of Satan the enemies of the true Church would gather against her and a final time of suffering would begin.

In the scheme of the seven trumpets this break came with the sixth trumpet.[22] As has been indicated, Foxe associated this particular trumpet especially with the Turks. A second meaning showed this trumpet to correspond in the history of the Church to the new freedom granted by the release of Satan to Antichrist, already firmly established in the Church in accordance with Paul's prophecies in Thessalonians.[23] At this time the fury of Antichrist increased greatly and

[19] *Dialogi Sex*, pp. 954-5. [20] *A & M (1583)*, vol. ii, pp. 724-7.
[21] Ibid., p. 724. [22] *Eicasmi*, p. 95.
[23] *A & M (1583)*, vol. iv, pp. 140-1; *Eicasmi*, pp. 107-11.

persecution became more frequent. Also at this time the preachers began to identify Rome with Antichrist and to prophesy the eventual fall of the papacy. The preponderance of Foxe's collection of prophecies of the Reformation dated from the fourteenth century. Especially telling was the prophecy made by Huss:

And first to begin with the prophecy of John Huss and Jerome [of Prague], it is both notable, and also before mentioned, what the said John Huss at the time of his burning, prophesied unto his enemies, saying: That after 'a hundred years come and gone, they should give account to God and to him'. Here is to be noted, that counting from the year 1415 (in which year John Huss was burned), or from the year 1416, (when Jerome did suffer), unto the year 1516 (when Martin Luther began first to write), we shall find the number of a hundred years expired.[24]

In his discussion of the same prophecy Jean Crespin had offered an alternative interpretation that by these words Huss meant to say that not even his persecutors would live beyond a hundred years, but must die and come to judgement for their acts.[25] It is clear which of these interpretations Foxe favoured.

Other prophecies in the Apocalypse contained specific references to the 'protestants' of the fourteenth and fifteenth centuries. The two witnesses stood as a general figure for all of them, but the three and a half days in which the witnesses were to lie dead in the streets of Sodom or Egypt referred specifically to the Council of Constance which had condemned Huss.[26] Foxe noted that this council had met from 8 December 1414 to 2 May 1418, or very nearly the three and a half years signified in the prophetical days. Then according to the prophecy the witnesses were resurrected, meaning that the teachings of Huss and Jerome would be taken up by others.

During the time of the sixth trumpet, the Angel appeared before John carrying a little book.[27] This book represented the Scriptures, and the presentation to John the restoration of Scripture to the Church. The agency for this restoration was the revival in learning, and especially the discovery of printing.[28] In Foxe's division of the pious members of the

[24] *A & M (1583)*, vol. iv, p. 253.   [25] Crespin, op. cit., Livre I, p. 80.
[26] *Eicasmi*, p. 181.   [27] Ibid., p. 106.
[28] *A & M (1583)*, vol. iv, pp. 252-3; *Eicasmi*, p. 107.

true Church from the impious followers of the beast three criteria appear to have been used. Martyrdom was certainly the first mark of the faithful, but learning or the recognition of Antichrist in the papacy also served to mark them. Following these criteria, Foxe assembled[29] such varied persons as Dante, Petrarch, Pico and Franciscus Mirandola, Lorenzo Valla, Reuchlin, Colet, Erasmus, as well as almost every well-known heretic from 1300 onwards, apparently without scrupulous distinction between those who expressed the views of orthodox Protestantism and those whose tenets were as much condemned by Protestants as they had been by Rome. This generosity was part of Foxe's temperament which led him in the course of his life to defend an adulteress and, even more shockingly, to plead for a group of London anabaptists.[30] If the horror of persecution opened his mind to one extreme, his love of learning extended his claims for the intellectual origins of Protestantism into unexpected quarters. Nevertheless, Foxe was not alone in thinking the revival of learning somewhat miraculous and not unconnected with reform of religion.

In another place Foxe selected from his long list three men as the predecessors of the Reformation, saying Luther had appeared only 'after Picus Mirandula, and Laurentius Valla, and last of all Erasmus of Rotterdam, had somewhat broken the way before'.[31] The most curious of these is undoubtedly Pico. Several aspects of Pico's interest and activities might qualify him. He challenged the established Doctors of the Church, and if he did not replace Aristotle's authority with Plato's he certainly considered Plato the equal of Aristotle. Foxe was not the first Protestant to express admiration for Pico. There were others, among them Osiander who used Pico's mystical calculations in his own conjectures.[32] Although he employed a kind of 'divine arithmetic' himself, Foxe was not an adept in those sciences of magia and Cabala studied by Pico. However, these interests were abroad in Europe and were making converts in some seemingly unlikely places. Renaissance neo-Platonism, Hermetic philosophy,

[29] A long list of learned Christian men appears in vol. iv, p. 253.
[30] Mozley, op. cit., p. 86.   [31] *A & M (1583)*, vol. iv, p. 259.
[32] See Chap. II, p. 62.

Hebrew Cabala, and their attendant practical arts, were all part of this turn of mind.[33] At root these philosophies were religious ones, so it should not be surprising to see their tendrils exploring the minds of Protestant reformers, especially of those who had been convinced by a study of prophecy that the Reformation was indeed a peculiarly blessed age. Foxe shows no more than a susceptibility to this kind of thought, but it would be well to remember its existence elsewhere. By the end of the century thoughts of this nature would surface, first in the commentary by John Napier, and in the first thirty years of the seventeenth century they would grow to even greater importance.

The seventh trumpet[34] indicated the Last Judgement still to come. Foxe did not predict a final year, but in the *Eicasmi* he expressed the opinion that the sixth millennium would be shortened, and in the *Acts and Monuments* he noted that the persecution of the second beast had by his time nearly equalled the 300 years given to the first beast to persecute the elect.[35] But nothing was known exactly, and Foxe was always careful to follow his own calculations with a disavowal of certainty. Like Bale, Foxe believed that prophecies could not be correctly understood until after their fulfilment, and therefore were properly the study of historians and not prognosticators.[36]

Foxe interpreted the story of the woman and the dragon in the traditional terms of the persecution of the primitive Church by the Roman emperors before Constantine.[37] When he reached Chapter 14, describing the 144,000 brought in victory before the throne, he launched into a discourse on

---

[33] These streams of thought are as important as they are complex. The works of Frances A. Yates are particularly recommended to anyone seeking an insight into the nature of the problems involved. See Biblio.

[34] *Eicasmi*, p. 195.

[35] *A & M (1583)*, vol. ii, p. 723, where Foxe speaks of the time from Satan's release to Antichrist's fall to be contained in 'these latter three hundred years now following' beginning in 1294, the date given in the inserted 'A Table containing the Time of the persecution Both of the Primitive, and of the latter Church, with the count of years from the first binding up of Satan to his loosing again, after the mind of the Apocalypse'. It appears Foxe intended his readers to compare the two persecutions both in character and duration, although he nowhere indicates this as a prediction.

[36] *Eicasmi*, p. 239.   [37] Ibid., p. 196.

the nature of the true and false churches and the difference between them.[38] This was reminiscent of Bale's *Image of bothe churches*. In a preface to the *Acts and Monuments* addressed to the true Church Foxe described the purposes of his history. Like Tyndale, Barnes, and Bale before him, he saw the need for a history of the Church free from monkish error and Roman bias. In places he echoed more than the sentiments of Bale:

This partial dealing and corrupt handling of histories when I considered I thought with myself nothing more lacking in the church than a full and complete story; which . . . should contain neither every vain fable . . . nor yet leaving out any thing necessary . . . but with a moderate discretion taking the best of every one. Which history therefore I have here undertaken, that as other story writers heretofore have employed their travail to magnify the Church of Rome, so in this History might appear to all Christian readers the image of both churches.[39]

Foxe's *Eicasmi* continued the commentary on the chapters of the Revelation to the seventeenth chapter. In all, the book ran to 400 pages, but after about the three-hundredth page the quality and clarity of his exposition decline steadily, eloquent if sad testimony to his determination to continue and to the pain he suffered in the final months of his life.

Much more could be said about Foxe's history in connection with the creation of the Protestant martyr, the function of divine providence as the rule of law, the illustration of the Christian prince as the guardian of religion, and so forth. All these things and more were important elements in Foxe's concept of history. Many can be traced in English Protestant historiography to themes in Tyndale and Bale, and several were to some extent allied to the apocalyptic tradition. Recent scholarship has sufficiently outlined most of these aspects as they appear in Foxe's history.

However, perhaps the most famous of the conclusions drawn from these studies, first made by William Haller in his *Foxe's Book of Martyrs and the Elect Nation* (1963), must be brought into serious question. Dr. Haller's thesis was that Foxe's book presented the Elizabethan public with an apocalyptic nationalism grounded in a study of the Book of Revelation, and that this led his contemporaries to regard England as the elect nation. Foxe is said to have 'set the apocalyptical

---

[38] *Eicasmi*, p. 276.   [39] *A & M (1583)*, vol. i, pp. xviii–xix.

conception of England which he brought back from exile at
the death of Mary in a valid historical perspective focussed on
the place and function of Kingship now devolving upon Elizabeth.'[40] This thesis has become known as the theory of the
elect nation, and a great number of studies, which, like Dr.
Haller's itself, have sought to explain the popularity and content of seventeenth-century millenarianism in England, have
traced its origin to the Elizabethan martyrologists, to Bale
and Foxe. In the absence of a thorough study of sixteenth-
century apocalyptic thought this theory did indeed seem
probable, for the seventeenth-century writers themselves
attributed it to their Elizabethan forerunners. However, both
they and their historians are guilty of reading into these
Elizabethan authors meanings that not only were not intended but also were flatly denied.

Unfortunately in his book Dr. Haller made no use of
Foxe's own commentary on the Book of Revelation.[41] Basing
his study upon the *Book of Martyrs* alone, where, inciden-
tally, no explicit passage can be found to support his thesis,
he was forced to argue that the connection between England
and the elect nation was implied (and implied so clearly that
none could fail to reach the conclusion Foxe himself did not
make). First, there arises the question whether Foxe intended
such an implication, and here the *Eicasmi* offers explicit evidence that he did not. Secondly, it should be asked whether
there were any other influential commentaries, perhaps from
those days of exile to which Dr. Haller points, which alerted
Elizabethans to an apocalyptic nationalism that could be
adapted to their own nation. Thirdly, had Elizabethan commentators contemporary with Foxe or immediately following
him independently generated such an interpretation of the
Revelation, into which Foxe's work could be said to have
fitted despite itself? My thesis is that no such interpretation
existed either before Foxe, in Bale or elsewhere, or in Foxe's
own work, or in the work of his contemporaries or immediate successors. Only one of his successors writing while
Elizabeth still lived saw in the prophecies types for confessional

[40] Haller, op. cit., p. 225.

[41] It is never mentioned in the text, or in the preface, or in any of the foot-
notes; yet it is in the catalogues and was described by Mozley in 1940.

allegiances in the way in which later writers and preachers would begin to speak of them in terms of nations and combinations of nations. He was Thomas Brightman; his commentary was not published until 1609, and it was published in Germany. His interpretation was not given a nationalistic reading until the early 1640s.

Foxe's *Eicasmi* is remarkable in many ways, especially for its insistence on the relevance of the prophecies to the study of history; but, in its interpretation of the Church and the promised kingdom and in its application of prophecy to all the kingdoms of the world, it is adamant in its support of a universalist meaning. In both the *Acts and Monuments* and the *Eicasmi*, Foxe's conception of the true Church is international and mystical, identifying the Church as the congregation of the elect. In the *Eicasmi* he denied to England as a nation a special place in God's promise to the elect:

Non Romae, non Angliae, non Franciae, regnum Christi divinaque obstringitur promissio. Ubicunque spiritus viget veritatis, ubi vera pietas, ubi evangelicae nullis fermentata erroribus institutio, ubi cultus summi numinis retinetur illibatus, ibi ecclesia est.[42]

In maintaining the universality of the prophecies of the kingdom of Christ, Foxe was not differing from his predecessors and contemporaries. None of the authors, either of history or of commentary, covered in the preceding chapters of this study, in England itself or in contact with the exiles abroad, shows any trace of disagreement on this matter.

A further study[43] of sixteenth-century interest in apocalyptic studies made by Dr. Bauckham covers an even broader range of Elizabethan theologians and churchmen, some of whom were interested in the historical implications of their work. There also, evidence for the existence of a belief that England was the elect nation was found to be conspicuous by its absence.

Nevertheless, there is much in Dr. Haller's book that is

[42] *Eicasmi*, p. 12.
[43] This is R. Bauckham's 'Interpretations of Prophecy', unpublished Cranmer Prize Essay (Cambridge, 1972) in which he agrees with the criticism of Haller's theory made in my doctoral thesis (Oxford, 1971) and adds further evidence which led him to the same conclusion. In the published version (*Tudor Apocalypse*, 1978) he notes that V. N. Olsen (Berkeley, 1973) has also advanced evidence against this theory.

confirmed by the studies that have followed his, and have taken seriously the influence of the Apocalypse upon the work of Foxe and the Protestant conception of history. The theory of the elect nation is seductive but also stimulating, for a genuine problem remains: how and when did English nationalism acquire apocalyptic overtones, and how much was this related to the study of prophetic Scripture? There is no simple answer. In a later chapter I shall suggest some ways in which, under new influences, the tradition altered in the seventeenth century so as to encourage both a futuristic and a nationalistic interpretation of the prophecies; but this alteration is probably not the whole answer.

Foxe's contribution to the development of the apocalyptic tradition in Protestant historiography was great. If Bale was the bridge between the continent and England, Foxe was the farther shore. He brought back from the Marian exile a knowledge of Protestant historiography and apocalyptic studies upon which he built his influential *Book of Martyrs*. That he did not bring with him an apocalyptic conception of England as the elect nation does not diminish the fact that he did place his nation, with other European nations, in a historical context bounded by the prophecies of the Revelation. His interpretation of the apocalyptic tradition differed from Bale's chiefly in his toleration for and even fascination with numerical and chronological methods. The closest Bale came to an expression of this was in his history of the papacy, where he referred to his use of the Apocalypse as the special mark and method of his book. Bale combined material collected by others with a scheme and argument based on the Apocalypse. For both Bale and Foxe the Apocalypse became the means whereby a collection of examples drawn from the past could be related one to another in the development of the argument of a whole history. Foxe, however, incorporated the tradition into his history, so that in the end it became essential to the argument giving form to the historical content.

The importance the apocalyptic tradition had assumed in English Protestant historiography can best be illustrated by a brief comparison of the methods of Tyndale, Barnes, Bale, and Foxe. Tyndale collected examples from history each of which illustrated the same theme without noticeable internal development and without connection in a greater historical context. Barnes connected his examples with a legal argument, again without a sense of development between examples; his method was to contrast one law at one time with another law at another time, illustrating legal discontinuity in the Church's teachings and actions. Barnes was closer to a Lutheran appreciation of history as the fortunes of doctrine, but his idea of church history was the approximation of each period to a static ideal. Bale's additions to Barnes's materials introduced the apocalyptic tradition by connecting Barnes's examples to show the rise and fall of the papacy. His additions were superimposed upon Barnes's material so that each man's work might stand alone: one as a smaller version of the *Image of bothe churches*, the other as a catalogue of examples of papal inconsistencies. Bale strove to unite the two into a single historical work, but this would have taken more than the addition of introductions at important places. Foxe was the first British author to write a Protestant apocalyptic history that attempted to explain changes in time in terms of an unfolding pattern of events.

IV

HISTORY AND PROPHECY IN SCOTLAND:
JOHN KNOX AND JOHN NAPIER

The Reformation in Scotland, like that in England, answered
demands for reform that sprang from both economic and religious unrest, but Scotland's position as a nation differed
from England's chiefly in her close relations with France.
From its early days the party of reform favoured a change of
alliance from one with France to one with England. At home
the Scottish reformers read the same books as their English
counterparts, and preached to congregations in English terri-
tory. Abroad in exile English and Scots shared the same congregations, elected one another as leaders, and argued freely
on issues that divided them not as nationals of one country
but as Protestants of differing doctrinal persuasions. To a
great extent Scotland's exposure to the new apocalyptic
thought and her contribution to it followed the English
pattern.

Although Scottish Protestant leaders worked mightily for
a break with France as much as with Rome, in matters of
culture and the education of the young the attraction of
France, of Protestant France, remained. The Scottish writers
in the tradition drew not only upon the teachings of returning religious exiles, but also upon their continuing association
with the intellectual changes occurring in the establishment
of Calvinist France, changes not only in Protestant theology
but also in the arts and sciences. These connections gave an
individual colour to the Scottish tradition and helped to encourage its originality.

One of the earliest pieces of literature to combine a plea
for the reform of Scotland with a warning from prophecy in
fact came from a writer who supported both France and the
Roman Church.[1] The author, who has not been identified,
was a lowland Scot living in France, and his work, *The Complaynt of Scotlande* (1549), was probably first published

[1] *The Complaynt of Scotlande* (1549), ed. James A. H. Murray (E.E.T.S.,
1872), Introduction.

there. Despite the allegiance of the author, the book echoed
Protestant tracts in its plea for reform and in its use of
examples from both Scripture and history to illustrate its
points. The author condemned the faults of negligence and
corruption, and showed how divine judgement fell upon
whole nations for the sins of their leaders. Unlike Tyndale,
whose method resembles this author's, he placed his argument against the background of a natural philosophy, empha-
sizing the natural rise and fall of empires according to the
workings of a divinely instituted law. When he came to a discussion of prophecy, his approach was as much through an
estimation of natural philosophy as through the written text
of Scripture.

The text was divided into three parts: the first was a discourse exposing the miserable state of Scotland and her
people and the causes of their suffering. The second part,
called the 'Monologue Recreative', related how the author,
much troubled by his thoughts, had walked into the country,
musing on the ultimate meaning of natural knowledge and
the laws of nature. While there, a vision appeared to him,
which became the third part of his work. He saw Dame
Scotia weeping. Her three sons came to her aid and promised
the destruction of her enemies, including the English invader.
A modern editor has commented how like one of Bale's
historical morality plays this part is.[2] Sadly, the author was
forced to conclude that all the world was under divine judgement for its crimes. This brought him to consider the question of the world's duration. His first thought was to follow
an opinion he attributed to Socrates that the world would
last 37,000 years, after which time all things 'sal retourne to
that same stait as thei began'.[3] This theory was based on the
calculation of the time taken to complete a full circuit of the
fixed stars and was usually identified as the great, mundane,
or Platonic year. By the early Middle Ages the figure was calculated, perhaps under Arabic influence, to 36,000 years. A
further supposition derived from this period by many was
that the return of the stars to their position at the Creation
would coincide with the Final Judgement. Some went further,

---

[2] *The Complaynt of Scotlande*, Introduction.
[3] Ibid. (text), p. 33.

to conclude that this return of the stars to their first state meant also the return of all nature to its original purity.[4]

Despite the strong natural argument for Socrates' opinion, the author could find no corroborative evidence in either theology or Scripture. At this point he turned to the Prophecy of Elias. He found much to recommend this prophecy, especially as it was expanded in the Christian idea of a world-week. Further, he argued that the present state of the world was so corrupt it did not seem possible it could last another 32,000 years. Therefore he would accept the calculations of Elias' Prophecy as he found it expressed in *Carion's Chronicle*: 'Nou, to confound the opinione of Socrates, and to confound al them that vil nocht beleve that the warld is neir ane final ende, i vil arme me vitht the cronikles of master jhone carion, quhar he allegis the prophesye of helie, sayand. . . .'[5] He quoted the prophecy from Carion and included the curtailment of the final 2,000 years.

His was the first reference I have seen in English to Elias' prophecy taken from Carion. The next time it appeared in Scotland was in Sir David Lindsay's poem the *Monarche*[6] which falls within the Protestant tradition. *The Complaynt of Scotlande* sprang from an unusual quarter. Most of the writers that followed were drawn to the tradition through the language of the Reformation and were Protestants who became convinced that Antichrist had appeared in Rome.

The outstanding personality of the Scottish Reformation, John Knox, took part in both the Edwardian Reformation and the Marian exile. Understandably then, Knox was the Scottish writer most influenced by the same forces that worked on the English exiles. In certain respects his experience was different. His residence in Geneva coloured his adaptation of the apocalyptic tradition. He was a man of conviction and dedication, characteristics that made him an

---

[4] The author here and David Lindsay in his *Dreme* both give the incorrect figure of 37,000 years, which suggests that they may have used a common source. The actual attribution of the opinion to Socrates appears to be false. Douglas Hamer, notes to *The Works of Sir David Lindsay of the Mount 1490–1555* (Scot. Text Soc., 1934), vol. iii, pp. 25–6. Modern calculations give a period of about 25,000 years for the complete circuit of the Zodiac.

[5] *The Complaynt of Scotlande*, p. 35.

[6] Douglas Hamer, op. cit., vol. iii (notes), p. 451.

admired leader and partisan historian. More than either Bale or Foxe, Knox arrived at his belief in the importance of prophecy in history from his personal experience rather than his reading or training. Knox came to believe himself a latter-day prophet. His progress towards this conviction began with his first encounter with Protestantism in the teaching and life of George Wishart.

Between 1530 and 1540, persecution of those who held Protestant opinions forced many Scots into exile, Wishart among them. He travelled to Germany, and spent some time in Cambridge, possibly at the invitation of Robert Barnes.[7] In 1543, Wishart returned to Scotland and prudently retired to his home, where from 1543 to 1545 he engaged in private study, perhaps reading books he obtained on his last journey to Switzerland. During this period he prepared a translation of the First Helvetic Confession (1537).

Knox, who became one of his disciples, provides the account of Wishart's career from his return to Scotland until his death in 1546. He praised Wishart in terms equal to those he later used to describe Calvin. Wishart was

a man of such graces as befoir him was never heard within this realm, yea, and as rare to be found yet in any man, nocht withstanding the great lyght of God that sence his dayes hes schyned unto us. He was not onlye singularlye learned, alswell in godlye knowledge, as in all honest human science; bot also he was so clearly illuminated with the spreat of prophesy, that he saw nott only thingis as some tounes and the hole Realme afterward felt, which he foir-spak, nott in secreat, but in the audience of many, as in their owin places shalbe declaired.[8]

Not least among the reasons why Knox admired Wishart was his ability as a prophet, not only as one who admonishes but also as a man given prescience by a special illumination. Knox introduced himself into the narrative after the death of Wishart and the assassination of Cardinal Beaton. He tells us that before being persuaded to enter the castle of St. Andrews he had desired to travel to the schools of Germany. The months from April to July 1547 were crucial to Knox's character and career. Having entered the castle in the company of his three pupils as their tutor, a position he had held

[7] Charles Rogers, *Life of George Wishart*, Grampian Club (London, 1876), p. 7.
[8] Knox, *History of the Reformation in Scotland*, ed. David Laing for the Woodrow Society, vol. i (Edinburgh, 1848), p. 125.

for some time, he was brought into a society of reformers eager for recruits. There he received his calling to active Protestant ministry. He was reluctant to begin a career as a preacher, but the leaders in the castle persevered, uniting in a plan to convince Knox of his calling. An appropriate sermon was given by one of them concerning the power of the congregation and the call of the preaching ministry. Finally, the call was announced:

Whairat the said Johanne abashed, byrst furth in moist abundand tearis, and withdrew him self to his chalmer. His conteanance and behaviour fra that day till the day that he was compelled to present him self to the publict place of preaching, did sufficiently declair the greaf and truble of his hearte, for no man saw any sign of myrth of hi, neyther yitt had he pleasur to accumpany any man, many dayis togitther.[9]

This was a personal and a professional crisis. The matters then brought to his attention, the decisions he made in the few days before his first sermon, and the content of that sermon, became associated in his mind with the purpose of his life and teaching.

John Knox gave another reason for his decision to enter the pulpit. It seems that one John Annand had 'long trubled' John Rough in his preaching, and Knox had undertaken Rough's defence in writing, and others hearing of this pressed him to preach as well as write. Knox had begun his defence with the intention to 'defyne the Church, by the rycht notes geven to us in Goddis Scripture of the trew Church', and distinguished a true from a false church. In so doing, he had employed the images of 'the immaculate spous of Jesus' against 'the Mother of Confusion' and the 'spirituall Babylon'. The Roman Church he called 'the synagog of Sathan'; the pope, 'the man of syne'. He concluded with the dedication: 'Yea I offer my selve, by word or wryte, to prove the Romane Church this day farther degenerate from the puritie which was in the dayis of the Apostles, than was the Church of the Jews, when thei consented to the innocent death of Jesus Christ.'[10]

During the interval between his vocation and his first sermon both the nature of the calling and the recent controversy must have been often in his mind. His first sermon took

[9] Knox, *History*, vol. i, pp. 186–8.   [10] Ibid., pp. 188–9.

this dedication for its thesis. He chose his text from Daniel 7:

And ane other king shall rise after thame, and he shall be unlyke unto the first, and he shall subdew three kings, and shall speak wordis against the Most Heigh, and shall consome the sanctes of the Most Heigh, and think that he may change tymes and lawes, and thei shalbe geven into his handis, untill a tyme, and tymes, and deviding of tymes.

His argument proceeded on three points:

(i) 'In the begynnyng of his sermone, he schew the great luif of God towardes his church, whom it pleaseth to foir-warne of dangeris to come so many yearis befoir thei come to pas.'

(ii) The second had two parts: first he reminded the congregation that the Jews were then in captivity in Babylon; secondly he rehearsed the four empires of Daniel's vision, 'in the destruction whairof, rase up that last Beast which he affirmed to be the Romane church; for to none other power that ever has yitt bein, do all the notes that God has schawin to the Propheit appertane, except to it allone . . .'.

(iii) 'But befoir he begane to opin the corruptions of the Papistrie, he defyned the trew Kirk.'

In the exposition of the last two points he gave the king in Daniel 7 his other names: 'the Man of Syn', the 'Antichrist', 'the Hoore of Babylon'. These referred not to one man but to a multitude of which the pope was head. The pope inspired his followers to sin, as Christ inspired his followers to justice. Next he reviewed the 'lives of diverse Papes, and the lyves of all scheavelynges for the most part'; showed their laws and doctrines to be contrary to Scripture, using justification by faith as an example, also using holy days, fasts, and celibacy. Knox then challenged any of his congregation to disprove him or dispute his use of 'scripture, doctour, or historye'. Present were John Mair, John Winrame, and several friars. If they came to him, he would show 'not onlye the originall whare my testimonyes are written, but I shall prove that the wrettaris ment as I have spokin'.[11]

Knox's pronouncements were given very early in the general history of the apocalyptic tradition, before Bale had published the whole of his *The Image of bothe churches*. Possibly Knox had a copy of Joye's *Exposition of Daniel* (1545)

---

[11] Knox, *History*, vol. i, pp. 189-90.

gathered out of the writings of several leading continental
theologians, or else access to some of the German authors
themselves. Another source could have been Frith's translation of Luther's *De Antichristo* (1529), a commentary on
Daniel 8 but not far in theme from Knox's interpretation of
the closing verses of Chapter 7. Wishart brought back with
him from Germany the Helvetic Confession and probably
other Protestant books. He was known to favour the Swiss
theologians, a tendency also noticeable in Joye. Wishart's
friendship with Barnes may well have resulted in his acquisi-
tion of the latter's *Vitae Romanorum Pontificum* (1535).
The combination of this work with either of the other two
would cover the main points of Knox's sermon. In the absence of the text of the sermon (Knox provides only the
outline), more positive conclusions are not possible. At least
one writer on John Knox's theology has expressed the
opinion that Knox originated this use of Daniel's prophecies.[12] However, although one cannot be quite certain that
Knox did not arrive at his thesis independently, by his own
admission he gathered his material out of Scripture, Doctors,
and histories, which seems very likely in the light of his
contemporaries' writings on this subject and the ways in
which he could have gained access to them.

One of the central arguments Hugh Watt gives for his
belief in Knox's originality is the surprise of the congregation. The sermon was a tremendous success and Knox reported that people wondered why they had never seen the true
interpretation of the prophecies before.[13] This reaction
simply shows that this approach to prophecy was new to
Scotland, not that Knox originated it. The success of this
sermon on the prophet Daniel, and later experiences in the
French galleys,[14] gradually convinced Knox that he, like
Wishart, had the gift of prophecy by special illumination, an
ability not only to interpret the word of God but also to
speak it. In 1565, after his victorious return to Scotland and
during the period in which he was engaged in writing his
history, he summarized his vocation in these words:

I decree to containe my selfe within the bondes of that vocation

---

[12] Hugh Watt, *John Knox in Controversy* (London, 1950).
[13] Knox, *History*, vol. i, p. 192.   [14] Ibid., pp. 228-9.

whereunto I founde my selfe especially called. I dare not denie (lest that in so doing I should be injurious to the giver) but that God hath revealed unto me secretes unknowen to the worlde, and also that he hath made my tong a trumpet to forewarne realmes and nations yea certaine great personages of mutations and chaunges, when no such thinges were feared, nor yet was appearing, a portion whereof can not the world denie (be it never so blind) to be fulfilled, and the rest (alas) I feare shall folowe with greater expedition and in more full perfection, than my sorrowful heart desireth.[15]

One particular revelation of God's will for which he became famous was the prohibition of rule by women. But the great stir this caused in Elizabeth's England should not blind us to Knox's belief that he was one of a series of prophets intended by God to reveal the pattern of coming events. This pattern of suffering followed by victory followed by destruction coming 'with greater expedition . . .' corresponded directly to the apocalyptic pattern's expectations for the present and immediate future.

One of Knox's audience at his first sermon was a man who had been among the conspirators who had forced him to undertake the vocation of preaching. This was Sir David Lindsay of the Mount, who was present in the castle as a go-between sympathetic to the reformers but anxious for agreement. Knox's sermon may have inspired Lindsay's poem the *Monarche*, which he began shortly thereafter and finished in 1553. This poem followed the history of the world from the Creation through the four monarchies to the promise of the kingdom. For the first half of the poem, Lindsay used a chronicle written in 1493, but for the second half he referred to *Carion's Chronicle*. There has been some discussion among scholars as to whether Lindsay used the original German version or a Latin or English translation. Albrecht Lange believes that Lindsay used the German version,[16] but more persuasively Douglas Hamer presents arguments for the English translation of 1550.[17]

There was nothing particularly unusual about Lindsay's

[15] John Knox, *A Sermon Preached by John Knox*, 19 August 1565 (Edinburgh, 1566), pp. ii–iii.

[16] Albrecht Lange, *Lyndsay's Monarche und die Chronica Carionis* (Halle, 1904).

[17] Douglas Hamer, notes to Lindsay's *Monarche*, *Lindsay's Works*, vol. iii, pp. 238–42.

choice of subject, but he presented it in a specifically Protestant form. Following the four usual monarchies he added 'the fyft Spirituall and Papall Monarchie', which intervened between the fall of Rome and the kingdom of Christ.[18] Lindsay traced the prophecy of this fifth monarchy to the part of Daniel 8 that Knox had quoted in his sermon.[19] Further, Lindsay expressed, both in this poem and in *Ane Satyre on the thre estates*, dread that 'the plaiges of Johnis Revelatioun | Sall fall vpon zour generatioun'.[20] He followed the Prophecy of Elias:

> Sum wryttaris hes the warld devidit
> In six ageis (as bene desidit
> Into *Fasciculus Temporum*
> And *Cronica Cronicarum*)
> Bot, be the sentence of Elie
> The warld devidit is in thre:
> As cunning Maister Carioun
> Hes maid plane expositioun. . . .
> So be this compt, it may be kend
> The warld is drawned neir ane end.[21]

When questioned about predictions of the Day of Judgement, Lindsay has Experienc˙ reply that

> Quharefore, perturbe nocht thyne intent
> To knaw day, hour, nor moment
> To God allone the day bene knowin
> Quhilk never was to none Angell shawin.

but

> Howbeit, be divers conjectouris
> And principall Expositouris
> Off Daniell and his Prophecie
> And be the sentence of Elie[22]

the duration of the world and its ages might be discovered. The ritual disclaimer of the possibility of true prediction, which had for Bale and many others signalled the end of their discussions of prophecy, was in other cases only the beginning.

The third part of Lindsay's *Monarche* dealt in great detail with the nature of the heavenly empire that would follow the

---

[18] *Lindsay's Works*, vol. i, pp. 238–42.   [19] Ibid., p. 353.
[20] Ibid., vol. ii, p. 133, 'Ane Satyre . . .', lines 1188–9; vol. i, p. 345, *Monarche* lines 4958–9 reads '. . . upon their generatioun', referring to the generation of Antichrist then living.
[21] Ibid., vol. i, p. 356, *Monarche* lines 5280–7, 5312–13.
[22] Ibid., lines 5264–71 (p. 355).

fulfilment of the prophecies in the Apocalypse. Two aspects
mentioned by Lindsay had become part of Protestant expectations associated with the prophecies of the Apocalypse.
The *Monarche* illustrated how at the end,

> The Hevin renewit salbe, than
> Rychtso, the erth, with devyse
> Compair tyll hevinlye Paradyse
> So hevin and erth salbe allone
> As menith the Apostill Johne.[23]

In the heavenly empire a thousand years would pass like an
hour because all those alive at the second coming would be
immortal and appear to be thirty-three years of age. As a
poet, Lindsay was allowed to dwell on the physical delights
of this second paradise, but in sober theology such preoccupation was greatly mistrusted. Nevertheless, these two aspects
of future expectation crept into writings of most serious
nature. The confession of faith of the Scottish Church under
the direction of John Knox expressed a belief in a cosmic
restitution and the immortality of those alive at the second
coming.

We believe that the same Lord Jesus shall visibly return for this last
Judgement as He was seen to ascend. And then, we firmly believe, the
time of refreshing and restitution of all things shall come, so that those
who from the beginning have suffered violence, injury, and wrong for
righteousness' sake shall inherit that blessed immortality promised them
from the beginning.[24]

In general, Lindsay referred to Daniel and the Prophecy of
Elias to describe the past and to the Apocalypse to describe
the future. His expression of the tradition in two of its three
main constituents was made before the Marian exile. Lacking
in this interpretation, but present in the English version after
Bale, was a historical rendering of the seven seals, trumpets,
and vials. Knox's sermon, by comparing Daniel's prophecy of
the vile person with John's of the whore of Babylon and finding both identified with Rome, began the Scottish approach
to the third constituent. This approach was hastened by the
Geneva Bible, and probably completed by Goodman's sermons. However, from the beginning the interests illustrated

[23] *Lindsay's Works, Monarche* lines 6055–9 (p. 377).
[24] Arthur Cochrane, *Reformed Confessions of the Sixteenth Century* (London,
1966), pp. 170–1; also Knox, *History*, vol. ii, pp. 102–3.

in the English experience by the efforts of George Joye received more sympathetic hearing in Scotland.

Knox's career after his first sermon took him first into French captivity, then to Edward's England, and finally into exile. During the years of the Marian exile, he joined the community in Frankfurt, led the more radical party of the controversy there, and then moved to Geneva. In both places he served as minister to the congregation, sharing his position in Geneva with Christopher Goodman. As an active minister, Knox's interests and concerns centred on questions of discipline, community reform, and duty to superior powers. In both interest and commitment, Knox was a man of the present. Increasingly during these years he turned for comfort and courage to the examples of the prophets, and increasingly found in their example his own vocation. One of his biographers, Jasper Ridley, traces from 1554 Knox's considerations of his own role in the solution of the problem of obedience to tyrants.[25] In epistles to the churches of England, Knox began to refer to the role of the prophets in the execution of God's judgements against tyrants, becoming particularly fond of Jehu's denunciation of Jezebel.[26]

His spirit of prophetic rebellion attained its most complete expression in his *First Blast of the Trumpet against the Monstrous Regiment of Women*. In this tract he likened his own pronouncement to those of the prophets before him, referring first to Jehu and secondly to Daniel.

The same prophets for comfort of the afflicted and chosen saintes of God, who did lie hyd amongst the reprobate of that age (as commonlie doth the corne amongest the chaffe) did prophecie and before speake the changes of kingdoms, the punishments of tyrannes, and the vengeance which God wold execute upon the oppressors of his people. The same did Daniel and the rest of the prophets everie one in their season.

. . . And further it is our dutie to open the truth reveled unto us, unto the ignorant and blind world, unless that to our owne condemnation we list to wrap up and hyde the talent commited to our charge.[27]

Knox brought to mind Daniel before all other prophets because he wished to make it clear that the prophet had not

[25] Jasper Ridley, *John Knox* (Oxford, 1968), pp. 177–8.
[26] Knox, *To Christ's Afflicted Church* (1556), in *Works*, ed. Laing, vol. iii, p. 247; *A Comfortable Epistle to Christs Church* (1556), ed. cit., p. 245.
[27] Knox, *The First Blast* (Crespin, Geneva, 1558), fols. 2–4ᵛ.

only the power of moral exhortation but clearly also that of prescience, a talent given of God which he believed he had himself received.

While Knox was in Geneva the exiles were at work on a new translation of the Bible. It is not known whether Knox took an active part either in the translation or in the writing of the extensive and powerful notes, but since he and Christopher Goodman were joint pastors of the congregation whose task it was, their influence was bound to be felt, and many of the notes express ideas known to be theirs.[28] The Book of Revelation was one of the most heavily annotated; in many places the notes are longer than the text itself. Even so, space was limited, and the Geneva Bible does not constitute a full commentary; it only highlights parts of the interpretation considered essential for understanding the prophecies. The points agreed upon are those common to most of the earlier Protestant commentators and no sources are given for the notes. Thus it is difficult to say whose influence is strongest. The most likely commentary to have been used by the exiles was Bullinger's *A hundred sermons*, both because the interpretations given are for the most part those he gave or repeated and because of the close association of the book with the exiled community. In some places it is possible to detect variances with Bullinger's views; for example in Revelation 20: 2 concerning the dating of the millennium, where the interpretation follows Bale's *The Image of both churches*.[29] These two works were the most popular during this period and the ones most often printed after the exiles returned to England.

The notes both attempted to indicate specific events and persons—the persecution under Domitian and the actions of Boniface VIII are assigned definite passages[30]—and avoided any specific periodization according to the order of the text or its images. The seven seals were recognized as indicating separate stages, but these were not identified with periods of years. Despite this, the introduction to the argument explained that in the book 'the livelie description of Antichrist

[28] Ridley, *John Knox*, pp. 288–90.
[29] R. Bauckham, 'Interpretations of Prophecy', chap. II.
[30] *Geneva Bible* (Edinburgh, 1579), fols. 118r, 122r.

is set for the whose *time* and power not withstanding *is limited*'.[31] The identification of the Antichrist with the papacy was maintained through the equation of the second beast with the usurpation of the empire by the papacy, and the scorpions and locusts were compared to the popish hierarchy. Because the Turks were not mentioned in these particular places,[32] the source is apparently closer to the view of Bale and Bullinger than to that of the early Lutheran commentators. The number of the beast was rendered as *Lateinos*. The Revelation was argued to contain both a description of Antichrist and clues to his historical identity. A growing interest in assigning particular historical settings to the prophecies was further illustrated in an insistence that parts of the text referring to future events did so in a historical sense. The treading of the winepress (Rev. 14) indicated the victory of the faith in 'a certain place appointed & not in heaven'. However obscure those parts of the text which remained to be fulfilled might be, they were, like those parts already past, part of a divinely ordained *procursus*.

The Geneva Bible was written by men who knew themselves to be the followers of Calvin in doctrine and discipline, and his influence upon the work as a whole is marked. However, because Calvin did not write a commentary on the Revelation, it would be misleading to assert that the Geneva Bible represented his views on this book. In one case a note echoed his argument for a historical Antichrist by referring the readers of Revelation 13: 8 to Paul's Epistle to the Thessalonians and the prophecy of a final apostasy. Calvin's followers were not hindered by his reluctance, and through the Geneva Bible and the other works of exiles like Knox and Goodman the apocalyptic tradition became part of British Calvinism. Nevertheless it ought to be clear that the apocalyptic tradition was not generated or perpetuated in a peculiarly Calvinist context.

In the two or so years during which the Geneva Bible was prepared Knox wrote a substantial defence of Calvin's

[31] *Geneva Bible*, ed. cit., Introduction to Revelation, my italics.

[32] The Turks are mentioned elsewhere in conjunction with the pope and Satan but their absence from the figure of the scorpions and locusts is significant.

doctrine of predestination against the anabaptists.[33] In this as
in the Bible, recourse to argument from the Revelation was
made in order to defend the master's views and to extend
them. Knox seems to have thoroughly imbibed Bale's two
images and then to have sharpened the dichotomy to suit his
own militant understanding of history, past and present. In
his hands the two cities of Augustine, transmuted through
Bale's two churches, became two armies.

For the first I say, that who so ever doth denie that from the beginning
there hath bene, this day are, and to ye ende shall remaine two armies,
bandes, or companies of men, whom God in his eternall counsell hath
so devided, that betwext them there continueth a battell, which never
shalbe reconciled, untill the Lord Jesus put a finall ende to the miseries
of his Church: who doth not understand the trueth of this (I say) doth
nether know God, nether his Sonne Christ Jesus. . . . The one of these
Armies, is called the Church of God the elect Spouse of Christe Jesus
. . . by ancient writters it is termed the citie of God. The other is called
the sinagoge of satan . . . And according to the divers natures, conditions, and endes of these two companies, doth the scripture pronounce
generall sentences, and universall propositions, which not withstanding
must be restreined to those of whom the holy Gost meaneth.[34]

The preordained battle could end in only one way; the condemnation of God delivered in the Apocalypse was irrevers-
ible. Not even repentance would save the false church from
utter destruction.

ye do not heare in all this revelation of John, that Babilon is exhorted
to repentance that the blasphemous beast is rebuked, ether of his
tyranny, ether of his blasphemie, with any promes made to him that he
will convert, he shall be receaved to mercie and favor. No the sentence
irrevocable is pronounced by the Angel, that he shall come to destruction.[35]

It is significant of the militant tone of the Scottish Reformation and of its Apocalypse-based assurance of success that,
when the Second Helvetic Confession issued from Geneva
containing the specific denunciation of any beliefs like those
held in Münster that in the last days the elect would slaughter
the reprobate and gain a temporal kingdom, the Scottish

---

[33] Knox, *An Answer to a Great nomber of blasphemous cavillations written
by an Anabaptist* (Geneva, 1560), hereinafter *Answer to an Anabaptist*, printed
by Jean Crespin. Ridley suggests Knox wrote it in the latter half of 1558 and left
it in Geneva in 1559 (*John Knox*, p. 290).
[34] Knox, *Answer to an Anabaptist*, pp. 398-9.
[35] Ibid., p. 256.

Church at first hesitated over accepting,[36] and then, when it was officially recognized, did not in 1567 or 1581 include this condemnation in its own confession.[37] The man appointed to interpret the Second Helvetic Confession to the Church Assembly was Robert Pont,[38] whom we shall meet again as an expositor of chronological prophecies, himself indicating a final date.

Upon his return to Scotland Knox began practising the doctrines he had preached in Geneva. His conviction that the world was divided into two armed camps stayed with him, and so too did the belief that the prophecies of Daniel and the Revelation had a peculiar significance for his own times and the troubles he faced in bringing the Reformation to Scotland. His history of the Reformation in Scotland occupied him over the years from 1559 to 1571. The second book in the final text was the first written. It covered events from May to December 1559. The third book continued the history to the return of Mary and dwelt on promises and signs of the coming victory. It occupied its author from 1563 to 1567. From about 1566 Knox began work on the first and fourth books. In these he traced his own career, illustrating his vocation as both preacher and prophet. Book One followed the beginning of the Reformation to Knox's conversion, calling, and early sufferings in exile; the last book showed how he as a prophet and instrument of God's purpose and judgement brought the Reformation to Scotland.[39]

Knox believed implicitly that as God had acted in the past so he continued to act in the present. The Bible was to him much more than a history of the faith. It was a handbook for the judgement of God upon nations and powers in the world. When circumstances matched, then similar conclusions

---

[36] The Church of Scotland to Theodore Beza, 4 Sept. 1556, *Zürich Letters*, Parker Soc., 1845, vol. ii, pp. 362-5. The Confession was received by Knox in March. The Assembly officially took exception only to the inclusion of certain holy days.

[37] The Second Scottish Confession of 1581 denied in strident tones the Roman Antichrist and all his works and dedicated Scotland to the extirpation of papistry. *Acts and Proceedings of the General Assemblies of the Kirk of Scotland from the Year MDLX*, Maitland Club (Edinburgh, 1839), Part I, pp. 515-18.

[38] Ibid., p. 90.

[39] Pierre Janton, *John Knox (ca. 1513-1572); L'homme et l'œuvre*, Études Anglaises (Paris, 1967), p. 428.

followed. By using the examples of Scripture he called down the same judgements upon his contemporaries that he found in Scripture. In doing this he only followed the example set by the prophets and messengers of God sent before him. Scripture contained such general sentences and revelations, but God also revealed to a small number of his elect certain special revelations applicable to any one age.[40] These special revelations placed a responsibility upon the receiver to declare and announce them to the congregation. Once this was done, God would fulfil the prophecy. On the prophet Jeremiah's premonitions, he wrote:

Was this I praye you a simple declaration? or was it not rather a sentence & decree so effectuall, that albeit nether Babylon, nether any other proud and whicked nation wold for that time beleve it, yet came it most effectually to pass? . . . The Prophet without feare did obey his commandement, and God did faithfully performe what so ever his messinger had pronounced.[41]

Knox felt that he had received a number of such revelations and that his sentences were uttered with the same force of inevitability.

Unlike most reformers, Knox did not write extensive commentaries on Scripture. In 1565 he explained that this was because he felt his vocation was to forewarn present nations of approaching mutations and judgements in God's name.[42] His mission as a prophet would be tried by his success in the world, in the effectiveness of his judgements in God's name. When he came to write his history he was to a certain extent breaking new ground. He wrote neither a commentary on the Apocalypse nor a history that dealt with the periods of the Church's history from the ascension of Christ, yet he cast the present into the apocalyptic context of the final battle between two armies. The 'general sentences' of the angel in the Revelation and the particular sentences of God's prophets down the ages to the Reformation were on the point of fulfilment. The history of the Reformation in Scotland declared not only God's purpose but also the means he chose to bring it about.

Although Knox used the themes of persecution and

[40] Knox, *Answer to an Anabaptist*, pp. 398-9.   [41] Ibid., pp. 374-5.
[42] *A Sermon preached by John Knox*, 19 Aug. 1565 (Edinburgh, 1566), pp. ii-iii.

martyrdom to illustrate the opening years of the Reformation in Scotland, he did not choose to model his history
solely upon the martyrologies of Crespin and Foxe. In his
interest in the contemporary history of religion and politics
he had more in common with John Sleidan. When he left
Geneva, Knox had left his work on predestination with Jean
Crespin, who was then working on an edition of Sleidan's
works. At the close of his book Knox recommended Sleidan's
Commentaries as 'written by that most faithful and notable
witness of thinges done in maters of religion, sithence the
beginning of the Empire of Charles the fifte untill the yere
of 1556'.[43] A year after leaving Geneva, Knox began recording the events of the Scottish Reformation for his own history. Later, as he wrote his preface, he echoed the purpose
declared by Sleidan in his preface to the *Commentaries*.
Sleidan's preface had read:

. . . but warlike matters, & suche other like affaires, I do not omit, for
that I mighte in no wise do. Yet have I not professed to to [*sic*] treat of
them expresly. For as I said a little before, this laboure was purposed
chiefly to the cause of religion. Therefore wold I have the reader
warned, that when he shal come unto such places, he loke for no long
discourse of those affaires. For nether is it mine intent, & they may
read it in other mens works, which have taken in hand to wryte of that
part, so much as herein shalbe wanting. An other thing that I said is to
be observed in a history, is fidelity or uprightnes, that is to wit, that
nothing be told of affection: which although it seme very harde,
because it is of few performed, and albeit that peraventure I shall not
perswade all men, that I have ben dilligently ware of the same, yet I
require them instantly, that I be not burthened with any suspition
before there be cause.[44]

And Knox wrote:

And yet, in the begynnyng, mon we crave of all the gentill Readaris,
not to look of us such ane History as shall expresse all thingis that have
occurred within this Realme, during the tyme of this terrible conflict
. . . for, with the Pollicey, mynd we to meddill no further then it hath
Religioun mixed with it. And thairfoir albeit that many thingis which
wer don be omitted, yit, yf we invent no leys, we think our selves
blamless in that behalf.[45]

Although he ostensibly adopted the same approach, Knox

[43] Knox, *Answer to an Anapabtist*, p. 408.
[44] Sleidan, *Commentaries* (London, 1560), Preface. The English edition published in 1560 is too late to have been used by Knox in Geneva.
[45] Knox, *History*, Preface, p. 4.

wrote a history that reads very differently from Sleidan's. In good part this was the result of differing versions of the prophetic tradition. Sleidan had had hopes that the Reformation would be accomplished through the agency of a great emperor whose reign was prophesied for the last age of the world.[46] Following in the steps of Bale and Foxe, Knox put his faith not in princes but in the small congregation of the elect. To this he added his own emphasis on the leadership of the prophets and messengers sent periodicially by God. Sleidan traced the fortunes of Protestant doctrine in the midst of error, but hoped in his dealing with individual persons that 'nothing be told of affection'. In contrast Knox viewed the struggle in terms of his two armies and wrote, 'Lett not thairfoir the reader wonder, albeit that our style vary and speik diverslie of men, according as thei have declared thame selves sometymes ennemyes and sometymes freindis, sometymes fervent, sometymes cold, sometymes constant, and sometymes changeable in the cause of God and of his holy religion.'[47] Both men looked for an institutional change, a church reformed by a temporal power. Both wrote their histories of religion as the opposition between the Roman and the Protestant faith, but for Knox that faith divided men into two armies locked in an apocalyptic struggle.

In the last years of his life Knox devoted much of his time to activities which show his continued interest in the application of prophecy to history. In July of 1571 he moved from Edinburgh to St. Andrews, where he lodged near St. Leonard's College. Every day he went to the church where he preached on the Book of Daniel, applying the text to current events and persons. The following summer he published the last of his pamphlets, *An Answer to a Letter of a Jesuit named Tyrie* (July 1572). Most of this had been written in 1566 in answer to a letter sent by Tyrie to his brother in Scotland. The brother had passed it on to Knox for his thoughts. At the time Knox decided not to publish his answer, but since then the Jesuit brother had begun publishing various propaganda

---

[46] Sleidan, *Commentaries*, Preface; see M. Reeves, *The Influence of Prophecy*, Part III, 'Antichrist and the Last World Emperor', especially the chapter 'Constellation of Prophecies: Charles V'.

[47] Knox, *History*, Preface, p. 5.

pamphlets in France.[48] Knox was provoked to reply and did
so paragraph by paragraph, using both histories, especially
Aventinus's (Johan Thurmair) history of Bavaria which
recounted the vices and crimes of popes during the Middle
Ages, and prophecies of Antichrist, referring with special
emphasis to Joachim's commentary.

Tyrie had argued that the Protestants were inconsistent in
condemning the Roman Church for seizing temporal power
and then proceeding, particularly in Knox's case in Scotland,
in attempting to do the same. Knox's very success in this
marked him by his own definition as a servant of Antichrist.
Tyrie had referred to an ancient writer of the twelfth century
who had shown that worldly success was the opposite of
spiritual success; Knox recognized a reference to Joachim and
prepared his defence to support the Protestant use of him. He
called to remembrance the time at which Joachim had
written and the original object of his criticism, the Roman
Church. Knox defined the time of Joachim's writing by
reference to the apocalyptic scheme: 'For then began the taill
of the Dragoun, to draw the starres from the heven to the
erth: Then began the fontanes which sometymes gave cleane
& holsome watter to become bitter: yea to be turned unto
blood, and yet did they prosper in all worldlie felicitie.'[49] To
support his interpretation that the Apocalypse applied to the
Roman Church alone, he directed Tyrie to read 'all wryters in
generall' who had written before the establishment of· the
Protestant churches.

And least that Maister Tyrie shal think that we put him to to much
pane, when that we send him to all wryters in generall, We shal releve
him somewhat, and appoint him to two only whome justly he can not
suspect to have bene corrupted by us. The one is Abbas Joachim, a man
sometymes of great authoritie and reputation amonges the Papists. The
other is Joanes Aventius historiographur, whose historie was prented by
command & with priviledge of the Emperour Charles the Fyft.[50]

Knox continued to quote Joachim's interpretation of the
Apocalypse, showing that Joachim had discovered in the
prophecies a denunciation of Rome. Lest this be interpreted

[48] Ridley, *John Knox*, p. 509.
[49] *An answer to a letter of a Jesuit named Tyrie* (St. Andrews, 1572), Dv^v;
see above, Chap. II, p. 44 and illustration p. 45.
[50] *Answer to a Jesuit*, Dvi^r.

to mean only the Roman Empire and not the Roman Church, he quoted Joachim as identifying the whore with the false Church in Rome which contrasted so completely with the poor pilgrims who came to her and were the true Church. Knox commented that here were portrayed the two distinct churches[51] that formed the basis of, and the excuse for, his uncompromising condemnation of Rome and his supremely partisan approach to the writing of history.

Unlike Foxe's *Acts and Monuments*, Knox's history did not introduce his readers to the systematic treatment of prophetic texts in order to construct a pattern of argument in history. However, it is evident that Knox based his treatment of the present upon assumptions about the past that were taken from the apocalyptic tradition. He added to this a strong personal conviction, lacking in either Bale or Foxe, that he had been given special powers of prescience. He saw himself as a successor to those special messengers and prophets of the Lord sent into each age. The martyrologists had shown how in earlier ages and in recent times these prophets had suffered at the hands of Antichrist and his army. So too had those who first sought to bring the Reformation to Scotland, but victory was promised to the army of Christ. The victory was not a martyr's victory of constancy in the face of affliction; it was the victory promised in the Book of Revelation, the utter destruction of the beast.

Until his death in 1572, John Knox dominated the Scottish Reformation. He continued to denounce Rome with the power and conviction of one who was certain he had both the prophetic gifts: the power to judge the present and the special enlightenment of one chosen to know the future. In the last year of his life Knox visited St. Andrews University to deliver a series of sermons on the subject of the prophecies of Daniel. The power of his attack is witnessed in the autobiography of James Melville who was a student at the time. Years later he wrote of 1571,

Bot of al the benefites I had that yeir was the coming of that maist notable profet and apostel of our nation Mr Jhone Knox to St. Androis. . . . I hard him teatche ther the prophecie of Daniel that summer, and the wintar following. I haid my pen and my litle book, and tuk away sic

[51] *Answer to a Jesuit*, Dvii[r].

things as I could comprehend. In the opening upe of his text he was
moderat the space of an halff houre; bot when he enterit to application,
he maid me sa to grew and tremble, that I could not hald a pen to
wryt.[52]

These sermons were as much a part of the course of study for
university students as any other series of lectures, and appear
especially to have caught the interest and fired the imagination of their hearers.

The impact of the Reformation upon the universities of
Scotland was quickly and sharply felt. Romish instructors
were expelled in great numbers and replaced by men of the
reformed faith. Emphasis was placed upon instruction in reformed theology; and to this end the sermons of both resident and visiting Churchmen were encouraged. The views of
John Knox or his colleagues were the stuff of politics and
events in the world at large. Their sermons were often the
most exciting events in the scholastic year. The young
students followed their course avidly, and many, like young
Melville, took notes.

Knox's influence did not wane with his death. Augmented
by the Geneva Bible and by his successors, his interpretation
of the present and the future gained in strength. Increasingly
events proved to the Scots that he had been right in condemning Rome utterly and in looking for evidence of God's
judgement in the life of nations. That the present was foretold in the prophecies of Scripture, in substance if not in
detail, was a conviction shared by the new generation and by
their king.

Both in England and in Scotland the events of 1588
provoked many to print their thoughts on the meaning of the
prophecies. Among them was King James VI. He wrote a
sermon on Revelation 20, 15, and 16, later published in
1616.[53] With a touch of royal arrogance James assumed the
persona of John in delivering his paraphrase of the prophecies,
but the message he delivered was that of Knox and the
Geneva Bible. He took the belief fostered by Knox that
prophecies dealt almost exclusively with affairs of state and

[52] *The Autobiography and Diary of Mr. James Melville*, ed. Robert Pitcairn,
Woodrow Soc. (Edinburgh, 1842), p. 26.
[53] Published in *The Works of the most High and Mighty Prince James* (London, 1616).

were therefore of especial necessity to princes. The Apocalypse revealed to him the historical identity of Antichrist
and his approaching defeat. James did not hesitate to name
particular happenings in his interpretation of the battle with
Gog and Magog. There he discovered an indication of the
treaty recently concluded between the Turks and Philip of
Spain, which had freed Philip to attack the rest of western
Europe.

And whereas the open enemie of God the Turke, was under bloody
warres with him [Antichrist] ever before is there not of late a truce
among them that the faithfull may be the more easily rooted out?
And are not the armies presentlie assembled, yea upon the very point
of their execution in *France*, against the Saints there? In *Flanders* for
the like; and in *Germanie* . . . ? And what is prepared to come forward
against this Ile?[54]

James had absorbed a good deal of the teaching of the
Protestant tradition. The open and the secret enemies, Turk
and pope, are there in his sermon; as are the two cities, two
peoples, and two armies. At the close he exhorts his readers
to call upon God and to have faith in his answer shown in
prophecies. Victory is assured and Scotland may take comfort in 'being in the tents of the Saints, & beloved city . . . as
warriors in one Campe, and citizens of one beloved city'.[55]
In his library he assembled several of the works important to
the apocalyptic tradition, including the *Magdeburg Centuries*
bought for him by an agent on the continent, Bullinger's one
hundred sermons, and *Carion's Chronicle*.[56] His sermon also
showed other aspects of his education. (The enemy, he
noted, revolved high upon the wheel of fortune and would
shortly fall.) But the chief influence upon him was that of
the established Protestant view.

In Scotland, easily the most important contribution to the
apocalyptic tradition provoked into print by the Armada and
succeeding events was the work of John Napier. A member of
the new generation who had listened to the sermons of the
reformers at St. Andrews, he came to the study of the
prophecies with a readily identifiable background, and yet he

[54] *The Works of the most High and Mighty Prince James*, p. 78.
[55] Ibid., p. 80.
[56] *The Library of James VI*, ed. G. F. Warner, Scot. Hist. Soc., vol. xv, Misc.
vol. I (Edinburgh, 1893).

brought with him much that was new. He was in his day as David Hume described him, 'the person to whom the title of Great Man is more justly due than any other whom his country had produced'.[57] He is remembered today almost exclusively for his contribution to the study of mathematics in the invention of logarithms, and since Mark Napier's biography[58] in 1834 no serious work has been done on any other aspect of his life or thought. Unfortunately even by then most of Napier's papers, except for some fragments on mathematics copied by his son and sent to Henry Briggs at Oxford, had been destroyed by fire,[59] leaving us uncertain about many things, including the extent of his correspondence and education. It is certain, however, that Napier regarded his work on the prophecies of the Apocalypse as his true vocation and the study of mathematics as the occupation of his leisure.[60] The two interests were not unconnected. His commentary shows the welcome influence of a logical and consistent mind, and his analytical method set a standard that many in the next century sought to equal.

In 1563, some years before James Melville trembled at the sermons of John Knox on Daniel, John Napier was sent to St. Salvator's College in St. Andrews and there came under the influence of Knox's old colleague in exile, Christopher Goodman. The sermons Napier heard had a powerful effect upon him. Years later he recalled the excitement he had felt:

being attentive to the sermones of that worthy man of God, Maister Christopher Goodman, teaching upon the Apocalypse, I was so mooved in admiration, against the blindness of Papists . . . that not onely bursted I out in continual reasoning against my said familiar [a Papist] but also from thenceforth, I determined with myselfe . . . to employ my study and diligence to search out the remanent mysteries of that

[57] Quoted in Mark Napier, *De Arte Logistica Joanni Naperi Merchistonii Baronis*, Maitland Club (Edinburgh, 1839), Introduction, p. iii.

[58] Mark Napier, *Memoirs of John Napier of Merchiston, His Lineage, Life and Times with a History of the Invention of Logarithms* (Edinburgh and London, 1834), p. 250.

[59] Mark Napier, *De Arte Logistica*, Introduction, p. iii.

[60] Mark Napier writes: 'it was the constant labour of his life to rend the fetters with which science was yet subdued. "In the course", he says "of devoting every moment of my leisure,"—doubtless from what he considered his great calling, the exposition of the Revelations [*sic*]. . . .' Ibid., p. xv.

holy book; as to this hour (praised be the Lord) I have bin doing at al
such times, as conveniently I might have occasion. . . .[61]

Goodman taught the identification of the Antichrist with the
papacy, and, like King James, Napier learned his theology
from the Geneva Bible and the thought of Knox and his
fellows. He joined the ranks of those who encouraged James
to see his duty as a prince in apocalyptic terms.

> Therefore, it is likewise the dutie of God's servants in this age, inter-
> preters of Prophecies, as well (according to the example of the
> Prophets) to incourage and inanimate Princes, to be ready against that
> greate day of the Lords revenge, as also to exhort them generally, to
> remove all such impediments in their cuntries and commonwealths, as
> many hinder that work, and prove Gods plagues.[62]

Napier remained true, at least in public, to his Scottish
Calvinist background throughout his life, and very little of
the content of his interpretation of the Apocalypse varies
from the expected. But in two things he exhibits influences
that are extraordinary: in his method and in his treatment of
the future.

It would be useful to know more about his education. It
seems very likely that some of it was gained abroad, but
Napier's biographer could find nothing conclusive in any of
what remains of his papers. It was the accepted thing for
young men of Napier's class to attend a foreign university,
usually in France; moreover, there exists a letter from
Napier's uncle to his parents suggesting that John should be
sent abroad.[63] When John was sent to St. Andrews in 1563,
the University had not fully recovered from the effects of
rapid reformation, and the quality of instruction in fields
such as mathematics had not been improved by the introduction of reformed theology. Even in 1571, as James Melville
illustrates in his autobiography, mathematics was taught in a
highly traditional manner. Students were taught 'the four
speaces of the Arithmetik, and sum thinge of the Spheare',
but the study of mathematics was considered less important
than that of Scripture and moral philosophy. Melville wrote
of his mathematics tutor 'bot the greatest benefit I had of

---

[61] John Napier, *A Plaine Discovery* (Edinburgh, 1593), 'To the Godly and
Christian Reader', fol. A6ʳ.

[62] Ibid., 'Dedication to James VI', fol. A3.

[63] Adam Bothwell to his sister, 5 Dec. 1560, printed Mark Napier, *Memoirs*,
p. 67.

him was his daylie doctrine at the prayers in the kirk, everie morning'.[64] Napier was in St. Andrews in 1563, but there is no record of his having proceeded to any degree in the following years,[65] and assuming that he had already by the age of fourteen shown an interest in mathematics it would seem likely that his parents would seek advice upon a suitable foreign university. Several possibilities exist. Mark Napier names Paris as a possible place, adding that both Buchanan and Craig, two friends of Napier's father, had been there themselves and would probably recommend it.[66] Other student contemporaries of Napier at St. Andrews were sent to Paris and Poitiers.[67] However, I think a more persuasive case can be made for considering the university at Guyenne, although certainty is not possible because again both fire (this time in 1862) and civil war have destroyed the college records for this period.[68]

When young John went to St. Andrews he lodged in the house of the principal of his college, John Rutherford, the Dean of the Faculty of Arts. Rutherford had himself been educated in France under Nicholas de Grouchy and both of them had taught at the Collège de Guyenne in Bordeaux. By a happy coincidence, that college was in 1563 just entering a period of great prosperity under the direction of Élie Vinet, the renowned scholar of Greek and mathematics. The future of Guyenne promised to be a return to the excellence known there in the late 1530s, when De Grouchy, Rutherford, Vinet, and George Buchanan had all taught there. Rutherford had left Guyenne in 1542 with Buchanan for Coimbra in Portugal, and Buchanan kept up a correspondence with Vinet partly through the Scots who arrived to study or to trade there each year. The historian of the college, Ernest Gaullieur, writes of the period from 1563:

[64] *Diary of James Melville*, ed. cit., p. 27.
[65] *Early Records of the University of St. Andrews*, ed. J. M. Anderson, Scot. Hist. Soc., 3rd series, vol. 8 (1926).
[66] Mark Napier, *Memoirs*, pp. 93–4; in *De Arte Logistica*, he again considered Napier's education abroad, presenting further indications: pp. lv–lxi.
[67] Andrew Melville went to both Paris and Poitiers, and Hercules Rollock went to Poitiers. The historians of Poitiers report that while Poitiers was well known for its teaching of law, Guyenne was more highly regarded for teaching the arts. *Histoire de l'Université de Poitiers* (1432–1932), ed. Boissonnade (Poitiers, 1932), p. 233.
[68] Ernest Gaullieur, *Histoire du Collège de Guyenne* (Paris, 1874), Preface.

Le nombre des élèves était très considérables, la Guyenne en fournis-
sait la plus grande partie; mais il en venait aussi des autres points de la
France et même de l'étranger: L'Écosse, tout particulièrement, en
envoyait chaque année quelques-uns: les marchands de cette nation que
leurs affaires attiraient à Bordeaux et dont certains apportaient à Élie
Vinet des nouvelles de son ancien collègue et ami Buchanan, étaient
heureux de confier leur fils à un homme dont la réputation de sagesse
et d'érudition était établie dans leur propre pays.[69]

Vinet had been a student at Paris at the same time as
Ramus, but unlike Ramus his career had not gained him any
enemies. Guyenne taught philosophy out of Aristotle, presumably with Vinet's blessing. The programme of studies[70]
he implemented during his years there stressed the study of
Aristotle and was as similar as he could make it to that
devised by André de Gouvea, the Portuguese humanist who
had directed the college when Vinet first arrived there. This
programme bore a resemblance to the one proposed by Jacob
Sturm in Strasburg.[71] In it the students were divided into ten
classes, of which the two highest pursued a course in which
the subjects of philosophy and mathematics were stressed, in
conjunction with a continuation of instruction in classical
languages and history. Vinet was also very interested in classical history, and the editor believes that the emphasis placed
upon its study reflected this, and was to his knowledge an
unusual aspect of Guyenne's programme.[72] The afternoon
public lectures, intended primarily for the upper two classes,
covered first the subject of Greek language, and secondly,
from 2 p.m. to 3 p.m., the study of mathematics. These were
Vinet's two particular arts, and he listed the texts he preferred to be used. First he suggested his own book, and a
more widely used text composed in the eleventh century by
Michael Psellos,[73] on arithmetic, music, and geometry. This

[69] Gaullieur, *Histoire du Collège de Guyenne*, p. 284.
[70] *Schola Aquitanica, Programme d'Études du Collège de Guyenne au XVIe*
siècle (first published by Élie Vinet, 1583), ed. Louis Massebieau (Paris, 1886).
[71] Massebieau, *Schola Aquitanica*, Preface, pp. viii–ix.
[72] Ibid., Preface, n. 48.
[73] Michael Psellos (1018–c. 1100) changed his name from Constantinos. He
was a leading Byzantine neo-Platonist who wrote works on history, medicine,
logic, and mathematics. The above work, probably wrongly attributed to him,
was edited by Archbishop Irsenius (Venice, 1532) and published thirteen times
during the sixteenth century. George Sardan, *Introduction to the History of*
Science (Baltimore, 1927), vol. i, p. 750.

was designed to give the pupils a grounding in the principles. Then followed the elements of Euclid and the Sphere. The book on the sphere may well have been the same as the one James Melville encountered at St. Andrews: a standard medieval work known as the *Sphere of Sacrobosco*, which Vinet had published in 1552 with a preface by Melanchthon.[74] This was followed by Greek and Latin authors of the lecturer's choice. When the lecturer was Vinet himself it is reasonable to suppose that most would be Greek and the mathematical content would be given competent attention.

Whether Napier's education was partly gained from experience abroad or if it followed the lines of Vinet's programme at Guyenne cannot be proven. However, at some point in his life Napier encountered the philosophy of Peter Ramus, and took to his method so completely that he incorporated it into his commentary on the Apocalypse. He could have learned this at Guyenne, or indeed at Paris, or he could have come by it in Scotland; for the reforms of Andrew Melville introduced into Scotland's universities the principles of Ramist method for the analytical treatment of Scripture. Melville began his career of reform in 1574 and enjoyed great success until well into the 1590s. During these years Napier, although in Scotland, was not living near a university. Melville encountered Ramism in Paris and carried back with him Ramus's hostility to Aristotelianism in all its forms. This hostility is one of the hallmarks of Scottish and also English Ramists.[75] But Napier made no such attack in his commentary.

At Guyenne, Vinet continued to teach Aristotle, and, in using the programme outlined by the brother of Antonio de Gouvea, probably showed his allegiance to one of Ramus's critics. Antonio de Gouvea believed that Ramus had oversimplified Aristotelian philosophy in his attacks, and worked to re-establish some aspects of Aristotelian thought within the context of Ramist method.[76] De Grouchey too had had

[74] Massebieau, *Schola Aquitanica*, Preface, n. 59.

[75] See Hugh Kearney, *Scholars and Gentlemen: Universities and Society in pre-industrial Britain 1500–1700* (London, 1970), chap. III.

[76] On Ramus and Ramism see Walter J. Ong, S.J., *Ramus: Method, and the Decay of Dialogue* (Cambridge, Mass., 1958), pp. 215–20. Nevertheless, Fr. Ong concludes that the 'Ramist method owes much to Gouveau—perhaps its very existence' (p. 218).

his doubts about Ramus,[77] doubts which may have reached Napier through his pupil Rutherford. At least one can say that Napier's position is consistent with that taught at Guyenne.

Napier's commentary, *A Plaine Discovery of the whole Revelation of Saint John*, was published in Edinburgh in 1593. After years of study he had still felt unready to publish his thoughts, but events following 1588 had so alarmed him that he abandoned his Latin version and hastened to publish in English so that those for whom his thoughts were chiefly intended might have them more quickly and in a language comprehensible to both English and Scots.[78] He may also have had a more personal reason for rushing into print. His father-in-law had been implicated in the affair of the Spanish Blanks and he may have felt that so soundly Protestant a work would remove him from any unwarranted suspicion. In both dedication and text he called upon King James and other princes 'without pitie, ruth, and mercie to procede with all possible extremitie against that devilish seat [of Rome] to the utter extirpation thereof'.[79]

He took his method from the Ramists, declaring he would handle the text 'as neere the analytik or demonstrative manner, as the phrase and nature of holy scriptures will permit'.[80] Ramus set out the principles of logical analysis in these words:

Logical analysis is the process by which a given example of discourse already composed is examined in terms of the laws of the art, the question is extracted, then the invention studied, and the place from which the argument was drawn looked for. This is the analysis of invention. Then the species of proposition used is gone into in the judgement of individual self-evident propositions: whether the simple proposition is common or proper, the composite compound or relative, connective or disjunctive; finally, by what truth whether of science or of opinion it is manifest.[81]

And Napier applied it to his commentary. Because he believed the Revelation to be above all a book of times containing dates and events hidden under the figures of prophetic

---

[77] Ong, *Ramus: Method, and the Decay of Dialogue*, pp. 160-2.
[78] John Napier, *A Plaine Discovery* (Edinburgh, 1593), 'To the Godly and Christian Reader'.
[79] Ibid., p. 222.
[80] Ibid., 'To the Godly and Christian Reader', fol. A6^r.
[81] Ramus, *Sch. in lib. art.* (1569), cols. 191-3; tr. Ong, pp. 263-4.

language, he used his ability and knowledge of mathematics to derive from the text a set of evident propositions, and applied to each of them in turn the analysis of invention. This analysis was completed in the first treatise, which Napier described as:

... the said introduction and reasoning, for investigation of the true sense of every chiefe Theological tearme and date contained in the Revelation, whereby, not only is it opened, explained and interpreted, but also the same explanation and interpretation is proved, confirmed and demonstrated, by evident proofe and coherence of scriptures, agreeable with the event of histories.[82]

In the second treatise, he discerned two types of discourse in the text: descriptive and prophetic; and as each case arose he applied to it the relevant propositions proved in the first treatise, showing the connections and disjunctions between the figures involved. The second treatise was divided into three columns: one for the text, a second for the analytical paraphrase, and a third for the truth of his interpretation as manifest in history. He followed the text 'Chapter by Chapter, Verse by Verse, and sentence by sentence'.[83] A favourite tool for illustration of argument used by Ramists of all sorts was the table. Napier's work falls naturally into such tables. He provided two which are reproduced here along with two sample pages from the second treatise. Careful study of each table will, as Napier promised, solve many questions which might arise in trying to understand his interpretation. The page selected as an example deals with a much-disputed section of the text. The principal divisions of the tables of the two treatises reveal how closely Napier followed the lead of earlier writers. Few of his identifications are startling; the most original aspect of his work lies in the form rather than the content. In the first table he divided secular or imperial history from church history; but then, in the second table and in the treatise following, the divisions are resolved into one continuous narrative. In this way, no symbol of the Apocalypse could have more than one referent. In order to decide the most likely candidate for each image or symbol, Napier looked first for the natural divisions of the text. In the first treatise[84] he discovered three stages of history. In

---

[82] 'To the Godly and Christian Reader', fol. A6^V.   [83] Loc. cit.
[84] *A Plaine Discovery*, p. 3 et seq.

A Table of the *Conclusions introductiue to the Reuelation*, and proued in the first Treatise.

The first Treatise is an introduction to the knowledge of the Reuelation, expounding by proofe and demonstration the meaning of

Dates and chiefe reckonings hid vnder tearmes,

Affaires and chiefe matters concerning

Vulgare and vsed, such as		New and strange, wherewith is dated		Gods seruantes. whole true and holie		Gods greatest enemies, as	
generally, a day for a yeare, a week for seuen yeares, a moneth for 30. yeares, and a yeare for a yeare of yeares. or three hundred & three score yeares, proued in the 1 proposition.	particularly 42. moneths 1260. propheticall daies: three great dayes and an half, and a time, times, and half a time, prooued to be all one date, proposition 15. and euerie one of them to meane a thousand, two hundred and three score Iulian yeares, proposition. 16.	the historie of S. Iohn his daies, vnder the tearmes of 7. seales, whereof the firste begins, An.Chri 29. prop. 8. the last An.Chri sti, 71. proposition 7. and euerie one of them indureth by the ninth proposition.	The prophecy to the worldes end, wherof The prophecie begins, An.Chri 29. prop. 7.vials which both ar proued to, be one of Gods 1. and euerie one of them doeth	The ende and last daies, are dated by 7. thunders. & 7. Angels of Gods harueast, both proued to be one,	Church with her contents is tearmed Gods Temple in heauen,Pro.20 and a woman cled with the Sunne, prop.22. The twenty foure books of the olde Testament are called the twenty foure Elders, propositi- fition 18.	Religion is tearmed God his throne in heauen, pro. 17. whereof the written word is testified by the two witnesses, prooued prop.21. to be the two Testaments, whereof The foure Evangels of the new Testament are called the foure beastes, propositi- on 19.	Sathan who is bound a 1000. yeares, be ginning An. 300. prop. 34. yet bond but only from raising of vniuersal wars, prop. 35.	Wicked kingdoms which are set out vnder the tearmes of Two nations, Gog and Magog prooued [by the thirtie & two proposition] to bee the Papistes and Mahometans, whose armies are all one with those of the sixt trumpette or viall, as is proued in the thirtie three propositi.

endure 245.yeares, gathered by the thirde and fourth propositions, and prooued by the fift proposition: and the first beginneth, Anno,Christi,71. proposition 6. and the last beginneth,an.Christ.1541. and ends Anno 1786.at the farthest.prop.10.

Christi,1541.prop.12. & euery one of the first three that goeth before the day of iudgement, to indure 49.yeares,prop.13. making the latter day to fall betwixt the yeares of Christ 1688 and 1700.by prop.14

The prophecie to be one, prop. 11. & to beginne Anno Christi,1541.prop.12. &c.

on, the whole Latine or Romane Empire, with the Antichrist descending of the same, of which Romane or Latine Empire,the seat and Metropolitane Citie,Rome, is meaned and represented by Babylon in the twentie three proposition. To this ten horned beast and Roman or Latine Empire[as is proued in the twentie seuen proposition] appertaineth

A ten horned beast, signifying, by the twentie foure proposition, Two Beasts. A two horned beast, signifying the Antichrist

only, by the twentie fiue proposition,who is proued to bee the rope,by the twentie sixe proposition,whose raign of a thousand, two hundred sixtie yeares, beginneth anno Christi 300. or 316. at the farthest,proposition. 36.

| An Image, prooued by the 28 proposition, to be these degenerate princes that onelie in name and shewe, are Romane Emperours. | A mark, prooued by prop. 30.to be the league of seruitude professed to the Romanes,by their subiects noted afterwarde by the Pope with visible marks,which, by the 31 prop.are $\chi \rho \varsigma$ & crosses of all kinds. | A name, prooued by the twentie nine poposition, to be the name of the Latine or Romane Empire, λατεινος | A number of *666*, assigned by the text. |

These Propositions ar set in this table after their natural order, but in the tretise following, they ar placed demostratiuely, to the effect every proposition may be proued by the former propositions.

(a) John Napier, *A Plaine Discovery of the whole Revelation of Saint John*, (Edinburgh, 1593) Table of the First Treatise

A TABLE DEFINITIVE AND
Diuisiue of the whole Revelation.

THe *Revelation*, is a difcoucrie of thofe notable matters that concerne the Chriftian Churche, from her beginning to the latter day, fet out by vifions, which Chrift hath fhewed to his Apoftle *Iohn* : And it containeth

A particular admonition, which as an Epiftle, is directed vnto the feuen Churches of litle Afia, and it containeth

A general difcourfe of all alterations, which generally doe concerne or intereft the Chriftian Church. from her beginning to the latter day, and it containeth

The preface, which fheweth the director, the receiuer, & to whome the meffage is directed, fet out fpiritually, cap, 1

The meffage directed particularly to the Churches of Ephefus, Smyrna, Pergamus, Thyatira, cap 2. And to Sardis, philadelphia and Laodicea, cap, 3. And it containeth

An orderly part, which deduceth fuccefsiuely, briefly, & in due order of time all alterations concerning the Chriftian Church: and it containeth

Ane amplificatiue part, wherein are more largely fet downe and expounded thofe greateft and moft notable maters, which wer ouer fummarlie, briefly, or obfcurelie expreffed in the orderlie part, & this forewarne h the eftate of the Elect

The reproofe of certaine pointes of their defection, threatning them to amendement.

The commendation of certain of their godly doings, exhorting them to perfeuerance.

A hiftorie of thofe thinges which

A prophecie, forewarning all notable accidentes, alterations and

on earth by commotions

in heauen, de fcribed cap.11. and 2 is vnder the terme of new Ierufalem.

wer accomplifhed before they wer written, expreffed cap. 4. 5. 6. 7. and beginning of the 8, vnder the termes of feuen feales.

Eccle fiafti cal, wherin are in are defcai bed, the Anti chriftian

Secu lare, which are intn tredu ced by pre face, cap 15

changes, that concerne the chriftian Church, betwixt S. Iohn his dayes and the latter day : and it is

& dilated in or der, cap. 16. vnder the termes of feuen Vials.

Secular, which forewarneth fuch mutations of earthlie kingdomes, and commotions of Empires as any way concerneth the Chriftian Church; & this is done in the reft of the 8. cap. & in the whole 9. chapter, vnder the termes of fixe of the feuen Trumpets. Hereafter followeth in the tenth chapter, an introduction to the feuen thunders, or feuen thundering Angels, which are myfteries of the feuenth trumpet and latter day.

Ecclefiaftical, which fimply and altogether forewarneth the oneconly progreff of Gods true church, & this is done Cap. 11.

beaftes ftrife with Gods Church cap, 12. and that Beaft his tokens and qualities cap. 13. and the progres of his falling, and the rifing of the Evangell to the latter day, cap. 14. and the interpretation of the Beaftes tokens cap. 17. & the decay of his citie and feat, Cap, 18. and the triumph alfo of Gods Church, cap, 19. And finallie is expounded briefly, cap, 20. how Gods publik and priuat enemies, ftriue againft other, and both againft his Church : but at length to their own wracke and confufion eternally. Amen.

THE

(b) John Napier, Table of the Second Treatise

who obeyed the dege-
nerate Princes thereof,
were fomtime plagued
and oppreffed by their
tyranny,and by the ty-
rannie of the thirty ty-
rants,that then raigned
vnder thé: Others,fom-
time were ouerrun by
ftrangers, through the
effeminate lenitie of
thefe Emperours,

3 Wherethrough,&
becaufe in the feconde
and next age , begin-
ning about the yeare
of God,316.the Empe-
róur *Conftantine* tráfpor-
ted the imperiall feat to
Conftantinople, it came to
paffe, thatthe towne of
Rome, and whole Penin-
full of *Cittim,* which is
(*ex Hieronymo de interpre-
tat.nominum*)interpreted
the gathering or tofsing
of the feas,,and nowe is
called *Italie* , is left a
praie to the *Huns,Gothes
Vandales,* and other bar-
barous nations , who
flewe and deftroyed of
the inhabitants of that
country at their plefure.

4 Then begins in the
yeare of God, 561. the
third age, in the which,
the wicked *Mahomet* a-

firft Vial, or age. *The fecond Viall.* *The*

316   561

out the cups of God
his wrath vpon the
great Empire of the
earth, & there came
a cruell and horrible
plague vpon al peo-
ple that profeffed o-
bedience to it , and
vpon them that re-
verenced that Em-
pire and the dege-
nerate Princes ther-
of.

3 And the Mef-
fengers of the fecód
age powred foorth
their cuppes of God
his wrath vppon a
certaine b fea coaft,
peninfull or lande,
named by the fea :
and that lande be-
came full of bloud-
fhed and murther :
and all the people,
that fometime liued
wealthilie in that
Peninfull , were for
the moft part flaine
and deftroyed.

4 And the Mef-
fengers of the tHird
age poured out their
cups of Gods wrath
c vpon the wholfom
floudes and liuelie
fountaines of pure
doctrin,and the do-

fell a noyfome
and a grieuous
fore vpon the
men, whiche
had the marke
of the beaft, &
vppon them
which worfhip
ped his image.

3 And the
fecond Angell
poured out his
viall vpon the
fea, and it be-
came as the
blood of a ded
man: and eue-
rie liuing thing
died in the fea.

4 And the
thirde Angell
poured out his
viall vpon the
riuers & foun-
taines of wa-
ters,

(c) John Napier, Sample page from the Second Treatise

the first, the prophecies referred to the time from the baptism
of Christ to the destruction of the Temple of Jerusalem, from
A.D. 29 to 71, and were hidden under the signs of the first
six seals. Each seal contained seven years. In the second, the
history from the opening of the seventh seal (A.D. 71) to
1541 was hidden under the terms of the seven trumpets and
seven vials, which he showed to be concurrent.

The proof of the concurrence of trumpets and vials was
central to his argument.[85] This gave him his first date. The
fifth trumpet spoke of a star that fell, and this he identified
as Muhammad, a prophet 'who fell from his former christian
profession and became an apostate'.[86] The fifth vial spoke of
a plague of locusts that would ravage the earth for five
months. This referred to the consequent rise of the heretical
Turks. The time of the sounding of the fifth trumpet and the
pouring-out of the fifth vial he set at 1051, or as he said at
about the time of the domination of the Turks under
Zadok.[87]

Napier then set forth a few numerical propositions to
prove that great alterations of kingdoms took place roughly
every 245 years.[88] He assumed that as the Hebrews had
measured history by Jubilees, periods of 49 years, so ordi-
narily should historical periods be measured. This law, however, had been altered by Daniel's prophecy to a period of
seventy weeks, or 490 years, as one day was generally taken
to signify one year. Alterations could then be thought to take
place every 490 years. Napier proposed this correction to
Carion and others who believed that the 'fatal period of
empires' was 500 years. The further revelation of John had
again altered the periodization, showing Napier that the
world would not last a full seven Great Jubilees, that is, a
full seven periods of 490 years each, or 3,430 years. To John
it had been revealed, and by Napier discovered, that the
periods would follow the seven trumpets and vials at intervals of one-half a Great Jubilee, or 245 years.

[85] *A Plaine Discovery*, p. 3 et seq.   [86] Ibid., p. 5.
[87] Foxe gives this account 'A.D. 1051. The first king of the Turks, called
Zaduke, began to reign in Asia and joined league with the Caliph of Egypt, and
there reigned till the conquest of Godfred and the Christians the space of forty-
six years.' *Acts and Monuments*, ed. cit., vol. iv, p. 117.
[88] *A Plaine Discovery*, p. 7 et seq.

By working forwards and backwards from the fifth trumpet and vial of 1051, Napier followed the fortunes of Empire and recorded at approximately 245-year intervals the alterations prophesied.[89]

1 trumpet and vial:	the destruction of Jerusalem	71
2 " " :	the translation of the Empire to the east (Constantine and Pope Sylvester)	316
3 " " :	Totila burns Rome	561
4 " " :	Charlemagne made Emperor	806
5 " " :	Zadok Dominator of the Turks	1051
6 " " :	Osman	1296
7 " " :	Reformation	1541

The third division or the last age began after the sounding of the seventh trumpet. This age appeared under the sign of the five thundering angels, each angel governing a Jubilee, 49 years.[90] The first three angels covered the years from 1541 to 1590 to 1639 to 1688. The fourth angel, 'even Christ himself', was due in 1688. Christ with three avenging angels would accomplish the Harvest between 1688 and 1786, when the last 245 years of history, from 1541 to 1786, were complete. It was uncertain whether after the second coming the final period would actually reach its conclusion. All this followed the Apocalypse very closely and advised people to expect great alterations in the kingdom or among kingdoms in 1590, 1639, and 1688. After 1688 the elect were assured rest and peace. Suffering would be limited to the reprobate.

On the subject of church history, Napier had less to offer that was new. Knox in his first sermon had noticed that the 1,260 days of the Book of Revelation were equal to the forty-two months, and that both could be said to equal the time and times and dividing of time [of Daniel]. Thus, a "time" taken as a day gave three and one-half days, which is three and one-half years or forty-two months, 1,260 days. All of these referred to the persecution of the true Church by Antichrist. Napier interpreted each image in numerical terms: the woman in the wilderness as 1,260 days, the time of persecution as 42 months, and the time the witnesses lay dead as

[89] *A Plaine Discovery*, p. 8.   [90] Ibid., p. 15 et seq.

3½ days, and he applied them all to the Roman Church. He
then counted the 1,260 years from the year 300 or from the
establishment of the papacy, and arrived at the particularly
appropriate date for Scotland of 1560 for the end of Roman
domination. He discovered the enemies of the Church to be
Satan and wicked kingdoms. Satan had been bound for a
thousand years. However, instead of equating this bondage,
as Foxe had, with the absence of persecution, Napier equated
it with the absence of universal wars.[91] Because of this limitation, all the wars during that time were, he said, of a minor
provincial character. With Knox, Napier believed in the image
of the two armies. After the year 1000 and before the release of
Satan, wars between the pope and Muhammad, between East
and West, began brewing. Both the pope and Muhammad were
enemies of the true Church, and were identified as Gog and
Magog. One enemy was secret, the other public, until the last
age when both would become known. The two beasts of the
Revelation were identified with the Latin Empire and the
pope. The pope was the two-horned beast because of his
presumption to the two swords, exemplified by Boniface
VIII. The Latin Empire was the beast with the ten horns
whose number was 666, proven by the value of the Greek
letters sounding the name, transliterated as *Lateinos*.

The story he told was familiar enough to any Protestant
who had made a study of his fellows' commentaries on Revelation. Unfortunately Napier did not burden his text with
detailed references to other commentators. He limited his
references to the text of either the Vulgate or the Geneva
Bible, and for the histories, in order not to appear to favour
the Protestants, he had taken his 'authorities and cited my
places either out of Ethnick auctors, or then papisticall
writers, whose testimonies by no reason can be refused
against themselves'.[92] He used pre-sixteenth-century chronicles, especially those generally favoured by Protestants, John
Baptista Egnati on the Turks and Platina on the popes.[93] The
few sixteenth-century works he used and cited were Carion

---

[91] *A Plaine Discovery*, pp. 62-3 et seq.
[92] Ibid., 'To the Godly and Christian Reader', fol. A7r.
[93] Egnati, pseud., Giovanni Battista Cipelli, *De Origine Turcarum* (Basle, 1533);
Platina, *Romanorum Principium* (Basle, 1518).

and Joseph Justus Scaliger, *De Emendatione Temporum*
(1583) for matters of chronology and computation, the former for material, the latter for method, and Castellio's Latin
edition of the oracles of the Sibyl (1555).

Before Napier, the study of the prophecies among British
Protestants had followed more closely the stream of interpretation that concentrated upon the development of a theme
through historical material. The type of interpretation
illustrated by Osiander in the early years of the tradition had
impinged more and more upon commentators, but its influence was still only slight. Conjecture of Osiander's sort was
no more than a curiosity and did not share the authority of
the more sober histories of Antichrist. When Napier applied
his own particular reading of Ramist method to the text and
found in the text itself propositions that resembled the old
practice of conjecture, he brought to this practice the
authority it had lacked.

If one accepts his propositions and follows his argument to
the construction of a schema of world history, it is hard not
to be persuaded also that his predictions carried an element
of truth. Until Napier, speculation about the future had been
held seriously in check. What could be known, it was argued,
was of too general a nature to be certain; in particular, *when*
the rest of the prophecies were expected was prohibited
knowledge. Of course that prohibition had not gone unchallenged.[94] Men of Napier's curiosity were not deterred.
From the start the influence of a conjectural method can be
traced through a very few British writers. Joye aped Osiander,
and even Foxe could not forbear to include a conjecture predicting the end of persecution.[95] Nevertheless, Napier is the
first to use this method extensively and to combine it successfully with the tradition evolved by the Marian exiles of both
nations. This appears, again, to be a closer connection with
continental thought than would be expected in a man who
had not travelled.

During the latter half of the sixteenth century, some
continental humanists whose religious allegiance centred on
the hopes for the Counter-Reformation began to remould

[94] For Osiander's answer see above, Chap. II, p. 62.
[95] *A & M (1583)*, vol. iv, p. 259.

Renaissance belief in *renovatio mundi* to express an evangelical fervour of their own. Many of these men were in contact
with Protestants, especially in the cities of Basle and Geneva.
Some moved as freely in the Protestant community as in the
Catholic. Castellio in Basle had such contacts, and his translation of the oracles of the Sibyl was one of his efforts to aid
students of prophecy. He firmly believed that the Age of
Gold lay in the future.[96]
Napier used Castellio's translation and even quoted a section of the prophecies at the end of his commentary on the
Revelation.[97] The inclusion of non-scriptural prophecy had
to be handled carefully, and Napier was quick to assure his
readers that such prophecies were mentioned not as certainties like the Apocalypse but as curiosities for speculation.
However, a truly inventive mind is always a prey to curiosity,
and there is some reason to believe that Napier had several
unorthodox interests he would not have been foolish enough
to display in print.[98]
   Guillaume Postel, another thoroughly strange writer on
prophecy with a firm conviction in its extensibility from the
past into a golden future, had been particularly active during
the years just before we suggest Napier may have begun his
education in ·France. Postel's career took him in and out of
the Jesuits. At one point he appealed to Melanchthon and
Bullinger for support and he was widely read by anabaptists.[99] Even Scaliger, whose position in the world of scholarship in his generation can be likened to Erasmus's in his,
thought highly of Postel.[1] In fact, as Marjorie Reeves has

[96] Reeves, *Influence of Prophecy*, pp. 481–3.
[97] *A Plaine Discovery*, fols. T1r–T4v.
[98] Mark Napier records an incident in which John appears to have employed
the art of magic in search of treasure (*Memoirs*, pp. 220–42).
[99] The fullest treatment of his views appears in William J. Bouwsma, *Concordia
Mundi: The Career and thought of Guillaume Postel (1510–1581)* (Cambridge,
Mass., 1957); and M. Reeves places him in the context of sixteenth-century
Joachimism.
[1] Philippe Tamizey de Larroque, *Lettres françaises inédites de Joseph Scaliger*
(Paris, 1879), p. 351; and *Scaligerana, ou bons mots rencontres Agreables et
Remarques Judicieuses & Sçavantes de J. Scaliger* (Cologne, 1695), p. 323. As a
young man Scaliger is said to have met Postel and offered him his bed during a
three-day visit Postel made to his printer over whose shop Scaliger was living.
Essays by the late Mark Pattison, coll. Henry Nettleship (Oxford, 1889), vol. i,
p. 202.

illustrated, material embodying a hope for a perfect future is
found fairly equally among Protestants and Catholics. Both
the Jesuit Order and the Second Helvetic Confession attempted a firm resistance to a belief in an approaching Golden
Age, but among a significant minority in both religious
camps the resistance crumbled.

In his commentary there are some hints that Napier expected the future he had predicted to be one in which knowledge of both divine and material science would be completed.
He was uncertain about the total perfection of creation, since
his study of Aristotle told him that perfection was not possible while there was yet movement and time, but certainly
the final age was a preparation for perfection.[2] In the character of this final age he had found the liberty for his curiosity.
He justified his belief that present knowledge (even in the
study of Scripture) outstripped the knowledge of past ages
(even that of the Apostles).

> Christ hath reveiled the same [the Book of Revelation] word by
> word, as it is written in the text, to his Disciple John, and now doth
> daylie by his holie Spirit, revile more and more the meaning thereof, to
> us in this our age, for the which it hath bene chiefly instituted.

> Of this booke of Revelation . . . onlie the historical part, to wit, the
> seven seals thereof, is opened by Christ and his Apostles to the primi-
> tive Church, in that that part was fulfilled in their dayes. But the text
> doth never show, that the book within is opened up, and offered patent
> to us, till now in this our seventh age, wherein Christ here (vers. 2) not
> only opens all the propheticall mysteries thereof, but also (ver. 9)
> offereth the same to the Church under the person of the prophet: as
> thirdly, ordaineth them to preach the same over and over againe, open-
> lie and patentlie to the whole worlde, wherethrow, without all ques-
> tion, this is the time of knowledge even presentlie, of which saith
> Daniel chap. 12.4 *Claude sermones & signa librum usque in tempus
> statutum.* Close up these speeches and seal the book untill the time
> appointed.[3]

During the seventh age all the secrets would become access-
ible to the human mind rightly directed.

Not only did Napier write more plainly than many of his
predecessors but he also greatly accelerated expectation. The
seventh trumpet had sounded in 1541 and had ceased in
1590. The present or 'the complete time of Revelation and
Knowledge'[4] was already come, and though dominated by

---

[2] *A Plaine Discovery*, p. 250.   [3] Ibid., p. 142.   [4] Ibid.

the trials of the five thundering angels they were to be succeeded by the second coming itself.

Napier was aware of the danger of being classed as one of the millenarians and added to his discussion of the future a paragraph refuting their opinions. Millenarians erred in expecting only a partially renovated kingdom, expecting it within time and history and without the re-formation of the elements of creation. Likewise they erred in their belief that such a kingdom would last for a set period of time of a thousand years.[5] Technically he avoided any taint of millenarian opinion, but his commentary had the effect of allowing others more ready to accept a worldly interpretation of the kingdom of the saints to see when it might be expected.

Napier's commentary was published three times in Edinburgh (1593, 1611, 1645) and twice in London (1594, 1611). His work gained its widest audience in the 1640s when it was abridged and reissued as *Napier's Narration* (London, 1641), *The Bloody Almanack* (London, 1643), and *A Bloody Almanack* (London, 1647). Each of these made good use of Napier's prophecies to reflect the excitement of the times. Between 1611 and 1640 it was more often published abroad: twice in Dutch, five times in French, and thrice in German. Abstracts were also made or his material used extensively in works published on the continent in 1610, 1623, and 1665.[6]

In the seventeenth century the apocalyptic tradition developed along lines alien to the tradition established by the Marian exiles. The beginnings of those changes can be traced to John Napier's method for evaluating the text of Revelation. In many ways Napier himself provides the pattern for a new breed of commentator. He was a layman, interested in science and mathematics, curious after antique lore, often dabbling with materials and texts that had remained at the outer bounds of theological respectability. The study of the Apocalypse engaged minds from many disciplines, and slowly these disciplines came to influence the form and content of the tradition.

---

[5] *A Plaine Discovery*, p. 143.
[6] Gathered from a catalogue of Napier's works by Wm. Rae Macdonald, as an appendix to his translation of *The Construction of the wonderful canon of logarithms* (Edinburgh, 1889), where the particulars are given.

V

CABALISTS AND TALMUDISTS:
HUGH BROUGHTON AND THOMAS BRIGHTMAN

Foxe died in 1586, and in 1587 his *Eicasmi* was published by his son. In 1588 the Spanish Armada attempted the invasion of England. In the years preceding 1588, speculation based on many prophecies about this particular year predicted calamities and terrors. Many of these prophecies came not from scriptural passages but from legendary or contemporary seers and prophets. The prophecies of Merlin, of Mother Shipton, or of Nostradamus were collected, compared, and spread abroad.[1] By no means all of England's inhabitants believed in these prophecies, but of those who did many were of what one critic called the 'more larned sort'. By 1587 speculation had reached such a pitch that this critic, John Harvey, the younger brother of Gabriel and himself a physician and astrologer, either took it upon himself or was invited[2] to write against false prophecies in general, and in particular against those believed to indicate calamities for the year 1588. His book *A Discursive Probleme concerning Prophesies*[3] drew a sharp distinction between those prophecies which by the 'surest rules, and directions in Divinitie, Philosophie, Astrologie, and other learning' might be credited, and those of uncertain origin unsupported by any of the rules of learning. Into the latter class fell many of those revered medieval mystics and prophets such as Hildegarde and Merlin whom Foxe had not hesitated to cite along with prophetic interpreters of Scripture. 'Alas', Harvey cried, 'is this wise world so simple, to beleeve so foolish toyes, devised to mocke apes, and delude children?'[4] Into this class also fell the prophecy of that unknown rabbi and 'Thalmudicall inventor' Elias, and with him to damnation went all the 'Thalmudicall or Cabalisticall doctrine'[5] that intrigued some

---

[1] See especially K. V. Thomas, *Religion and the Decline of Magic* (London, 1971), pp. 461–516.
[2] Garrett Mattingly suggests that Elizabeth may have requested it to suppress rumours of disaster: *The Defeat of the Spanish Armada* (London, 1959).
[3] (London, 1588).   [4] Harvey, op. cit., p. 2.   [5] Ibid., pp. 10, 15.

students of prophecy. Harvey averred that the Prophecy of Elias could be supported neither by reason nor by divine authority, and that the world must forgive him for not crediting anything but that which 'either humane reason shall probably persuade, or divine authority canonically enforce.[6]

Divine authority did support the prophecies of Daniel and John. Harvey thought that there was something hidden under the terms of the sevens in the Apocalypse, although in his opinion none of the expositors had as yet discovered the full explanation;[7] and Daniel 'above all other prophets had most special and singular revelation of such things, and events as should behappen the church from the very time that it was in captivity untill the last daies of the world'.[8] Although he had planned to omit any discussion of the sibylline prophecies because their antiquity had somewhat disposed him to think more of them,[9] the revival of Catholic interest in the Tiburtine Sibyls[10] required some answer. Harvey was evidently well versed in the continental Catholic interest in prophecy, for he sought to disprove an interpretation that granted a special reforming significance to Charles V, an idea that had entranced Guillaume Postel for a number of years.[11] Postel was not mentioned in this connection, but his name appears a few pages later, where Harvey wonders 'whether he deserve the reputation of an upright and sound christian or no'. In any case events had adequately disproved the prophecies attributed to Charles V.[12]

Although the prophecies that suggested a significance for the number eighty-eight and therefore for the year 1588 were not founded in the apocalyptic tradition as it has been defined,[13] the expectation of cataclysmic alteration for whatever reason could easily be made concordant with scriptural prophecy. Despite his disdain for the foolishness of

[6] Harvey, op. cit., p. 4.   [7] Ibid., pp. 24–5.   [8] Ibid., p. 33.   [9] Ibid., p. 41.
[10] They were given a Catholic interpretation and, Harvey says (p. 41), presented to the pope. A copy was included in a late sixteenth-century manuscript collection of prophecies which may well have belonged to Archbishop Laud. Bodleian Library, MS. Laud Misc. 588.
[11] Reeves, *Influence of Prophecy*, pp. 381–4.
[12] Harvey, op. cit., p. 125.
[13] Harvey said it derived from Regiomontanus, i.e. Johann Müller of Königsberg, a fifteenth-century mathematician and astronomer. Mattingly discusses the prophecy, pp. 159–63. See Bauckham, op. cit. pp. 162–184.

common fables, Harvey believed that a tragedy of universal
proportions was near at hand.

> yet for mine owne simple opinion, I am undoubtedly resolved, and
> fully persuaded, according to good warrants of learning, that this 88
> shall at the uttermost proove but the *Prologue* therof, howsoever in
> some other yeere not far hence . . . there may perhaps, some shrewd
> *Epilogue*, or at least some perillous issue of such troublesome and
> tragicall actes finally be expected.

When the time came it would be known 'by physicall and
mathematical conjectures, rightly drawn from the due observation of certain fearefull *Eclipses* . . .'.[14]

The Armada and its failure left an impression on the minds
of Englishmen of proof of God's special providence and, implicitly, of the validity of prophecy. William Lilly, whose
copy of Harvey's book[15] I read, wrote on the final pages
'Harvey lived to see him selfe fooled by writing this discourse,
for wee all know 1588 was annus terribilis; wittness ye
Spanish Armado/'. Very likely this was the general reaction
to Harvey's attacks on the idiocy of belief in common
prophecies.

One particularly notable aspect of Harvey's attack was his
vehement dislike of 'Thalmudizers' and 'Cabalisticall' interpreters. Remembering Bale's opinion of the Talmud,[16] and
Foxe's presentation of Jewry,[17] this attitude is not surprising.
What is surprising is that Harvey should have had by then sufficient provocation for his attack. The history of the philo-
Semitic movement in Europe at the time has not yet been
written, but when it is it will contain such names as Postel
and Scaliger and the Englishman Hugh Broughton. Since the
days of Reuchlin and his edition of the Talmud the study of
Hebrew had snowballed from a simple interest in a biblical
language necessary for textual reconstruction into a passion
for the wisdom and traditions of the first race. Since Reuchlin's controversy with Pfefferkorn in the early sixteenth
century there had been two broad approaches to the proper
use of Hebrew wisdom; one was to treat it and the Christian
revelation separately, the other to attempt to reconcile them.
Like Reuchlin, Scaliger was firmly committed to the former
approach, but Broughton became devoted to the latter.

[14] Harvey, op. cit., p. 130.   [15] Bodleian Library, ref. Ashm. 637.
[16] See above, p. 46.   [17] See above, p. 94.

Consequently, although each respected the other's learning, neither could respect the other's use of that learning.

With the Reformation, the study of the biblical languages in England improved. Among the continental scholars entertained by Thomas Cranmer during the reign of Edward was a Hebraist, Antoine Chevallier, who became the princess Elizabeth's tutor in French. Chevallier's fortunes were soon entangled with the English Reformation, and in 1553 he fled from England to live in Strasburg, where he became professor of Hebrew. Later he moved on to Geneva and Caen, but by 1569 he had returned to England to become lecturer at Cambridge. There he taught Hugh Broughton, who during the 1570s enjoyed fellowships at St. John's, and later at Christ's College, [18] and the patronage of Sir Walter Mildmay. By 1588, however, Broughton had resigned his fellowship and moved to London, where he became known as a Puritan preacher and was said to have predicted the defeat of the Armada. [19] There he lived with the Cotton family, and later in the same year his friend John Speed saw his *A concent of scripture* through the press. This book was immediately controversial, and both John Rainolds of Oxford and Edward Lively of Cambridge attacked it. Broughton, who did not take criticism kindly, began to lecture in his own defence in St. Paul's. This practice of self-defence continued to interrupt his other works and dominate his correspondence for many years. *A concent of scripture* was to him more than a contribution to learning, it was a statement about the method and ends of all learning, a position on the nature of Scripture. When his appeals to have the book debated by Whitgift and Aylmer failed, he left on a tour of Germany, there to argue against popery and to dispute with the Jews. In 1591 he returned to England and again tried to get some sort of official approval of or recognition for his *Concent*; but, meeting with no success, he left in 1592 for a much longer period.

A concent of scripture took for its primary thesis the assertion that the Bible contained within itself the clues to a divinely established chronology, and that after thorough

---

[18] Both colleges were known to house many of the more radical divines and supporters of Ramism. Kearney, *Scholars and Gentlemen*, chap. III.

[19] *D.N.B.*

study of the Hebrew texts the agreement not only among all
the books of the Old Testament, but also between them and
the books of the New Testament, would be abundantly apparent. There were five interlocking 'chaines', a progression of
rules which clarified history from Adam to Christ. From
these rules Broughton prepared a table which illustrated how
dates could be gathered from genealogical information and
from the patterns revealed in prophecies. The printed version
of this table is cluttered with his commentary, but the manuscript version,[20] entitled 'A Sinai Sight', left room for the
commentary outside the tables and charts. There the patterns
are more readily apparent, especially his use of Daniel's
seventy weeks. He maintained that these weeks equalled 490
years, covering exactly the period between Daniel and the
birth of Christ. The problem of the seventy weeks (Daniel 9:
24) was one to which nearly all biblical chronologers or students of Hebrew contributed either new theories or arguments for or against established ones. Broughton chose with
few reservations to side with the Huguenot writer Matthew
Beroaldus.[21] Broughton's opponents chose to oppose Beroaldus. Ralegh like Broughton would defend him.

Like Beroaldus, he believed Scripture was an exact representation of truth. Its authority was final and unassailable in
all respects. The Old Testament could not be interpreted or
corrected by reference to documents or literature originating
outside the Hebrew tradition. In matters of history and tradition, where pagan sources contradicted Scripture, the pagan
sources were to be discounted. In cases where Scripture
apparently contradicted itself, the answer was to be found
either from sources within the Hebrew tradition or by re-
interpreting or translating the Hebrew text.

Along with the growth of interest in the literature and
mysticism of ancient Judaism, there seemed to go a denigra-
tion of ancient pagan culture, of the Greek and Latin authors
so diligently revived and admired by earlier generations.

---

[20] Bodleian Library, MS. Bodley 950, fols. 6^v-7^r.

[21] Beroaldus (Matthew Brouart), b. 1520 in Paris, d. 1576 in Geneva. In about
1574 he became for a time the pastor of the Walloon Church in London. (Haage,
La France Protestante.) Broughton published Beroaldus's thoughts in *A short
view of the Persian monarchie, and of Daniels weekes: beeing a peece of Beroaldus workes, with a censure in some points* (London, 1590).

Resistance to the ideas of Beroaldus and Broughton came not only from those who took another view of the nature of Scripture, but also from those whose expertise and livelihood lay in Latin and Greek and not in Hebrew or who saw a danger that the classical civilizations might again be lost. The great Scaliger had shown how an admiration of Jewish learning could be combined with classical knowledge and the whole body of knowledge subjected to critical evaluation in the search for historical and chronological truth. His methods were employed by those like John Napier who nevertheless believed that the Scripture would be shown to be accurate, and by those who hoped to counter the claims of those like Beroaldus.

Hugh Broughton may not have been an easy man to get along with, but the antipathy he stirred up against himself in Oxford and Cambridge owes something to the threat his position posed to resident classical scholars. Edward Lively's attack upon his presentation of Beroaldus's work on the Persian monarchy was written both to defend the ancient classical writers and to ridicule the Jewish texts. The very first words of Lively's text are 'Cicero says'. Later in the book he exclaimed, 'It is not to be spoken, how much and how clear light the diligent study and reading of Latin and Greek writers: yeeld to the knowledge of holy scripture.'[22] Scaliger's name appears everywhere to his praise, and Lively informs the reader on his title-page that his work is intended 'against the frivolous conceits of Mathew Beroald'. In a short discussion of the value to chronology of rabbinical knowledge, Lively expressed the greatest scorn for Jewish learning. He asked, 'who can reade the chronologies of the Rabines, their Seder Olam Rabba, their Seder Olam Zuta, their Historicall Cabbala without laughing'.[23] Broughton could. He went so far as to entitle one of his works on chronology *A seder olam that is, order of the worlde: or yeares from the fall to the restoring* (1594).

Broughton attracted criticism from several sources. The universities and the church thought little of him, and Scaliger

[22] Edward Lively, *True Chronologie of the times of the Persian Monarchie* . . . (London, 1597), p. 15.
[23] Ibid., p. 36.

whom he met abroad thought him 'furiosus et maledicus'; in
his estimation Broughton was 'fort versé dans la langue
Hebraique, mais un peu fou'.[24] Nevertheless, Broughton
found friends among the Jews of Europe, and his work influenced the more attractive personalities of Thomas Brightman and Sir Walter Ralegh.

In later life Broughton did not move from his first premiss
that Scripture was the final authority, each book agreeing
entirely with the others. He used his skill in Hebrew to
extract more and more possible meanings, but he neither
doubted the text nor allowed it to suffer in any comparison
with non-biblical sources. The apocalyptic tradition presented him with a ready-made scripturally based pattern for
chronology. The key prophecies that ordered and directed
his chronology were those of Elias, Daniel, and John. In
order to maintain the constancy of his truth, God had provided the Church with 'Prophecies in every age, the first larger,
the latter narrower, all briefly told, all for event fully recorded'.[25] In order to prove this, God had endowed Scripture
with a marvellous agreement of names and places covering
the whole earth. To illustrate the universality of Scripture,
Broughton carefully drew and coloured a map of the world
with Hebrew place-names gathered from the Old Testament.[26]

The three prophecies were indicative of a progression from
the more general to the more particular. Elias' prophecy gave
the general boundaries of historical time, which, although he
does not mention Elias by name, Broughton did not transgress; Daniel spoke of the world monarchies (Broughton later
altered this to mean those who had held power over the Jews
only); and the Apocalypse made a particular prophecy of the
birth and history of Antichrist. Broughton's account of the
period from the birth of Christ to the Reformation followed
the usual Protestant version. The dates indicated were for
specific prophecies rather than the result of the application

[24] *Scaligerana* . . . (Cologne, 1695). Broughton gives his view of their differences in 'To the Right Reverend Fathers, the Governours of Oxford', *A require
of agreement* (1611), pp. 89–92.
[25] Broughton, *A concent of scripture* (London, 1588), Dedication to Queen
Elizabeth.
[26] MS. Bodley 950, fols. 12^v–13^r.

The Whore of Babylon

One of the six plates from Broughton's *A concent of scripture*. An earlier identification of the Locust with the Turk had been replaced more generally by one with the Jesuits. The identification here with 'the belly God clergi' betrays a Puritan hand.

of patterns; so that whereas Napier looked for changes every
245 years as each trumpet sounded, Broughton like Foxe discovered in an event the fulfilment of one part of the text.
Broughton's times were not the equal periods of Napier, but
unequal links in a chain. Because as time passed the prophecies narrowed, links were more frequent in later ages. The
time from Christ to the end was predicted under the seven
trumpets which indicated such persons and events as Phocas
and Boniface, Charlemagne, and Muhammad. The sixth trumpet he allocated to the Saracens and Turks.[27] In fact Broughton's commentary on the history of the Church was no more
original than Napier's. By this time the events alluded to in
the prophecies had become very standard stuff indeed.
Interest was rapidly turning to either end of the pattern: to
Genesis and to the Apocalypse.

During his second stay abroad, Broughton wrote his commentaries on Daniel (1596) and the Revelation (1610). His
departures from past Protestant tradition were the result of
his two new-found preoccupations: his controversies with the
papists and his discussions with the Jews. As has been indicated, Catholic interest in the Apocalypse, especially among the
Jesuits, had been quickening of its own accord. It was not,
however, until Cardinal Bellarmine took it upon himself to
refute Protestantism that British Protestants at home became
truly aware of Jesuit activity in this direction. Broughton's
commentary on the Apocalypse shows marked influence of
the Jesuit interpretation. Without abandoning the discovery
of Antichrist in the papacy, Broughton managed to absorb
into a Protestant context new elements taken from the
Jesuits. His commentary on Daniel, on the other hand, was
controlled by his desire to appear reasonable to the Jewish
community.

Jewish tradition as Broughton encountered it in Germany
held that Daniel's prophecies applied to the Jews alone.[28]
The fourth beast, which had been identified by Christians

---

[27] *A concent of scripture*, Hiii^r.

[28] Calvin had encountered this same Jewish interpretation but had minimized
the importance of Antiochus Epiphanes, declaring that the real significance of
Daniel's prophecy lay in the prediction of the Messiah. *Commentaries on the
Book of the Prophet Daniel by John Calvin*, ed. Thomas Myers, Lecture XLIX,
chap. IX: 24, p. 197.

with the Roman persecutors of Christianity and more recently by Protestants as the papal tyranny, was held by the Jews to be Antiochus Epiphanes Longimanus (176-164 B.C.), the Seleucid king whose persecutions led to the Maccabean rebellion. Broughton, who often referred to himself as a 'Thalmudique' and cherished the praise he received from learned Jews,[29] sought their conversion by turning their own learning back upon them. His view of Daniel's prophecies accepted Antiochus Epiphanes as the fourth beast,[30] and based its argument upon the prophecy of the seventy weeks.[31] In this way he hoped that the Jews, seeing their own learning respected, would be more ready to see the fulfilment of prophecy in Jesus. His interpretation of Daniel raised a storm of protest among his Protestant countrymen, who were loath to see any scriptural indictment of the pope go to waste. Of course James I had declared himself in favour of Knox's application of the prophecy in question to the papacy. Broughton's interpretation did not succeed in winning much support; but the question had been raised, and later writers took the trouble to review the claims of Antiochus Epiphanes before either dismissing them or reconciling them by employing a theory of repetitive types for Antichrist, and thus, while apparently agreeing with Broughton, reserving some connection between the text and the Roman papacy.

While abroad Broughton involved himself in a scheme to convert the Jews of Constantinople. The story as Broughton repeatedly told it[32] began with the arrival of a mysterious letter via Mr. Edward Barton, Queen's agent in Constantinople, requesting a learned teacher of Christianity. The letter was sent to Alderman Stapers, who conveyed it to Broughton in Basle for translation. Broughton had it printed with his

[29] See especially his report of his dialogue with the Rabbi Elias on the Apocalypse in *A require of agreement* (1611), pp. 44–50.

[30] *Daniel His Chaldie visions and His Ebrew* (London, 1596), The summe and graces of Daniel, Aii–Aiv; *A revelation of the holy apocalypse* (Amsterdam?, 1610), p. 161.

[31] *Daniel His Chaldie visions and His Ebrew*, The summe and graces of Daniel, Aii–Aiv.

[32] Recounted in *Two epistles unto Great Men of Britaine in the year 1599* (2nd impr. 1606), Civ–Ciiv; *A revelation of the holy apocalypse* (1610), pp. 12, 24–5, 137, 138.

translation and response[33] and tried to interest the Queen's Privy Council, the Archbishop,[34] or the Turkey Company[35] in sponsoring the teacher requested—presumably Broughton himself. It was thought in England that Broughton had forged the letter.[36] He of course denied this as hotly as he pleaded for opportunity to convert the Jews.

In one of his letters he outlined his plan of attack, indicating those tasks he believed most likely to improve the appeal of Christianity to the Jews. The first task echoed his thesis in *A concent of scripture*: 'There remayneth a laboure of longe winges, for joyning of all the bookes [of Scripture]; from theyr beginning with the creation of the world, unto the end of the last book: which is called the Revelation of S. John, which sealeth up all.'[37] Of all the books of Scripture so joined, three were especially important: 'And three bookes specially are full of the brightnes of Christ, & beames of his glory: the book of Daniel, The forework Gospell, & the vision of S. John.'[38] In 1610 he published his commentary on the Apocalypse. It was immediately apparent that he hoped the Jews would be among his readers. In the dedication to King James he compared the Bible and the Talmud and praised Moses Maimonides. In the letter of the author to the reader he took up the old matter of his *Concent*, and also referred to the Constantinople affair. Part of what he would have done had he been sent was to preach the text of the Apocalypse in Hebrew, the language he continued to find more appropriate to its meaning. Evidently he still at least pretended to hope that the Turkey Company would finance the venture: 'I have turned the Apocalyps into Hebrew: and so I would expound it: if the Turky merchants would pay the charges. If they refuse, I will leave them to try whether strange shipwrack shall revenge them.'[39] Later commentators also tended to substitute the Hebrew terms for the Greek; with the less familiar and more 'original' language a certain divinity was possible, as well as considerable latitude for interpretation.

---

[33] (Amsterdam, 1606).   [34] *Two epistles* (1599).
[35] *A revelation of the holy apocalypse*, p. 12.   [36] Ibid., pp. 24–5.
[37] *Two epistles*, Biii^V.   [38] Loc. cit.
[39] *A revelation of the holy apocalypse*, p. 12.

Part of Broughton's interest in the Apocalypse sprang from his recognition of similarities between it and Jewish tradition and his hope that by being told of these similarities the Jews might be converted. Unlike his predecessors, who had more often been drawn to Daniel for support of an interpretation of the Apocalypse, Broughton intended to prove the Apocalypse a Gentile version of Daniel: 'So *John* expoundeth *Daniel*, into Salvation of all Jews of grace.'[40] Broughton approached the New Testament as a Talmudist.

The most interesting aspects of Broughton's commentary are those in which he mirrors the Jesuits. His passion for the conversion of the Jews (always a key event in the apocalyptic tradition in general) united in his mind with the requirement for the universal preaching of the gospel before the end. Jesuits such as Bellarmine often cited the absence of the universal preaching to discredit Protestant expectation of the last days, while other Jesuits busied themselves with missionary zeal to accomplish this task of the true Church. Broughton's convictions about Scripture, as evidenced in his world map, led him to derive the entire world's population from the tribes of Israel. He became increasingly excited by news of the New World, imagining the language of the Indians perhaps to be derived from Hebrew: 'And for Cethem of Ophir, this honoreth Israels travelling far. I asked a simple mariner which had ben in the west Indians, what they called gold there; he said Cethem, just the scripture terms.'[41] Indians were part of the Jews in need of conversion. This was the great task of the seventh trumpet: 'And with the seaventh Trumpet the last state shalbe to shew Gods mercy, to *Iocktanes* sonnes the *Indians*, and to you miserable Jewes: who for your zeal *Rabbi Elias*, as I hope shall finde mercy.'[42] He was unhappy to see the Jesuits more active in this task: 'The best learned Jesuites wished my poore skill in the Thalmudique of the new Testament: saying, that so they might soone turne the Indians: and many spake and dealt in equall maner. And now the Jesuites despising idler monches condemning the other

---

[40] *A revelation of the holy apocalypse*, p. 13.
[41] *A require of agreement* (London, 1611), 'Dedication to the Merchant Adventurers'. A2ᵛ.
[42] Ibid., pp. 69–70.

Locustes begin to have some skill in Ebrew and Greek. . . .'[43]

Marjorie Reeves has shown how the Jesuits revived the Joachimist prediction of a mediating order and united with it a version of the apocalyptic tradition. Nearly all her evidence for the Jesuit revival comes from the period 1590 to 1620, at about the time that Protestants began to react specifically against the appropriation by the Jesuits of a book that they had come to consider their own. The Jesuit leaders in this rediscovery were predominantly Spanish or Portuguese.[44] For us, the interesting aspect of the Jesuit revival is not its roots in medieval Joachimism but its parallels with the Protestant tradition. Miss Reeves outlines a Jesuit interpretation of the Order's place in history given in a sermon by Osorius in 1595. Ignatius Loyola was likened to the angel of the fifth trumpet at whose blast the star (Luther) fell from heaven and with him his army of locusts (Protestant heretics). This interpretation was officially recognized at the Council of Tatra in 1602.[45]

This was only one of several Jesuit versions. Others were less subjective and closer to the Protestant interpretations of periods either of the early Church or of the future. The conversion of the Jews was one future event that both parties in the early seventeenth century agreed was of well-founded importance. Another was the postponement of the second coming to judgement until after the universal preaching and the establishment of some form of true Christian world hegemony. Neither of these preoccupations had been apparent in the version propounded by the Marian exiles; but Broughton's long stay abroad and his disputations with continental Jesuits and Jews gave him ample opportunity to encounter both of

---

[43] *A require of agreement*, pp. 69–70.

[44] The leading English Jesuit, Robert Parsons, published an attack on Foxe which restated Harpsfield's objections against Foxe's 'pseudo-martyrs' and also used some of Bellarmine's arguments against the identification of Antichrist with the Roman Church. However, Parsons did not take seriously Foxe's chronological and apocalyptical computations, or indulge in any himself. A biting attack on 'the first dreame of John Foxe in his bed' based on the passage quoted above (p. 89) appears in Parsons, *A Treatise of Three Conversions of England from Paganisme to Christian Religion* (St. Omes, 1603), Bk. ii, chap. 8, nos. 14–16, pp. 467–9. He was answered by Matthew Sutcliffe in *The Subversion of Robert Parsons* in 1606.

[45] Reeves, *The Influence of Prophecy*, p. 276.

them. Broughton's later works were greatly influenced by the Jesuits he sought to displace.

On the other side, the arch-controversialist Robert Bellarmine was extremely well schooled in Protestant apocalyptic historiography. He shared many of his Protestant contemporaries' preconceptions about world history, and several of their enthusiasms, particularly their interest in biblical chronology. He accepted the Prophecy of Elias as probable,[46] and likewise accepted a version of the theory of the four monarchies.[47] He studied the *Magdeburg Centuries* very closely in order to refute it. Traces of its influence are visible throughout his works, and it seems he was much influenced by the work he sought to destroy.[48] In the *Controversies*, published in three volumes in 1581, 1582, and 1593, he defended the pope against the charge of being Antichrist, by referring to the Antichrist legend. In 1589 he wrote his *De Translatione Imperii Romani a Graecis ad Francos, adversus Matthiam Flaccium Illyricum*,[49] in which he presented his own interpretation, which will be discussed later.

As before, impetus for change came from abroad. Broughton published several of his works in London; but all his grand schemes, for example for the conversion of the Constantinopolitan Jews or for a new version of the Bible (the King James), either came to nothing or were given into other hands. English Protestants at home really awoke to the Jesuit challenge only after the turn of the century, becoming at James's insistence increasingly active in controversy. King James established a new college in Chelsea devoted to controverting the papists and Jesuits, to which were invited many notable Protestant scholars, both foreign and domestic. Controversial theology became intensely popular among aspiring divines of all sorts, so much so that Ralegh felt it necessary to ridicule the absurdity of petty disputants, calling them 'Commedians in religion'.[50]

[46] E. A. Ryan, *The Historical Scholarship of Saint Bellarmine* [*sic*] (Louvain, 1936), pp. 69-72 with reference to Bellarmine, *De Romano pontifice*, Bk. III, chap. 3.
[47] Ibid. Ryan refers to Bk. III, chap. 5 and to Bellarmine's *Chronologia Brevis*.
[48] For a more complete evaluation of Bellarmine's dependence upon the *Centuries* see Ryan, *Historical Scholarship of Saint Bellarmine*.
[49] (Antwerp, 1589).
[50] Ralegh, 'History of the World', *Works* (Oxford, 1829), vol. ii, Preface, p. xxxii.

One of those to enter the field against the Jesuits was Thomas Brightman, writing from his country parish in Bedfordshire. His was not one of the great intellects encouraged by King James, but that of a well-educated Puritan of his generation. He became much more famous after his death than he ever was before. As far as is known he never went abroad, although his commentary was first published in Frankfurt. His life and training come near to being typical of the English Puritan of his day. He was born in 1562 and educated at Queens' College, Cambridge, entering as a pensioner in 1576 and becoming a Fellow in 1584. He completed his B.D. in 1591. He shows all the signs of having shared the prevailing sympathies of his university. He hoped to see further reformation in the Church and admired the example of Geneva.

While Brightman was at Queens' College, Ramism became popular among the more radical Puritan Fellows.[51] Brightman was certainly affected by this vogue, but not in the way or to the extent that Napier was. His talents and interests were linguistic rather than mathematical, and for this reason he is more typical of the British adaptation of Ramism to scriptural studies. Like Napier, he adopted the use of the analytic method, and occasionally provided tables of the texts which he proposed to treat. One of these appeared in his commentary on the Song of Solomon,[52] in which he discovered that the type of the New Jerusalem was a prophetic sign of the reformed church.

At Cambridge he made friends with John Osborn, the son of Peter Osborn who had been Keeper of the Privy Purse to Edward VI. Through this friendship, Brightman was preferred to the rectory of Hawnes in 1592. He was renowned for his saintly life, and died suddenly in 1607 while travelling with John Osborn.[53]

In the preface to his *A revelation of the revelation*,[54]

[51] Kearney, *Scholars and Gentlemen*, pp. 60-7.

[52] Thomas Brightman, *A commentary on the Canticles of the Song of Solomon. Wherein the text is Analised, the Native signification of the Words Declared, the Allegories Explained, and the Order of times whereunto they relate Observed* (Amsterdam, 1644).

[53] *D.N.B.*

[54] First published in Latin (Frankfurt, 1609). All later editions were in English.

Brightman apologized for writing yet another interpretation of the Apocalypse. However, he explained that there were still some parts in need of exposition and that the works of the Jesuits needed answer. His words reveal the surprise and anger with which Protestants greeted Jesuit competition.

For when as I had by chaunce light uppon Ribera,[55] who had made a Commentary upon this same Holy Revelation; Is it even so (said I) doe the Papists take hart againe, so as that Booke which of a longe tyme before they would scarce suffer any man to touch, they dare nowe take in hand to intreate fully upon it? What? Was it but a vaine image or Bugge, at the sight whereof they were wont to tremble a fewe years since, even in the dimme light, that nowe they dare be bold to looke wishly upon this glasse in this cleare sunshine, and dare proclayme to the World that any other thinge rather is pointed at in it then theire Pope of Rome? O wee sluggish and lazie creatures, if wee suffer that. I thought it fit therefore that the crokinge of theis fellowes should be somewhat repressed. . . .[56]

Brightman's book was addressed to the reformed churches of England, Germany, and Switzerland; but apart from his respect for the Genevan model his sources and exposition were explicitly English. Although he had read the *Magdeburg Centuries*, he reserved the higher praise for Foxe's *Acts and Monuments*. Foxe was 'our countryman of blessed memory'.[57] Brightman applied the Apocalypse to the Church's past, but chose nearly all his examples from British history. For his discussion of the rise of the monks in the west he followed Bale's *The actes of Englysh votaryes*. When he reached the Reformation he applied the prophecies even more closely to England alone, discovering the angel's predictions of Thomas Cromwell and Thomas Cranmer. His lists of learned men who had written histories included Carion, Melanchthon, Sleidan, and the Marian exiles Bale and Foxe. He was firmly grounded in the tradition springing from the exiled communities of the 1550s, admiring above all others the commentaries of Bullinger and Beza. However, he added to his list of favourite expositors of Scripture the name of Hugh Broughton.

[55] Francis Ribera, *In Sacram Beati Ioannis Apostoli & Evangelistae Apocalypsin Commentarii* (Salamanca, 1591), edition consulted: Antwerp, 1603.
[56] Brightman, *A revelation of the revelation* . . . Wherein the sense is declared out of the scripture, the event also of thinges fore told is Discussed out of Church-Histories (Amsterdam, 1615), 'To the holy Reformed Churches', fol. A4r.
[57] Brightman, *Rev. of Rev.*, p. 318. This is followed by Foxe's account of the prophecy of Hildegard.

Broughton and Brightman had been to Cambridge at about the same time. Both were Puritan, and they shared the same convictions about Scripture. But whereas Broughton fell foul of established learning and found it impossible to re-establish his position in England from his self-imposed exile, Brightman apparently never wandered far from the beaten track, except in his commentary on Revelation, which was published posthumously abroad. Not having been subjected to the same pressures that Broughton had encountered abroad, Brightman was better able to reconcile some of Broughton's more unusual interests with the tradition he inherited from the Marian exiles. Brightman wrote his commentary after Broughton had written on Daniel (1596) but before he had written on the Apocalypse (1610). It must be remembered, however, that most of Broughton's interpretation of the Apocalypse derived from his views on Daniel.

Brightman's interpretation of Revelation was a grand and convoluted superstructure, in many ways the opposite of Napier's systematic simplification. The differences, however, were more a matter of temperament than of method. Brightman began clearly enough, with the analytical division of the text into three sections: the letters to the churches, the description of the universal church, and the seven seals, trumpets, and vials. But once into his commentary Brightman confronted the problems posed in the text armed with an indefatigable love of invention. The first of his inventions was the most important. In the letters to the seven churches he saw both 'panes' and 'counterpanes': the seven referred not only to themselves as named, but also to certain periods of church history from Christ to the present. The church of Ephesus had a 'counterpane' in the apostolic Church to the time of Constantine. Smyrna corresponded to the time from Constantine to Gratian, 382. Pergamum corresponded to the next period to 1300. The beginning of this period was obviously a problem. On one page he gives the date of 380, on the next he alters it to 400.[58] Elsewhere he seems to have given the date as 506 and as 607.[59] Since Pergamum was the type of the corrupt Roman Church, confusion about this date was symptomatic of the attempt to sever apostolic from antichristian

[58] Brightman, *Rev. of Rev.*, pp. 62-3.   [59] Ibid., pp. 322, 288.

practices. Thyatira corresponded to the period from 1300 to 1520, Sardis to the German Reformation, Philadelphia to the Genevan churches, and Laodicea to the Church of England.

Brightman was much intrigued by the repetition of the number seven in the prophecies. This seemed to indicate a relationship between the outer heavenly sphere in which *Ursa Major* was seen to contain seven stars and the inner human sphere in which there were to be seven periods of history.[60] (Even John Harvey had thought there was something hidden in the sevens of the Apocalypse.) He also believed that time and space were intimately connected. The distances of the churches from Ephesus were indicative of the lengths of their ages, and the direction from Ephesus in which each lay also indicated an approach to or a recession from purity. Movements to the north were recessions, movements to the south were approaches. Brightman traced the movement northwards to Pergamum, and thereafter southwards. At each point on the southward movement, he found a parallel with a point on the northward movement.[61] Thus, Thyatira was in opposition to Pergamum, which represented the opposition between the heroes and martyrs from 1300 to 1520 and the Roman Church; giving a new expression to the theory of the two churches. Sardis was parallel to Smyrna; the partially corrupted church to the incomplete reformation in Germany. The damning fault of the German Reformation was the belief in consubstantiation. Philadelphia was parallel to Ephesus, and was the new apostolic Church.

The church that remained, Laodicea, had no 'Parallele to match here, as beinge a peereless Paragon'.[62] Laodicea stood for the potential Church of England, which if she once fulfilled her destiny might parallel the first church of all, the Garden of Eden.[63] This was the first reference to a special significance reserved for England based upon and delivered within the context of an interpretation of the Apocalypse.

[60] Brightman, *Rev. of Rev.*, p. 6.
[61] N.B. These categories of thought were of course endemic in educated Elizabethan society. Notice especially the use of cartographical information to explain mystical relations. It is not far from this to Ralegh's map of Eden. Notice also the semi-mathematical or geometrical relationships indicative of neo-Platonic and Pythagorean influence.
[62] *Rev. of Rev.*, p. 124.   [63] Ibid., pp. 139, 50, 51.

Brightman's expression of this special election was given more in the terms of hope than conviction, for to him England appeared bogged down in Laodicea's self-complacency and unwilling to realize the full reformation that was her destiny. This part of Brightman's commentary was the most clear and forceful and was the most often abstracted or quoted in the later pamphlets that proclaimed him a true prophet of the new reformation.[64]

Behind the mysterious relationships hidden in the sevens of the Apocalypse lay the natural law of universal decay, which helped to explain the falling-away from purity of the medieval Church. This process must inevitably work 'unless God doe sometimes beyond the order of nature make light to shine out of darknes, as nowe for a good while he hath done in this last age of the world'.[65] In the Apocalypse the Church was assured of the special nature of the final age. For the present God had reversed the process and turned decay into renovation. The ideal figured in the New Jerusalem and prophesied historically in the counterpane of Laodicea (the Church of England) could be attained. One need not merely approximate the apostolic Church, one could hope to equal— even, since Laodicea had no parallel in the past—surpass it.

The second section of the text presented 'an Universall Type of the future Church'.[66] This was the fullest revelation of the true Church in all ages, and with the apostolic Church provided a guide to the organization and government of the Church. Moreover this type had one advantage over the apostolic Church in that it was not tied down by particular historical circumstances; in particular the change from heathen emperor to Christian king did not alter it.[67]

The third section of the text dealt with the events of church history. Brightman took up the story in the age of Domitian. The four horsemen, the altar, and earthquake concerned the period to Constantine when the seventh seal opened. The silence that followed corresponded roughly with the counterpane of Smyrna. The seven trumpets Brightman, like Foxe, applied to the raising-up of the Church's enemies

[64] e.g. *A Revelation of Mr. Brightman's Revelation* (London, 1641), *Reverend Mr. Brightman's Judgement on Prophecies* (London, 1643).
[65] *Rev. of Rev.*, p. 140.   [66] Ibid., p. 166.   [67] Ibid., pp. 173–4.

beginning in about A.D. 300. The first four trumpets were called the 'lesser', the last three the 'greater'. The first four sounded before the year 607, the latest date Brightman allowed before Antichrist took complete control of the Church. The fourth trumpet was concurrent with the 'flying angel' that represented Gregory the Great, an exception 'out of the rabble of many Popes', who had prophesied the appearance of Antichrist.[68] The fifth trumpet, the first of the greater trumpets, indicated both the apostasy of Muhammad who fell like the Star from heaven, and at the same time the dealing of Boniface III with the Emperor Phocas.[69] The locusts also had two meanings. In the east they represented the Saracens and in the west the monks. The sixth trumpet, said to last from 1300 until 1696 at the most, added the Turkish Empire to the list of enemies and foretold its rise and fall.[70]

The three greater trumpets were so called because they contained another of Brightman's inventions, 'double events'. One series prophesied the enemies of the Church, the other the fortunes of the elect; in effect, the two churches.[71] As usual the true Church was persecuted and forced into hiding. The two beasts represented the papacy; the first arrogated to himself the supreme spiritual power, the second, beginning with Boniface VIII, assumed temporal power.[72] The woman symbolized the Church from 300 to 1300. She was served by angels who were both specific reformers—Huss, Wyclif, Luther, and Calvin—and generally taken to mean princes and magistrates.[73] Brightman made two changes in the interpretation of this section: all reference to the first beast as the pagan Roman Empire was dispensed with in favour of a heavier concentration of images around the papacy; and Christian magistrates were shown to have an equal role with princes in the maintenance of true religion.

[68] Brightman, *Rev. of Rev.*, p. 283. This interpretation began as early as Bale's *Acta Romanorum Pontificum* (1558) in which as here Gregory becomes the Angel in the midst of the heavens.

[69] Ibid., p. 288. Brightman knew that Muhammad lived many years after Boniface III, but 'though yet I suppose that others doe more rightly referre him to some years after for the summe of the matter there is no difference.' Foxe might agree to this; Napier would not.

[70] Ibid., pp. 322-7.   [71] Ibid., pp. 287-8.   [72] Ibid., p. 430.   [73] Ibid., pp. 480-8.

The more significant novelties in his interpretation began
with his version of the Harvest and the Vintage, which he
took to mean the Reformation. 'The Harvest was in Germany
and hath brought us to the year 1530. This vintage was in our
Realme of England, being so mervailously jumping with the
matters that were done here, both in the course of time, and
in agreement of the whole matter, that it is not to be
doubted, but that the Holy Ghost hath pointed his finger to
these Grapes.'[74] From this point onwards most of the
prophecies were seen to be fulfilled in England. Thomas
Cromwell was identified as the avenging angel with the scythe
in his hand,[75] and Thomas Cranmer as the soul from out of
the altar.[76] The seventh trumpet blew in 1558.[77] The vials
began under Queen Elizabeth in 1560.[78] The seventh trumpet and the first vial overlap. In four vials[79] Brightman
covered the time remaining to his own time, showing how
each vial worked to the defeat of papistry.

1. Vial (1563) Elizabeth dismissed many of the papist
    clergy
2. Vial (1564) The Council of Trent meeting for many
    years confirmed errors which effect the
    damnation of many
3. Vial (1581) Act of Parliament against the treason of
    papists
4. Vial (his present) 'this boiling heate of the Sunne is
    nowe every daye to be loked for, that is,
    some more cleare opening of the Scriptures,
    whereby the man of sinne may be more,
    vehemently scorched.'[80]

The last three vials remained in the future. The fifth prophesied the destruction of Rome,[81] and the seventh Arma-
geddon.[82] The sixth vial concerned the future conversion of
the Jews. References to the re-calling of the Jews were not
absent from the earlier Protestant writings; Bale cited the
conversion of the Jews as one of the most certain signs of the

[74] Brightman, *Rev. of Rev.*, p. 502.   [75] Ibid., p. 503.   [76] Ibid., p. 504.
[77] Ibid., p. 388.   [78] Ibid., pp. 510–11.   [79] Ibid., pp. 524 et seq.
[80] Ibid., pp. 542.   [81] Ibid., pp. 773–4.
[82] Ibid. and described in detail pp. 836 et seq.

end. However, by this Bale often meant the conversion of papists to the true biblical Christianity of the Protestants. The martyrs sent forth in the fiery chariot of persecution were the new Eliases preaching to the Gentile Church. The elect were Jews by adoption, as Paul had said, and the actual Jews were of little importance. The gathering of the remnant of the Jews out of all nations meant simply the founding of congregations of Protestants.[83]

Brightman began his commentary with the same attitude. Early in his text, in the discussion of Philadelphia and its counterpane, he made it very clear that by 'Jews' he meant 'the Papists':

In the Counterpane, they are Jewes . . . such as are the Romanists at this day, that glory no lesse in Peeters Chayre, then the Jewes of old did in there Temple. . . . Some of these Jewes therefore are given to this holy Philadelphia, when there are many every day, whome God of his singular mercy pulleth out of the jawes of Antichrist . . . who beinge first of the Popish Religion, were afterwardes converted to the truth.[84]

He first used the word Jews to signify the Jewish people in his answer to Bellarmine, in what was virtually an independent treatise wedged between two sections of his commentary on Revelation.[85] One of the chief reasons for his writing on the Apocalypse was to answer the Jesuits, especially Bellarmine and Ribera whose commentary had so angered him. Although Foxe had foreseen the general nature of the Jesuits' counter-attack and had given several pages to averting it,[86] his commentary had been published only once in England, and actually had little influence on the later writers. Brightman looked to this contemporaries for guidance in his answer to the Jesuits. He found his defence in an extension of some of Broughton's ideas about the Book of Daniel.

Ballarmine's defence of the papacy[87] against the charge of being Antichrist drew heavily upon the many details concerning the latter; these were often gathered from the apocryphal books which the Council of Trent had received into the canon. Nearly all the details had some connection with the Jews. Bellarmine stated that Antichrist could not be said to

[83] Bale, *Image*, p. 137.   [84] *Rev. of Rev.*, p. 116.
[85] Comprising pp. 622-770.   [86] See above, pp. 99-101.
[87] Bellarmine, *Controversia*, Bk. III, 'De summo pontifice', quoted in Brightman, *Rev. of Rev.*, p. 623.

have come before all the following conditions had been fulfilled: (i) Enoch and Elias must come again to convert the
Jews; (ii) Antichrist must be born of the tribe of Dan and
reign in Judaea from Jerusalem; (iii) the gospel must have
been universally preached. None of these conditions had been
met, and therefore Antichrist had not come and could not be
the Pope of Rome.

Ribera's commentary differed from Bellarmine's defence
in that Ribera was not solely a controversialist but was
writing and responding within the frame of the Catholic
tradition. He split the seven seals into two sections, five to
cover the early Church to Trajan and the last two to cover
the end of the world; thus avoiding the present and the
medieval past altogether. On the subject of Antichrist he
agreed with Bellarmine.[88] This interpretation particularly
irked Brightman, as it must have many Protestants who since
the beginning of the Reformation had laboured to destroy
the papists' 'triennial Antichrist'.

In his answer to Bellarmine, Brightman wished to demonstrate that the calling of the Jews followed rather than preceded the defeat of Antichrist. In this context for the first
time he meant the actual Jews. 'At the callinge of the Jewes
. . . shall Antichrist utterly bee destroied. . . . For after the
throne of the Beast is Darkned the way shalbe prepared for
the kings of the East: that is, the Jewes shalbe called straight
after Rome is destroied. . . .'[89] Support for this order of
events came from the Book of Daniel. Instead of restricting
the prophecies of Daniel to the time before the birth of
Christ as Broughton had done, Brightman allowed them to
refer to the entire history of the Jews. Broughton had called
the Apocalypse a Gentile version of Daniel; Brightman regarded Daniel as a Jewish version of the Apocalypse. Therefore
Daniel contained the history of the Jews until the second
coming[90] established the New Jerusalem, and the Apocalypse

[88] Ribera, *In Sacram Beati Joannis . . . Apocalypsin Commentarii* (Antwerp, 1603), chap. 7, no. 10; chap. 20, no. 6.

[89] Brightman, *Rev. of Rev.*, 'Against Bellarmine', p. 711.

[90] Brightman, *A most Comfortable Exposition of the last and most difficult parts of the Prophicie of Daniel* . . . wherein the restoring of the Jews and their calling to faith of Christ, after the utter overthrow of their three last enemies is set forth in lively colours (London, 1644), p. 920: 'it is the purpose of the spirit

contained the history of the Gentile Church until the same final event united both churches in the kingdom. Since the kingdom must be founded after the defeat of Antichrist, the restoration of the Jewish Church must also follow upon Antichrist's defeat.

In order to maintain this interpretation of Daniel, Brightman had to reject the identification of the fourth beast with Antiochus Epiphanes. This he did by declaring that Antiochus had not fulfilled the entire prophecy of Daniel, and so by default the beast must be found in the next universal empire after the Greek, i.e. the Roman. As Calvin had said, the little horn pointed directly to the fall of the Roman Republic, when, Brightman added, the Romans had forgotten the gods and the magistrates of their fathers.[91]

In his commentary on Daniel, Brightman outlined the history of the Jews as he found it prophesied. Rome persecuted the Jews and destroyed the Temple; then the Saracens in 630 and the Turks in 1300 had invaded their lands.[92] In fact, the history of the Jews paralleled the history of the 'new elect'. They lay hidden during the reign of Antichrist; they were always few in number; and with the new elect they would be summoned into New Jerusalem, a land between the seas, the 'darling' of the Lord.[93] Both Broughton and Brightman interpreted this land as Judaea, between the Mediterranean and the Euphrates. In the last days the Kings of the East would defeat their enemies and enter the New Jerusalem.

Brightman's new interpretation of Daniel held several consequences for his view of the final chapters of the Revelation. The fight against Antichrist would take place on two fronts, one in the east where the Jews would defeat the dragon (i.e. the Turk) and one in the west where the Protestants would defeat the Roman Antichrist.[94] Since 1558 Brightman had observed the success of new Christian kingdoms whose

---

in this place, to comprise in a short abridgement, the whole estate of the people of the Jewes, in a continuall orderly succession, even to the second coming of Christ.'

[91] *On Daniel*, pp. 910–11.   [92] Ibid., pp. 920–2.

[93] Ibid., pp. 932–3. In *Rev. of Rev.* (pp. 851–2) he writes about the future Kingdom of the Millennium: 'We must also waite for some time longer, before our brethren the Jewes shall be converted to the faith.'

[94] *Rev. of Rev.*, pp. 836–8.

establishment he called 'a peculiar prerogative of this time'. These kingdoms were part of the true kingdom of Christ which 'should never be obscured so againe as the former Kingdoms were, which came to an utter ruin in process of time. For so it is said and he shall reigne for evermore'.[95] This was further proof that God's special providence had reversed the natural law of universal decay. These new kingdoms were the small beginnings of the final kingdom of Christ. In the wars facing east and west, the west need not necessarily be led by Christ himself; perhaps he would raise up 'some excellent man, in whose person he may present a visible Michael'.[96] Obviously the battle would take place where the Church was the most pure, for against that Church would Antichrist rage his fiercest.[97] By implication from his scheme of the seven churches, this would happen either in the Genevan churches or in England.

By 1650 Rome would have been defeated, and at that time the Jews would be restored (Brightman meant in their own land). By 1695 the dragon would have been defeated by the Jews in the east, and the way would be prepared for the New Jerusalem to come down from Heaven. Brightman wrote 'The Prophecy proceeds no furder then to the finall and Universal slaughter of all the enemies, & the full restoring of the Jewish nation.'[98] The New Jerusalem when established 'shalbe eternall and shall never be broken of again, and discontinued, and . . . it shall be translated at length from earth into heaven'.[99] And then 'Can it be doubted any longer, but then shall be indeed that golden age, and highest top of holy felicity and happiness.'[1]

In fairness to Brightman it should be stated that these opinions are widely scattered throughout his two commentaries: nevertheless, taken together they represent beliefs specifically condemned by the Helvetic Confession of 1566. That confession condemned 'Jewish dreams that there will be a golden age on earth before the Day of Judgement, and the pious having subdued all their godless enemies will possess

---

[95] *Rev. of Rev.*, p. 388.   [96] *On Daniel*, p. 937.
[97] *Rev. of Rev.*, p. 557.   [98] Ibid., p. 559.   [99] Ibid.
[1] *On Daniel*, p. 968 (misnumbered 966).

all the kingdoms of the earth.'[2] Brightman did condemn millenarians but by their heresy he seems to have meant only antinomianism.[3] Napier and even Ribera also expressed their condemnation of millenarianism in the same terms.[4]

Like Napier and many continental authors before him, Brightman believed in a future Golden Age which would see not only the perfection of religion but also the completion of knowledge. The progressive revelation of divine mysteries throughout history as seal after seal and then trumpet after trumpet was opened or sounded led to the final knowledge possible only after the seventh trumpet. During the last three trumpet-periods from 1300, knowledge had so increased that ancient languages and histories had been recovered. The men of the sixth trumpet from 1520 to 1560 had been particularly important in these tasks: Church historians such as Carion, Melanchthon, and Sleidan. 'Who compiling the Histories of the times past, did set before us the outward estate of the Church in their writings as in a mappe. And indeed the Prophecy was nowe at last to be added of necessity.'[5] Prophecy could not be understood until the sounding of the final trumpet. As it sounded in the mid-sixteenth century the centuriators and Foxe had led the way in showing that in Scripture 'thou shalt see the perpetuall tracke in which thou has sett thy footesteps even from the Apostles tymes, so lively described that thou canst require no more lightsome & notable History'. And Brightman adds, 'Surely this addition [of the Apocalypse] with the rest of the Apostolike writings, beinge joyned to the old Testament, doe sufficiently furnish thee with the Historyes of the world from the first beginninge of it to the last end in which regard this invaluable treasure ought to be most deare to every one.'[6] A true understanding of the past could not have been had before the final

[2] Arthur C. Cochran, *Reformed Confessions of the Sixteenth Century* (London, 1966).

[3] Brightman (*Rev. of Rev.*, pp. 852-3) thinks some bodily pleasure will be allowed but no excess.

[4] Napier, *A Plaine Discovery*, p. 240, and Ribera, *In Sacram Beati Joannis*, chap. 20, no. 17, p. 606.

[5] *Rev. of Rev.*, p. 349.

[6] *Rev. of Rev.*, 'To the Holy Reformed Churches, A3^v–A4^r and p. 397 (misnumbered 367).

consummation was at hand. This was not only because men had lacked the proper intellectual tools, but also and primarily because the appointed time had not yet come.

Nowe it (the Historye) is reserved for this time because there could not be a full understanding of these things before the last trumpet. The events came forth by little and little, and point by point, to the knowledge of which the world attained severally & by leasure—like, as when hangings are unfolded, but nowe when al things were at last accomplished, it was a fit time to see the whole garment displaid at once.[7]

Brightman's commentary is only one of several that illustrate the same changes in emphasis after the turn of the century. Patrick Forbes in Scotland wrote a commentary, published in both London and Middleburg,[8] which was similar in its emphasis upon the conversion of the Jews[9] and its use of the letters to the seven churches to illustrate a succession of ages. However, unlike Brightman, Forbes did not identify the later churches with national or confessional allegiances. Sardis symbolized the early reformed Church, but Philadelphia and Laodicea stood respectively for the love of reform and lukewarmness throughout the entire reformed community.[10]

Answers to Bellarmine occupied at least one generation, engaging both professional scholars and learned clergy. Brightman, writing from his country parish a book which was first published abroad, could not be said to have remained always at the heart of the academic community. An attack other than his but as fully involved with the Protestant apocalyptic tradition came from the pen of Robert Abbot, the elder brother of George, who was then professor of theology at Balliol. Abbot was widely known for his Puritan sentiments and for his learning, in which he was recognized as his brother's superior.[11] His *Antichristi Demonstratio*[12] appeared in 1603, in ample time for Brightman to have

---

[7] *Rev. of Rev.*, p. 397 (misnumbered 367).

[8] Patrick Forbes, *An exquisite commentarie upon the Revelation of St. John* (London, 1613); used here is the corrected version *An learned commentarie . . .* (Middleburg, 1614).

[9] Forbes, op. cit., p. 162. One of his sources was Broughton on Daniel, cited p. 231.

[10] Forbes, op. cit., p. 3.   [11]*D.N.B.*

[12]*Antichristi Demonstratio, contra Fabulas Pontificias, & ineptam Roberti Bellarmini de Antichristo disputationem* (London, 1603).

consulted it before his death in 1607. Abbot's answer called forth many of the same arguments used by Brightman. Abbot ended his discussion with two longer chapters in which he discussed the life and actions of Antichrist and the final apostasy; both subjects had roots in the earliest English involvement. His sources included Bale's *Acta Romanorum Pontificum*,[13] Foxe's martyrology,[14] *Carion's Chronicle*,[15] Sleidan's *Commentarii* and *De quatuor summis imperiis*,[16] and the *Magdeburg Centuries*.[17] He mentioned the works of Ribera.[18]

Forbes and Abbot presented an interpretation of the Apocalypse more moderate than either Napier's or Brightman's. Forbes set out to avoid the extremes as he saw them.

The first, is of these, who typing themselves to more strait rules of interpretation then the holy Spirite hath laid to them, wil needes have these seven Seales, as also the Trumpets & Vials to bee so many knots or periods of time exactlie cutted, within which, the accommodation of each is to bee sought; whereas they are no knots of time but types of distinct matters; and the whole matter comprehended in seven Seales. . . . The other extremity, is of these, who well perceiving the absurdity of the first neglect ih [*sic*] the accommodation, all consideration of distinct time, so jumbling Seales, Trumpets and Vials, to the confusion of al order, and light of Story, which in this Prophesie is most orderly set downe, with speciall relation to distinct events.[19]

This is a fairly accurate description of the two extremes and the moderate position. The kind of prediction Napier indulged in was disparaged; but on the other hand the text held within it a periodization which, although it might not be reducible to natural law, was nevertheless divinely established and evidenced by history itself. The key lay in the order of the text and the strict relationship of the seals, trumpets, and vials. Another development to which Broughton had pointed the way was the belief that later prophecies narrowed their application and became more specific, sometimes foretelling particular persons: Thomas Cromwell and Thomas Cranmer are examples from Brightman's commentary. The great apologist Hooker expressed credence in

[13] Cited, pp. 94, 137, 138, 139.
[14] Cited, pp. 95, 109-10, 111.   [15] Cited, p. 132.
[16] *Commentarii* cited, pp. 143, 172; *De quatuor summis imperiis*, p. 59.
[17] Cited, pp. 180, 182, 189, 190, 200, 203, 221.
[18] p. 78.   [19] Forbes, op. cit., p. 39.

particular prophecies of this sort, which served as a Protestant substitute for miracles in maintaining faith. In Scripture, he declared, God had together with doctrine 'mingled prophecies of things both civil and ecclesiastical, which were to come in every age from time to time, til the very last of the latter days, that by those things, wherein we see daily their words fulfilled and done, we might have strong consolation.'[20]

The moderates themselves did not write often on the Apocalypse, not from any lack of belief in its relevance, but because with Calvin they felt its obscurity and difficulty made nothing sure, or at best very little. Even the politic historian John Selden, although he had harsh words for the 'unlimited liberty' and 'trifling boldness' of the commentators who had 'grounded themselves rather on their own rash fancies, or depraved judgements, than on the careful and impartial examination of the holy text, or of the true and false church',.was of the opinion that the Apocalypse might have an interpretation so long as it were 'made according to the analogy of the scripture and the church story . . . which is the exactest rule of interpretation of it'.[21] The historical method that underlay Selden's *History of Tithes* (London, 1618) was not much different from analytical commentary on Scripture. In the *History of Tithes* itself Selden attacked the improper interpretation of the Apocalypse.[22] James, who sought to uphold the Protestant version of the Roman Antichrist, called upon Selden to clarify his position. In answer Selden skilfully compared his position to that of Calvin, and acquiesced in the King's opinion that 666 did very likely stand for *Lateinos*. His greatest criticism of commentators had been their lack of philological accuracy,[23] and that they gave in too easily to fanciful thoughts. Selden believed in trying evidence 'by storie and synchronisme'. This sort of criticism was much taken to heart by later commentators. The prime example of a first-class philologist with his own use of synchronisms in the apocalyptic tradition is of

[20] Richard Hooker, *The Works of Mr. Richard Hooker* (Oxford, 1850), vol. ii, p. 758.
[21] John Selden, *Of the Revelation, Opera Omnia* (London, 1725), vol. iii, pt. ii, pp. 1402-3.
[22] John Selden, *The History of Tithes*, ibid., p. 1081.
[23] Ibid., p. 1073.

course Joseph Mede, whose reputation surpassed that of all his predecessors.

By the end of the first decade of the seventeenth century, the apocalyptic tradition had not only been firmly absorbed into British Protestantism, but had also become the subject of quite sophisticated study. The mysteries of divine prophecy could be probed successfully only by those skilled in the arts of philology, chronology, and history. History in this context indicated only a severely restricted art, which because of its derivation from the greater art of rhetoric amounted in fact to little more than a method for obtaining and ordering examples from past experience to meet present needs. Both philology and scientific chronology were recognized then, as they are today, as great servants of historical truth. In the apocalyptic tradition sacred and universal history were inextricably bound together; the exposition of Scripture and prophecy was the exposition of history as God had eternally ordered and judged it.

In Ralegh there was a bit of everything: a little of the English Hebraist, the French universalist, the Machiavellian politician: but before all else there was an attitude to Scripture in full accord with both Broughton and Beroaldus. The next chapter begins with the influence of the apocalyptic tradition upon his *History of the World.*

VI

APOCALYPSE AND PROVIDENCE:
WALTER RALEGH AND GEORGE HAKEWILL

Time and again in his history Ralegh appears to rush head-
long towards the brink of innumerable inconsistencies only
to avoid it by a deft turn of phrase. This very ability has
earned him a fine literary reputation, but must prove frus-
trating to those who seek to uncover and weigh the importance of contemporary influences upon his thought. There are
few basic propositions that Ralegh was prepared to defend to
their logical consequences; perhaps only one: the absolute
authority of Scripture. All other systems of thought and categories of belief which appear and disappear among his pages
were subject to an extremely personal eclecticism. Not long
ago, historians debated the unfruitful question, whether
Ralegh was the typical Elizabethan. Nearly every thought he
expressed has been expressed by one contemporary or
another, so he is typical in the sense that he was essentially
unoriginal. However, taken as a whole his selection was so
personal as to be untypical of anyone but himself.

Ralegh will always present this sort of problem. In asking
how far Ralegh's history was influenced by the apocalyptic
tradition we shall be looking among a personal collection of
opinions for expressions or constructions of inference typical
of it, and will not be asserting that because Ralegh used the
apocalyptic tradition he was not also influenced by other,
even rival, traditions.

Among Ralegh's many interests were two arts that helped
to prepare him for his task of writing the history of the
world: mathematics and Hebrew. His achievement in both
was modest, but it did provide him with some discipline to
apply to his subject. The books in his library[1] included many
on biblical chronology, among them works by Beroaldus[2]

---

[1] Walter Oakeshott's discovery of Ralegh's library list is the single most important addition to our knowledge of Ralegh in recent years. *The Library* (Dec.
1968), 5th series, vol. xxiii, no. 4.

[2] Matthew Beroaldus, *Chronicum* (Geneva, 1577); Oakeshott, entry 400.

and Broughton.[3] They believed as Ralegh did in the unassailable truth of Scripture, and Ralegh turned to them for more
than their dates and sums. Although he proposed to cover the
whole of world history, he managed to complete his work
only to A.D. 130. In the apocalyptic tradition to this date he
need only have dealt with the prophecies of Elias and Daniel.
Although he was very interested in medieval and modern history, interests clearly illustrated by his collections of chronicles and modern histories, it is impossible to know how he
would have explained the later periods, or how he would
have structured his periodization. There are, however, indications that he was influenced by the tradition through the
period he did cover, and in other of his works there appear a
few tell-tale phrases taken from the New Testament prophecies and applied to medieval and modern events.

In his history Ralegh sought to uphold two general propositions, the authority of Scripture and the rule of providence.
The first cause of all events must be taken to be the will of
God. In order to write a history one needed a beginning, and
Ralegh chose the Creation. He wished to make it quite clear
that he began with literal belief in creation *ex nihilo*, and that
such a belief was the only possible one for a Christian. By a
single act of will God had created the world and then limited
its duration. 'For the same action of his will which made the
world for ever, did also withhold the effect to the time ordained.'[4] He wished not only to support a definite moment
of creation but also to posit an equally definite if unknown
moment of re-creation. 'The first point, That it was not for
ever, all Christians confess, the other they understand no
otherwise than that after the consummation of this world,
there shall be *a new heaven and a new earth*, without any
new creation of matter.[5] The Christian had in Genesis a revelation of the beginning and in the Apocalypse a revelation of
the end. Both were or were to be historical events. The connection between providence and Scripture was a very close
one because Scripture was quite simply the revealed will of
God. Universal history must deal with divine judgements; the

[3] Broughton, *A Concent of Scripture* and *Daniel*; Oakeshott, entries 443, 444.
[4] Ralegh, *History of the World, Works* (Oxford, 1829), vol. ii, Preface, p. lii.
[5] Ibid.

universal historian's first task was to refer 'all to the will of God, I mean, to his revealed will',[6] that is to Scripture, as history, or as prophecy of history, or by analogy of situations.

There are a few things to notice in this usual expression of the general Christian theory of universal history. The movement is from Creation to restoration or renovation, not to judgement and destruction. There is also the implication that Ralegh is going to develop the idea that Scripture is sufficient to reveal the preordained will of God.

Ralegh kept within the bounds of Elias' prophecy, setting the date of creation in 4031 B.C. He described three great periods of world history, before the law, under the law, and under grace.[7] The final era began with the Messiah and contained within it 'the promise of an everlasting kingdom' that he found described in the Apocalypse. However the crucial prophecies for him were those of Daniel and the Apocalypse. These two were so interdependent as to be a single prophecy of succession of empires and the rise of Antichrist. 'St. Paul', he said, 'describeth Antichrist out of Daniel, and the Revelation is wholly an interpretation of Daniel's visions.'[8]

The prophecy of Daniel was especially important as the justification for the connection Ralegh wished to make between sacred and profane history. Until the time of Daniel, Scripture apparently dealt with the history of the Jews alone. The section of the history[9] in which Ralegh proposed to shift his attention from the Hebrews to the ancient world in general contains a long passage in defence of Daniel as a true prophet of history. The purpose of this defence was twofold: to maintain the authority of canonical Scripture, and to bring a united and universal chronology under its aegis alone. Daniel had performed a connective function long before this: *Carion's Chronicle*, for example, had at the mention of Daniel's prophecy left biblical history for the history of four monarchies; and Hugh Broughton had altered his chronological table in the same direction. The difference between

[6] Ralegh, *History*, Bk. ii, chap. XXI, sec. vi; vol. iv, p. 613, 'a digression wherein is maintained the liberty of using conjecture in histories'.

[7] Ralegh, *History*, Bk. II, chap. IV, sec. xi; vol. iii, p. 122.

[8] Ralegh, *History*, Bk. iii, chap. I, sec. i; vol. v, p. 5, 'Of the connection of sacred and profane history'.

[9] Ibid.

Carion in 1532 and Broughton in 1588 lies entirely in the latter's extension of the authority of Scripture beyond its role as a guide to interpretation and towards a position of supreme chronological authority. Carion dated his events in three ways: in the year of the world, in Greek olympiads, and in years after Christ; ways which held equal authority. Broughton, however, and Ralegh after him, distinguished between divinely established chronology which could never err and pagan systems which could and did. This is an attitude towards Scripture which must take problems in the chronological interpretation of prophecy very seriously indeed.

For Ralegh the most important aspect of Daniel's prophecy was the justification it provided for extending his view of providential history beyond the bounds of biblical times without abandoning the basic proposition that Scripture revealed all. It provided an explanation for the eclipse of the Jewish nation and the progression of pagan empires down to the time of Christ and the new election. At the time of Daniel it became 'convenient briefly to shew by what means and circumstances the history of the Hebrews, which of all others is most ancient may be conjoined with the following times, wherein that image of sundry metals, discovered by God unto Nebuchadnezzar, did reign over the earth when Israel was either none, or an unregarded nation'.[10]

This vital connection must at all costs be maintained. Ralegh's defence of Daniel included a warning against too close an inspection of prophecy and a mockery of those students of his time, like Lively and Rainolds, whose efforts to solve such problems had found so many ways to uncover the sun that they had obscured the true and simple belief in the clarity of Scripture. Whenever possible, Ralegh maintained that prophecy should be interpreted literally and its authority should not be questioned. He was a great reader of commentaries on Scripture and not a true student of the Hebrew texts, and no doubt the problems seemed to him both trivial and divisive. Disagreement over pagan dates and chronologies was unavoidable, but disagreement over divine chronology was wicked.

[10] Ralegh, *History*, Bk. iii, chap. I, sec. i; vol. v, p. 2, 'Of the connection of sacred and profane history'.

This disagreement is found, not only in the reigns of heathen kings and princes, but even in computation of those times which the indisputable authority of holy scripture hath summed up; as in that of Abraham's birth; and after in the times of the judges, and the oppressions of Israel; in the times of the egression to the building of Solomon's temple, in the Persian empire, the seventy weeks; and in what not?[11]

The problems Ralegh lists here are very complex, and several involve the interpretation of prophecy. He was of the opinion that the prophetic books were as accurate as the historical, and that if a prophecy was given in clear words it was not necessary to pry too closely into the circumstances surrounding its fulfilment, because any discrepancy so found would reflect not on the truth of the prophecy but rather on the sources for the discrepancy. 'But it stands with little reason that we should seek the interpretation of prophecy out of circumstances, when the prophecy is such as doth expound itself.'[12] An example of the sort of conclusion this led him to may be found in his section entitled 'That Egypt was conquered by Nebuchodonosor contrary to the opinion of most authors: who following Herodotus and Diodorus, relate it otherwise'. There he cites the prophecies of Isaiah, Jeremiah, and Ezekiel, and says that this must have happened otherwise 'was it vainly done of the same prophet [Jeremiah] (which God forbid that any Christian should think, seeing he did it by the appointment of God himself)'. In fact Ralegh will go further: if Nebuchednezzar did not conquer Egypt, 'yea, then was that prophecy no other than false'.[13] Such a thing is unthinkable, and therefore false. In every case of this nature Ralegh's first concern was the reputation of Scripture. By doubting part of Scripture 'the reputation of the whole story might perchance bleed thereby, were not the testimony of the scripture supreme so as no objection can approach it'.[14]

Ralegh's profound literalism is important in a discussion of the influence of the apocalyptic tradition primarily because it makes no distinction between prophecy and history: prophecy is history of the future. Whatever he may have imagined to the contrary, Ralegh did not refer all to Scripture. He referred

[11] Ralegh, *History*, Bk. ii, chap. XIII, sec. ii; vol. iii, pp. 386-7.
[12] Ralegh, *History*, Bk. iii, chap. I, sec. iii; vol. v, p. 6.
[13] Ralegh, *History*, Bk. iii, chap. I, sec. viii; vol. v, pp. 27-31.
[14] Ralegh, *History*, Bk. ii, chap. I, sec. vii; vol. iii, p. 21.

to commentaries on Scripture, and there he found the additional materials needed to fill in any gaps or to explain any
difficulties. Ralegh's natural, philosophical, and historical
interests in the Creation especially took the form of inquiry
among contemporary commentaries on Genesis. Arnold Williams amply illustrates the aggregation of numerous notions
and traditions around the story of Genesis and Ralegh's use
of many of them.[15] Ralegh rarely refers to Scripture itself,
preferring to cite his commentaries and biblical chronologies.

Ralegh owned a few commentaries on Daniel, but, according to his list, none specifically on the Apocalypse. From his
statement that John's Revelation is an interpretation of
Daniel, it appears that he regarded the Apocalypse as a fuller
and more particular account of the Antichrist predicted by
Daniel. This interpretation, given among others by John
Knox, ties in with the version of the theory of the four
monarchies generally adopted by Protestants in Britain. This
theory was somewhat different from the German one propounded by Matthias Flacius, debated by Bellarmine, and
rejected by Jean Bodin during the course of the sixteenth
century. Ralegh most certainly rejected the German version,
but shows a readiness to reach conclusions that would support the British version.

By the time Ralegh had reached the prophecies of Daniel
his subject was empire. Thence by Daniel's prophecy he proceeded through the four monarchies to Rome. In his concluding pages he wrote:

By this which we have already set down is seen the beginning and
end of the three first monarchies of the world, whereof the founders
and erectors thought they never have ended. That of Rome, which
made the fourth, was also at this time almost at the highest.

Since the fall of the Roman empire (omitting that of the Germans
which had neither greatness nor continuance) there hath been no
state fearful in the east, but that of the Turk; nor in the west any
prince that hath spread his wings over his nest, but the Spaniard....[16]

[15] Arnold Williams, *The Common Expositor: an account of the Commentaries
on Genesis 1527–1633* (Richmond, Va., 1948). This is a comprehensive study of
Renaissance interpretative techniques and of authors on Genesis. References to
Ralegh illustrate his dependence upon Pererius and Zanchius, and his essentially
unoriginal comments on Genesis. Pererius and Zanchius appear in his library;
Oakeshott, entries 259 & 266, p. 342.
[16] Ralegh, *History*, Bk. v, chap. VI, sec. xii; vol. vii, pp. 898–9.

Ralegh concluded that there was yet no true successor to
Rome. Instead the Empire was split between two states, both
enemies of the Christian religion. 'These two nations, I say,
are at this day the most eminent, and to be regarded; the one
seeking to root out the Christian religion altogether, the
other the truth and sincere profession thereof. . . .'[17] One
enemy is open, the other more subtle. The apocalyptic tradition in Britain usually held that, following the fall of the
fourth monarchy, a false empire of Antichrist had succeeded
in deluding the world. This empire took the guise of the two
beasts, or of Gog and Magog, representing the Turk in the
east and the pope and his minions in the west.

Gog and Magog first appear in the prophecies of Ezekiel.
Dealing with them there, Ralegh chose to follow Mathew
Beroaldus's[18] opinion that this nation is identifiable in the
first instance with a tribe in the vicinity of Israel in Ezekiel's
time. There is, however, a sense in which Gog and Magog
prefigure a later situation. Ralegh told the story in such a
way that the parallels with his own time would be apparent.

By which prophecy of Ezekiel, it appeareth that God purposed to
gather together his people, to give life to dead bones, and to rule them
by one prince. For to that purpose it is written, *And David my servant
shall be king over them, and they shall have one shepherd*; that is, they
shall be united as they were in David's time. Hereupon in the 38th
chapter, Ezekiel prophecieth against those nations which should seek
to impeach this union, and disturb the people of Israel, whom God purposed to receive to grace, and promised to restore. And so in the same
chapter are those nations coupled together, which infested the Israelites after their return, and sought to subject them; all which were the
subjects or allies of Gog, prince of the Magogians. . . .[19]

James I is represented by David, the pope by Gog, and the
pope's allies, principally Spain, by the Magogians. Ralegh
does not explicitly make these comparisons, but he follows
the above description by a definition of Gog and Magog
which points ahead to the time of Antichrist. 'Gog signifieth
in the Hebrew, saith St. Jerome, *tectum* or *covering of a
house*; and Pintus upon Ezekiel affirmeth, that by Gog is
meant *antichrist*; for saith he, *Antichristus erit Diaboli*

---

[17] Ralegh, *History*, Bk. v, chap. VI, sec. xii; vol. vii, pp. 899–900.
[18] 'Who hath laboured herein with great diligence, and whom (of all that ever
read) I find most judicious', vol. ii, p. 260.
[19] Ralegh, *History*, Bk. i, chap. VIII, sec. iv; vol. ii, p. 261.

tegumentum sub specie humana; that "antichrist shall be the covering of the Devil under human form".'[20] Ralegh sought to strengthen the connection between the Magog of old and the antichristian Magog through the application of historical conjecture. It seemed to him that Spain was not only prefigured by the nation of Magog, but quite possibly descended from it. 'For without any repugnancy of opinions, it may be granted that in process of time these people might from their first habitation pass into the countries near the Euxine sea, and from thence in the after-ages into Spain.'[21]

The identification of Magog was just one example of the use of conjecture in writing universal history. Ralegh's defence of conjecture had two major lines of argument. The first claimed that the reasons for an action given by other historians did not preclude influences like those of the passions and predispositions of the persons involved. In exercising this kind of conjecture the historian was borrowing from the poet. 'Yet all this, for the most part, is not enough to give assurance, howsoever it may give satisfaction.'[22] There was, however, a second form of conjecture which could offer assurance as well as satisfaction: conjecture based upon the written and revealed will of God in Scripture. The best form of conjecture was based upon prophecy.

Ralegh developed this line of argument throughout his digression on conjecture in history. In attempting to write a history that mounted to the first cause, he had discovered how few of his predecessors, and therefore his sources, had attempted the same task. 'For all historians do give us information of human counsels and events, as far forth as the knowledge and faith of the writers can afford; but of God's will, by which all things are ordered, they speak only at random, and many times falsely.'[23] Ralegh was faced with random witnesses which he must order according to the revealed and written will of God. That was his task and it was impossible without the liberty of conjecture.

The problem that provoked his digression concerned the

[20] Ralegh, *History*, Bk. i, chap. VIII, sec. iv; vol. ii, p. 261.
[21] Ibid., pp. 264-5.
[22] Ralegh, *History*, Bk. ii, chap. XXI, sec. vi; vol. iv, p. 614.
[23] Ibid., p. 612.

Persian wars waged by Darius and Xerxes. He had referred to the prophecies of Daniel for guidance in his narrative but had found that, apart from predicting the wars themselves, they gave no information about their meaning or any illustration of the example they were to present to the Church. Ralegh had been forced to make conjectures concerning the divine will and intention in the history of Xerxes' expedition. He would rather have had a prophet to guide him, but since he had none he was forced to write about second causes. All this is evident in his own words.

Had the expedition of Xerxes (as it was foretold by Daniel) been written by some prophet after the captivity, we may well believe, that the counsel of God therein, and the execution of his righteous will, should have occupied either the whole or principal room in that narration. Yet had not the purpose of Darius, the desire of his wife, and the business at Sardes, with other occurents, been less true, though they might have been omitted, as the less material: but these things it had been lawful for any man to gather out of profane histories, or out of circumstances otherwise appearing, wherein he should not have done injury to the sacred writings, as long as he had foreborne to derogate from the first cause, by ascribing to the second more than was due.[24]

From this it should be obvious that Ralegh considered the biblical prophets the best historians. They best met his requirements in ascribing all to the first cause and in dealing with the moral implications of God's judgements in history.

Ralegh also wrote a few short treatises. In one of these[25] he introduced a homily in the manner of the early reformers on the rights of kings to resist papal intervention, with a collection of historical examples of the treacheries of the past. In this section he compared the Turk with the pope, finding them remarkably similar in their abominations. He spoke of the Turks as locusts and called Muhammad the false prophet.[26] He upheld the initial purity of the English faith before the arrival of Roman missionaries. In a description of the importance of his voyages to Guiana[27] he emphasized the

[24] Ralegh, *History*, Bk. ii, chap. XXI, sec. vi; vol. iv, p. 617.
[25] Written between 1614 and 1616, this treatise, *A Discourse of . . . War*, is one which LeFranc lists as authentic. Pierre LeFranc, *Sir Walter Ralegh écrivain: l'œuvre et les idées*, pp. 54–6; published in *Works* (Oxford, 1829), vol. viii.
[26] *Works*, vol. viii, p. 256.
[27] *Out of Voyage for Guiana* [British Library, Sloane MS. 1133], printed as an appendix to Hakluyt Soc. edn. (1848) of *The Discovery of the Large, Rich, and Beautiful Empire of Guiana*, ed. Robert Schomburgk, pp. 135-53.

division of the world into those who preached the false doctrines of Rome, especially the Spaniard, and those who
preached Britain's role as the representative in the New World
of the reformed faith.

Ralegh's *History* is at least as significant in those parts of
the apocalyptic tradition he chose to omit or evade as it is in
those he chose to incorporate. Most historians in the apocalyptic tradition as it was conceived by the Marian exiles Bale,
Foxe, and Knox had adopted some form of the theory of the
two cities. Ralegh would seem to have expressed this in his
suspicions about the origin and nature of the Spanish
monarchy opposed to his own nation and her religion, but he
avoided giving them a basis in the two cities. He admired
Augustine's *De Civitate Dei* and often referred to it in his
history, but his interpretation of it was nearer to Augustine's
intentions, for he applied it first to the individual soul. He
was aware that others, for example Calvin and Beza, had
extended the theory to indicate two separate societies; but
for his own reasons he preferred to remain undecided. The
question of the two cities fell under the general category of
predestination. Predestination certainly governed individual
election or damnation, but the full extent of its application
was known only to God.[28] Ralegh was more than uneasy
with the doctrine of predestination, fearing it might lead to
the abdication of moral responsibility. Predestination and
citizenship in the city of God were a private matter between
a man and his God; the truly active power of God in history
was providence.

By providence Ralegh, paraphrasing Augustine, meant a
foreseeing, a caring for, and an ordering of all things. All this
was witnessed in the Scriptures and observable in nature.
Sacred history was not for him the history of the Church or
the faith, but the story of the successes and failures of men
in fulfilling the universal moral law imposed by divine will
upon the world for its direction. In the past this attitude had
led historians to amass many examples of moral actions re-
warded or judged by providence. The Bible presented the
basic permutations of situations, and later history was a repetition of them. Ralegh recognized this use of the Bible by

[28] Ralegh, *History*, Bk. i, chap. I, sec. xiii; vol. ii, pp. 34–7.

his predecessors, 'the first divine histories being nothing else but a continuation of such examples'.[29] However, he wished to claim more for divine history than mere pre-eminence in moral instruction. The bulk of Ralegh's history followed precisely this construction: example, law, judgement. At those points where he wished to claim more for sacred history he verged on the apocalyptic tradition. Immediately following the avowal of his intention to do more than present examples, he began his attack on both the Aristotelian belief in the eternity of the world and the Platonic belief in the pre-existent image of the world at the time of Creation. Both the content and the position of this discussion are important. In this section Ralegh proved that God had set limits in both time and matter upon his creation, and that these limits were described in Scripture.

Providence worked through natural influences, or second causes. Instead of elaborating the theme of predestination, Ralegh explained: '. . . God worketh by angels, by the sun, by the stars, by nature or infused properties, and by men as by several organs, several effects; all second causes whatsoever being but instruments, conduits, and pipes, which carry and disperse what they have received from the head and fountain of the universal.'[30] The concept of the universal replaced the two cities, societies, or armies of some earlier Protestant historians. It did not, however, entirely replace the concordant belief that God had preordained an order of time revealed in Scripture and prophecy. The most important single question arising from Ralegh's dual desire to support the Scriptures as the revelation of God's will in the limitation of creation and its history and to confine predestination enough to allow an absolute moral responsibility (especially for princes) was the question of the cause of the rise and fall of empires. Did they fall because from the beginning they were fated to do so or because of the sins of their princes and peoples?

This perennial problem of historiography was then exercising the minds of many of the historians represented in Ralegh's library. Among these were several French lawyer-

[29] Ralegh, *History*, Preface, vol. ii, p. xliii.
[30] Ralegh, *History*, Bk. i, chap. I, sec. x; vol. ii, p. 25.

historians and theorists in history. In their works we see the
same concern for the universal approached by theories of
secondary causes. Ralegh had works by La Popelinère[31] and
René de Faucigny-Lucinge.[32] These two disagreed as to
whether the historian ought to raise the level of his discussion
from secondary causes to the first cause. Ralegh came down
decidedly on the side of La Popelinère. He had no respect for
'the wise men of the world who raise these effects no higher
than to second causes, and such other accidents which as
being next their eyes and ears, seem to them to work every
alteration that happeneth'.[33] The question still remained,
how did the divine will control history: by special intervention, or by Providence, setting down 'the date and period of
every estate, before their first foundation and erection'?
Having posed this question, Ralegh at first evaded it: 'But
hereof I will give myself a day over to resolve.'[34] He never
returned to answer it.

In practice he used both explanations. God had delivered
prophecies of the rise and decline of empires, as in Daniel's
prophecy, had most fully described Alexander's victories
over the Persians, and through his prophets had uttered sentences as irrevocable in Ralegh's mind as they had been in
Knox's. But God was also free to intervene in the world's
affairs at any time to punish gross immorality, often judging
nations by their princes.

Among the books in Ralegh's library was one arguing for
a regular periodicity in the rise and fall of empires which
combined both 'natural' and 'divine' laws. This was Robert
Pont's little treatise[35] which owes so much to Napier's *A
Plaine Discovery*. Robert Pont (1524–1606) had a long and
distinguished career in the Scottish church. At the first
General Assembly of the reformed Church on 20 December

---

[31] La Popelinère, *L'histoire des Histoires avec l'idée de l'histoire accomplie . . .*
(Paris, 1599); Oakeshott, entry 70.

[32] De Faucigny-Lucinge, *De la naissance, durée et cheute des estats* (1588);
Oakeshott, entry 79.

[33] Ralegh, *History*, Bk. ii, chap. XIX, sec. iii; vol. iv, p. 564.

[34] Ralegh, *History*, Preface; vol. ii, pp. vii–viii.

[35] Robert Pont, *A newe treatise of the right reckoning of the yeares, and ages
of the world, and mens lives, and of the estate of the last decaying age therof, this
1600 year of Christ . . .* (Edinburgh, 1599); Oakeshott, entry 445.

1560 he was designated as one of the twenty pastors quali-
fied to teach.[36] He often sat with Christopher Goodman
hearing cases brought before the Church Assembly. He translated the Helvetic Confession of 1566 and presented it with
his explanation to the Assembly.[37] His son married one of
John Knox's daughters. He was particularly famous for his
learning in astrology and was reputed to possess some
prophetic insight.[38] His treatise, published in 1599, seven
years after Napier's *A Plaine Discovery*, illustrates several of
the trends that have been noted among the English Hebraists
of this period, especially the preoccupation with history from
the Creation through biblical times and with systems of universal chronology.

The title-page reveals something of the nature of the content; it lists the major subjects treated and quotes the same
verse in Scripture[39] that had formed the basis of one of
Osiander's conjectures. The emphasis is on the natural bases
for chronology, but it is combined with and tested by scriptural prophecy. Pont concurred with Scaliger's date for the
Creation but demonstrated it as the outcome of systematic
interpretation of prophecy, following a combination of
propositions and working backwards through Scripture to the
date of 3947 B.C. 'In the which counte of yeares (albeit by
an other manner of reckoning) I agree with the learned
Josephus Scaliger, & some others more auncient then he.'[40]

Pont's system of universal chronology centred on the exposition of 'sevens', one of his main propositions being 'That
there is a merveilous sympathie of periodes of times, in
reckoning by sevens. . . .'[41] The two central prophecies were
Daniel's seventy weeks and John's seven angels and trumpets.
Daniel's prophecy held until the birth of Christ, but times
thereafter were hidden in the sevens of the Apocalypse. For
those times he referred his readers to Napier: 'whereanent,
who would know further, let them read that learned and

[36] *D.N.B.*

[37] *Acts and Proceedings of the General Assemblies of the Kirk of Scotland
from the year MDLX*, Part I, pp. 60-1, 90.

[38] *D.N.B.* He was said to have known instantly of Elizabeth's death.

[39] 'Luke 17:— As it was in the dayes of Noe, so shall it be in the dayes of the
Sonne of man.'

[40] Pont, p. 21.   [41] Proposition 6, Preface.

divine worke of JOHN NAPER, in the exposition of the *Revelation*, the 5, 6, 7, 8, & 9 propositions'.[42]

Napier had not considered pre-Christian times or the rival systems of universal chronology. Pont brought both of these to Napier's explanation of history from Christ to the end, and in doing this also discussed some Elizabethan notions about the progress of history. He began by giving a summary of all the prophecies considered important revelations of the course of history. The Prophecy of Elias came first; because it had been written by an unknown rabbi it lacked authority by itself, but because there was Christian confirmation of it in the idea of the world-week and in Augustine's six ages, Pont recommended it as one of the systems most simple to understand. To this could be added the division used most often by poets and astrologers: the four metals as in Daniel's vision. This also had some authority because it was based on Scripture. Others divided ages into periods dominated by the seven planets or by the seven ages of man. The last pattern was the least reliable because it did not deal specifically with either scriptural prophecy or the heavens.[43] Like Napier, Pont felt that the stars were not only instruments for the telling of time but also, by their continual movement, the second cause of temporal change. When they stopped, time would stop.

Pont proposed his own synthesis of the most useful of these notions. There were to be seven millennia. Six followed Augustine's six ages of the world: (i) the Creation to Noah; (ii) Noah to Abraham; (iii) Abraham to Solomon's Temple; (iv) the Temple to Christ; (v) Christ to 1056 when Antichrist's kingdom reigned supreme; (vi) 1056 to the end soon approaching. If a millennium was shortened, then a prophecy was given to guide chronologers; for example, Daniel's seventy weeks and John's seven angels and trumpets. The seventh millennium was the millennium of the kingdom. To this pattern Pont added a version of the four metals. The first age was golden. The fourth age, containing as it did Daniel's prophecies, went through all four metals with the four

---

[42] Ibid, p. 17.
[43] Ibid. pp. 35–41. He reviews all the ways of periodization and presents the most compact summary of the alternatives I have encountered.

monarchies. With the advent of Christ began a second Golden Age, but this soon decayed to the present state of things. However, with the expected second advent of Christ would come also a third Golden Age.[44] Here is expressed a common but strange mixture of despair and hope that the world was in the last stages of decay but held also the promise of new glory.

Following Napier's interpretation, Pont designated the year 1600 as the sixtieth of the seventh trumpet. The end could not be far off, and already the heavens were giving signs foretelling both the trials of the last days and the promise of the second coming. The comet of 1572 he likened to the Star of Bethlehem, and the eclipse of 1598 would, he expected, be followed by another in 1605. These signs portended a worsening situation in Europe, attended by the wars of the last days. England and Scotland would not be immune from these conflicts, for both were guilty of proud ambition[45] and insincerity in religion. The future held both warning and promise. Although he had included Napier's discussion of the hints in Scripture of a fatal period of empires of 490 years, and had found that in the past such great changes had occurred at approximately this interval, he held that as yet not enough was known to enable confident prediction.[46] His implication was that more had to be learned about the movement of stars before any exact rule could be found. An inquiry into the periodicity of empires was for him in the nature of a natural science, rather than the interpretation of Scripture.

We have no way of knowing exactly what Ralegh thought of Pont's hypotheses. He did combine a strong sense of the universal decay of all nature with an optimistic attitude towards the achievements of his own time. This may have been merely the expression of a proud man under sentence of death, or it may have had some connection with a certain conception of the present that was available in his reading materials and to which he appears occasionally to allude. He certainly did not expect the imminent destruction of the world when he spoke of the generations to follow him into death, but then neither did Broughton, who expected the

[44] Pont, pp. 78-9.   [45] Ibid., p. 103.   [46] Ibid., pp. 67-8.

struggle with the papacy to continue for several hundred years more, until the universal preaching had been accomplished. Broughton had his eyes on the conversion of the Jews in the east and Indians in the west. Ralegh believed the opportunities of the New World were at least partly spiritual, that economic success might be at least partly dependent (the judgement of God being always at work) upon the recognition of a duty to convert the Indians to the true faith.

Pont belonged very much to the older generation of reformers, and shared their opinion that 1600 would be a very important date. Luther and Melanchthon thought the world would not last much beyond then; Foxe, Napier, and Pont, that it must mark at least the beginning of a quick series of events completing the prophecies of the Apocalypse and preparing the world for the kingdom or the Last Judgement. Broughton, Brightman, and Ralegh, all of whom wrote their most important works after 1600, delayed the completion of history, Broughton for some hundred of years to come, Ralegh indefinitely; and Brightman offered two alternatives to destruction, a radical spiritual change of some kind, or the raising-up of an agent of the kingdom, a 'visible Michael' or a perfect church, not necessarily the return of Christ himself. The revelation of Antichrist had not immediately led to his complete destruction. The later generation believed the earlier not to have misjudged the nature of the times, but to have underestimated the strength of the beast and the effort and warfare necessary to defeat him. Also, Broughton and Englishmen after him would add that they had been unaware of the extent of the tasks that remained to be completed. The focal point of the struggle was Europe, but other races and other continents had also to be considered. This is something of a new spirit, arising out of the older one and inheriting from it the outlines of history in the apocalyptic tradition first formulated to support the contention that the end was indeed near at hand.

The apocalyptic tradition has been shown to arise out of the combination of three major prophecies. By the turn of the century changes had occurred in the reputation and interpretation of at least two of them. The Prophecy of Elias was brought forward, partly because it was interpreted to mean

that the final 2,000-year period would be shortened out of
God's mercy towards the elect. The idea that the world
would last for 6,000 years found support in the world-week
of Creation and did not necessarily require the corroboration
of an unknown rabbi, unless this final curtailment were the
point. References to the Prophecy of Elias became fewer in
learned works, though not in popularizations of earlier
writers, while its origins among the writings of the Talmud
were noted more to its discredit than otherwise. In Britain,
John Harvey openly disbelieved it, and Robert Pont subsumed it under the general heading of the world-week. It
maintained its importance in suggesting the date of Creation
to have been about the year 4000 B.C.

As early as 1565 Jean Bodin had ridiculed the prevalent
belief in Elias' prophecy and had challenged the theory of the
four monarchies. His book *Methodus ad facilem historiarum
cognitionem* set out to demolish many such pet theories and
replace them with a kind of universal history based on ideal
and precedent. Bodin's profession was law; his favourite type
of history was civil history. His personal religion has
remained something of a mystery to historians. It was certainly unusual, combining with Christianity elements of
Judaism and cabalistic astrology. Bodin was probably wise in
maintaining silence concerning the full extent of his departure from tradition.

In England Bodin became well known after the publication
of his *Republic* and his visit between 1579 and 1581. His
Republic was more often discussed than his *Method*. L. F.
Dean, who searched for references to the *Method* in England,
could find none before 1580.[47] It was principally on the
strength of the reputation of the *Republic* that people read
the *Method*.[48] In Scotland, Andrew Melville brought the
Method home to his nephew James, who reports that they
read and discussed it together.[49] The only impression it
appears to have made on James was one of Bodin's sagacity
in matters connected with civil policy and history; James

[47] L. F. Dean, 'Bodin's *Methodus* in England before 1625', *Studies in Philology*, 39 (1942), pp. 160–6.
[48] Ibid.
[49] *The Autobiography and Diary of Mr. James Melville*, ed. Pitcairn, p. 46.

went on to hear Knox on the prophecies of Daniel without a word of comment about the conflict of opinion. Thomas Brightman referred to Bodin's *Method* at one point,[50] but only as the source of information on a minor matter concerning the organization of the city of Geneva.

One of the reasons for this lack of impact on the treasured belief in Daniel as a prophet of empire was the way in which Bodin phrased his attack. He wrote:

> A long-established, but mistaken, idea about four empires, made famous by the prestige of great men, has sent its roots down so far that it seems difficult to eradicate. It had won over countless interpreters of the Bible; it includes among modern writers Martin Luther, Melanchthon, Sleidan, Lucidas, Funck, and Panvinio—men well read in ancient history and things divine. Sometimes, shaken by their authority, I used to think that it ought not to be doubted. I was stirred also by the prophecy of Daniel, whose reliability it is a crime to disparage, whose authority it is wicked to question. Yet afterwards I understood that the obscure and ambiguous words of Daniel could be twisted into various meanings; and in interpreting the prophecies I preferred to take the formula of the courts, "it doth not appear", than recklessly to agree with anyone because of the opinion of others which I did not understand. I thoroughly approve the reply of Calvin, not less polished than sagacious, when he was asked his opinion about the book of the Apocalypse. He candidly answered that he was totally at a loss regarding the meaning of this obscure writer, whose identity was not yet agreed upon among the erudite. Similarly, I do not see how we are to relate the wild beasts and the image discussed by Daniel to those empires which flourish everywhere now-a-days and have flourished for so many centuries.[51]

His specific denunciation was reserved for the German version[52] of the prophecies and he expressed himself as one anxious to protect the authority and reliability of Daniel. Further, he attacked not so much the idea of a spiritual translation of divine interest as the restriction of the number of empires to four. Few Englishmen had supported the full German version, preferring the idea that the pope's usurpation of the Empire had been more complete and the Empire replaced . by Antichrist. Bodin was arguing for the validity of the use of the word 'empire' in a civil sense. He cited several nations that deserved to be called empires: the Spanish, the Turks,

---

[50] Brightman, *Rev. of Rev.*, p. 111.

[51] Jean Bodin, *Method for the Easy Comprehension of History*, trans. B. Reynolds (New York, 1945), chap. VII, p. 291.

[52] He cited Melanchthon.

the Arabs, the barbarians who invaded Rome, and the Tar-
tars.[53] All these had figured in one form of the apocalyptic
tradition or another, not as true empires defended by God
but as the nations of the empire of Antichrist, plagues sent
to try the elect or punish the wicked. It would be quite
possible to read Bodin and agree with him that one could use
the word 'empire' thus in civil speech without abandoning a
special significance for the four mentioned by Daniel and an
apocalyptic interpretation of non-Christian or papist successors.

Despite his expressed concern for Daniel's authority,
Bodin was ready to discount Daniel when there seemed too
much evidence against him. Some carried their defence of
him so far that 'they think that there ought to be only five
kings of the Persians, because Daniel said that there would be
only five kings to come. But the unanimous verdict of all
writers places the minimum at eight; some even at ten, on
account of seditions and civil wars.'[54] Some fifty years later,
Ralegh would not allow Daniel's reputation for truth to
suffer in any comparison, nor could he have accepted Bodin's
position that some parts of Scripture could be so obscure or
ambiguous as to defy interpretation.

Of the traditional notions about history attacked by Bodin
two received the excited attention of some Englishmen.
Bodin attacked the notion of universal decay and the idea
that the Golden Age lay far in the past. While Bodin was still
in England, Gabriel Harvey wrote with evident excitement to
Edmund Spenser, 'You suppose the first age was the goulde
age. . . . It is nothing soe. Bodin defendeth the goulde age to
flourish nowe. . . .'[55] This idea captured the imagination of
many and resulted in the first expression of what some historians[56] are pleased to report as a nascent theory of progress.
In fact, as illustrated by Pont, Napier, and even Brightman,
theories of universal decay and the return of the Golden Age
were not mutually exclusive. Whatever Bodin himself may

[53] Bodin, ed. cit., p. 296.   [54] Ibid.
[55] Harvey to Spenser, 1579–80, *Letterbook of Gabriel Harvey*, ed. E. J. L.
Scott, Camden Soc., New Series 33 (1884), p. 86.
[56] Ernest Lee Tuveson, *Millennium and Utopia: A Study in the Background of
the Idea of Progress* (New York, 1964). This thesis needs qualification if it is not
to be misunderstood.

have believed, his readers in England appear to have seized upon those aspects conducive to the apocalyptic tradition and rejected those that worked against it.

On the subject of universal history Bodin and Ralegh had much in common. Bodin's emphasis upon the universal found expression in an understanding of the importance of law with which Ralegh was in full agreement. To Ralegh, however, God was more than the fount of the universal; he controlled the world through providence. Ralegh's paraphrase of Augustine's definition was not really sufficient to explain the complexities of so important a doctrine. By 1627 a full discussion had been written by George Hakewill.

Hakewill accepted Bodin's rejection of the theory of universal decay and his opinion of the Golden Age, and was also an avid believer in the power of divine providence. He was able to combine these positions with an acceptance of the apocalyptic tradition as it applied to the past and the present. In the preface to his *Apologie* he informed the reader that a great part of his book would be spent 'in proving that *Antichrist* is already come from the writings of the *Romanists* themselves . . .'.[57] Bellarmine was still finding his opponents.

In the first book he set out to dispose of the idea of universal decay and similar fancies. One of his candidates for extermination was the prophecies of the Sybil. He rejected them because they were not scriptural, but still believed them to be true.

That the *Sybils* clearly foretold many things touching the name, the forerunner, the birth and death of *Christ*, the coming of *Antichrist*, the overthrow of *Rome*, & the consummation of the world, which notwithstanding, (as *Causabon* hath learnedly observed) seemes to be contrary to the word of God, that so profound mysteries should be revealed to the *Gentiles*, so long before the incarnation of *Christ*.[58]

No serious writer in the tradition had given the Sybilline texts equal authority with Scripture: none had claimed more than that they were true and could rightly be interpreted to signify the Roman Antichrist.

In the fourth book Hakewill dealt with some aspects of ecclesiastical history, touching upon the Reformation and the

---

[57] George Hakewill, *An Apologie of the power and providence of God in the Government of the World* (Oxford, 1627), C1^r.

[58] Ibid., Bk. i, chap. I, sec. iii, p. 6.

idea that the last days of the world would be the worst. He described the Reformation as a 'special providence' of God.[59] One of his arguments against universal decay actually strengthened the apocalyptic tradition in some of its newer emphases.

But I would demaund how it can hang together, that we should expect the *subversion* of *Antichrist* & his kingdome, & the *conversion* of the whole Nation of the *Jewes* to the saving knowledge of the truth, before the end of the world, and yet withall affirme or beleeve, that the whole world still hath, & doth, & shall to the end thereof grow worse and worse?[60]

On the subject of the history of Antichrist, Hakewill found a way to turn Bodin's rejection of the theory of the four monarchies into an argument to support a version of the theory commonly held in Britain. Agreeing with Bodin that such a fabrication was meaningless to present-day civil history, he pointed to the patristic commentators and others who had maintained that only one thing restrained the appearance of Antichrist in the world, the power of the Roman Empire. As long as Rome could be said to stand, Antichrist could not be born. But, Hakewill continued, nothing was left of Rome but a shadow and a title. 'I would demaund then, whether a name, a title, a shadow can hinder the comming of *Antichrist*, or be divided among ten Kings, and shared into ten kingdoms? if it cannot, then is *Antichrist* undoubtedly already come into the world.'[61]

Although Carion and Melanchthon had argued for the validity of the translation of the Empire through Charlemagne to Otto and the Germans, Protestants since Calvin had been developing another version in which Rome had fallen and been succeeded by the papal usurper, and so the four monarchies had passed into history. Bodin had attacked Melanchthon by name in his denial of the theory, and Bellarmine for his own purposes had specifically denounced Matthias Flacius and the German translations but had maintained the theory of the ten toes. Hakewill attacked both German and Jesuit theories, but apparently still maintained the Protestant version which held that Rome had fallen totally to the Antichrist and therefore no legal successor remained. History had

---

[59] Hakewill, *Apologie*, Bk. iv, chap. XII, sec. i, p. 432.
[60] Ibid., sec. ii, p. 434.   [61] Ibid., sec. iv, p. 440.

finished with the four monarchies and entered the times of the Apocalypse.

Hakewill took Scripture to mean by the 'last days' all the times after Christ, not simply those during which Antichrist would rage. With something of the spirit of the early English reformers Tyndale and Bale, Hakewill noted that in St. John's time there were already Antichrists about, 'fore-runners no doubt and harbengers, as it were to the great *Antichrist* that was to come' and that St. Paul had said 'even then *the mystery of iniquity began to worke*'.[62] If these were the last days and Antichrist had already come, as Hakewill believed he had, then the identification of him should be possible. He did not intend to make the identification of Antichrist his main subject, but he could not help noting that no more likely candidate could be found than the pope of Rome, who he said had usurped the imperial power.[63] However, he had less certain views about the time of the end or the nature of the kingdom to come. John had described in the Apocalypse a new heaven and a new earth, but 'it cleerely appeares (whatsoever *Bright-man* dreame to the contrary) that he there describes the state of the Saints after the day of judgement'.[64]

George Hakewill was no millenarian, and it is interesting to note that by 1627 Brightman had gained the reputation of being one. The bulk of Hakewill's *Apologie* was devoted to a comparison of the ancients with the moderns, showing that in every way the moderns equalled and in some things surpassed the ancients. By a Golden Age Hakewill did not mean the kingdom of the millennium. The world would certainly have a definite end, and towards that time Antichrist would be entirely defeated and the Jews converted, but the date of these things was known only to God. Although he accepted what the apocalyptic tradition told him about the past, and some of its implications for the present and future, he did not wish to push the matter further, especially in the direction indicated by Brightman.

By the time we reach 1630 several things are clear. The tradition as it appeared in a certain view of the past, especially

[62] Hakewill, *Apologie*, Bk. iv, chap. XII, sec. iv. p. 438.
[63] Ibid., p. 440.   [64] Ibid., sec. vi, p. 452.

in church history, has gained nearly universal acceptance. Even those like Hakewill, who were willing to do away with such things as the theory of the four monarchies when the subject was civil history, invoked ideas dependent upon it when the subject was ecclesiastical history. The attacks that had been made upon the Prophecy of Elias, the theory of the four monarchies, and the prophecies of the Sybil had none of them completely expunged the history these were supposed to prophesy. Seeking dates for actual events, students of divine chronology embodied Elias' prophecy and debated the correct interpretation of Daniel's seventy weeks and other of his chronological or numerical utterances. However, outside the field of biblical chronology some of the main props of the tradition were being questioned. Of what authority, asked John Harvey and Hakewill, were such things as the prophecies of an unknown rabbi or the treacherous utterings of the pagan sybils? As yet, however, only the props and not the tradition itself were under fire.

With this as a general background, the apocalyptic tradition now developed in two different directions. One led where Brightman had pointed, towards a millenarianism of simple and potent form expressed in sermon and pamphlet and occasionally in parliamentary speech. Those who seek in this literature for reasoned expression of a new intellectual trend, for its origins or its development, will be sorely disappointed. Brightman's 900-page commentary is reduced to ten pages purporting to present his views. Napier and others receive the same treatment. It is no wonder that historians seeking to evaluate the importance of this literature find it shallow, its main purpose declamatory.

Curiously, as the popularity of apocalypticism increased among some sections of the community, it was on the wane among the more educated. In a way the tradition had become top-heavy, weighed down by too many theories attempting to cover too much material. The refinement of the tradition had become a study so sophisticated that only the greatest minds could comprehend the complexities of language, history, chronology, and divinity necessary to pursue its development. At the same time and apparently without it being suspected, little by little the main props which from the first had supported the tradition were being weakened by continuous reinterpretation, always toward the more symbolic. The works of Broughton and Brightman are early indications of this process. Broughton delayed the approaching end of the world until after some hundreds of years, and emphasized the tasks of further reformation, the conversion of the Jews and the universal preaching. Brightman's use of repetitive types, double events, panes and counterpanes had considerably weakened the simple idea of a historical progress through the prophecies in their textual order. The ease with which Hakewill dispensed with some of the supporting arguments for the tradition without dispensing with the tradition itself illustrates an attitude that also tended to weaken the possibility of further development. The tradition as it applied to all but the most recent period of history had become static. The only additions made to it were either apocalyptic images to suit more recent events such as the continental wars, or a new systematic arrangement of the images dealing with the past which more clearly expressed the given tradition. Joseph Mede did both these things and his new way to express the old order remained standard throughout the century. Newton was perhaps the last of the hyper-sophisticated minds to wrestle with the complexity inherent in this study, and in matters of interpretation he hardly ever varied from the path set for him by Mede.

The fact that Newton takes up the study again near the end of the century is itself an eloquent indication that the tradition was never wholly refuted. It was merely abandoned. The reasons for this are theological, historical, and historiographical. The next chapter will show how Mede's achievement of a standard work brought with it a new millenarianism and the effect that had upon the historical tradition.

VII

THE MILLENNIUM AND THE ECLIPSE OF
THE HISTORICAL TRADITION

Since the days of the Marian exiles there had been many
subtle changes in the apocalyptic tradition, but even greater
alterations were made in the first decades of the seventeenth
century. The single most important alteration was the introduction of a new spirit of millenarianism. In part the historical tradition of the previous century had prepared England
for this, but the real source for the change lay abroad.

Early in the new century Thomas Brightman had warned
England against the lukewarmness of Laodicea and called
upon the English church to work more closely with the
Protestant churches of Europe for the cause of the New
Reformation. In the years preceding the Thirty Years War the
desire to see Britain more actively involved in the protection
of international Protestantism was voiced by many on the
continent. Hopes rose with the marriage of James I's
daughter Elizabeth to the Elector Palatine, but were dashed
by events in Bohemia and with the outbreak of war. European Protestants sought a saviour again in Gustavus Adolphus
and always sought the aid and the refuge of Britain. Encouraged by John Dury and Samuel Hartlib, the ideas of men
such as Johann Valentine Andreae, John Henry Alsted, and
John Amos Comenius were brought to the attention of
Englishmen.[1]

The intellectual history of the period is no less complica-
ted than the political. The names of Andreae and Comenius
figure prominently in the aggregation of ideas that form what
Frances Yates has described as a Rosicrucian culture.[2] The
interplay between such streams of thought as Christian
Cabala, Hermeticism, angelology, and alchemy helped to
drive an engine of thought in directions compatible with a

[1] G. H. Turnbull, *Hartlib, Dury, and Comenius: gleanings from Hartlib's papers* (London, 1947).
[2] Frances A. Yates, *The Rosicrucian Enlightenment* (London, 1972); Paladin edition (St. Albans, 1975) consulted.

brand of apocalypticism. Any attempt to come to grips with the bewildering array of ideas that make up the matrix of European thought during this period is bound to raise nearly as many questions as it hopes to answer. In her admirable work Miss Yates noticed that there were both similarities and dissimilarities between the Rosicrucian pattern and the Baconian.

One of the important similarities here is a belief in the possibilities of an 'advancement of learning', of a new age of knowledge. Bacon's 'great instauration' of science was, as Miss Yates says, 'directed towards a return to the state of pure and sinless contact with nature and knowledge of her powers'.[3] The apocalyptic tradition shares with the Rosicrucian movement and Baconianism something of the same background in Renaissance thought. Especially in that stream of the tradition which was first noticed in the German Lutheran Osiander, in George Joye, in the author of *The Complaynt of Scotlande*, in the work of John Napier, and finally in Thomas Brightman who died in 1607, there are signs of a similar conviction about the nature and potential of the present age. Despite hints along these lines, none of the principal writers in the tradition had openly identified the present or a time that was close approaching with the millennium.

In terms of the apocalyptic tradition Francis Bacon would be classed as a cautious moderate. In *The Advancement of Learning* of 1605, he addressed himself among other things to the nature of the study of history. There were three kinds of ecclesiastical histories, of which the third was the history of providence.

The second, which is history of prophecy, consisteth of two relatives, the prophecy, and the accomplishment; and therefore the nature of such a work ought to be, that every prophecy of the scripture be sorted with the event fulfilling the same, throughout the ages of the world; both for the better confirmation of faith and for the better illumination of the Church touching those parts of prophecies which are yet unfulfilled; allowing nevertheless that latitude which is agreeable and familiar unto divine prophecies; being of the nature of their author, with whom a thousand years are but as one day; and therefore are not fulfilled punctually at once, but have springing and germinant

[3] Yates, *The Rosicrucian Enlightenment*, p. 156.

accomplishment throughout many ages; though the height or fulness of them may refer to some one age.[4]

He added, 'This is a work which I find deficient; but is to be done with wisdom, sobriety, and reverence, or not at all.' Nevertheless, he recognized it as a branch of study and recommended a way of approaching it that is easily recognizable as supporting the Protestant position on the relevance of the prophecies to the past, present, and future of the church with the added provision that the 'height or fulness of them might refer to some one age'. The third kind of ecclesiastical history was that of providence, which alone of the three was static, being a collection of 'notable events and examples of God's judgements, chastisements, deliverances, and blessings'.

Few Baconians who were also students of prophecy, or who became followers of the millenarian foreigners, would come to think that their fascination with the Apocalypse debarred them from working also for the advancement of learning and society. Two such were that remarkable partnership for international Protestantism, Samuel Hartlib and John Dury. Through their efforts, as Professor Hugh Trevor-Roper has shown, a new social philosophy, in part derived from the ideas of Bacon and in part supplied by Comenius and other foreign thinkers connected with him, won adherents in Britain and eventually found its way into the revolutionary parliaments. Professor Trevor-Roper observed also that one of the abiding interests that united them and distinguished them from purer Baconians was an overwhelming fascination with the Apocalypse.[5]

Three men stand out as formulators of the millennial ideas that reached England: Andreae, Alsted, and Comenius. Andreae provided one of the models for the Utopia envisaged by Hartlib and his friends. Alsted was one of the first open millenarians and one with whom Joseph Mede came substantially to agree. He was also the teacher of Comenius, who combined a utopianism like Andreae's with a millennial fervour. In each case the new enthusiasm was built upon the

[4] Bacon, *The Advancement of Learning*, ed. William Aldiss Wright, 5th ed. (Oxford, 1926), Bk. 2, III (2), pp. 99–100.

[5] H. R. Trevor-Roper, 'Three Foreigners' and 'The Fast Sermons', both in *Religion, the Reformation and Social Change* (London, 1967).

foundations of the historical apocalyptic tradition as it had developed on the continent.

In 1620 Andreae published his *Christianopolis*,[6] a Utopia which was less the result of the application of reason to the government of society than a prophetic vision of the future. His city was patterned on the description of the New Jerusalem in Revelation, and although he acknowledged that his work was an imagination of something that remained a mystery in his day, he emphasized that he had followed the clues laid in Scripture and prophecies.

His preface summarized the past, following the apocalyptic tradition. He believed there were two kinds of men in the world: conservatives and ameliorists. Of the former kind 'Antichrist gave us the clearest example when he oppressed the Church of Christ with wicked burdens'. The conservatives allowed Antichrist his way 'until, as men's minds became enraged with the indignity of the thing an impulse was given to restore light and dispel darkness'. Then came Luther to raise up the second sort of men. Despite Luther's Reformation, Andreae still saw too many men of the world and so he was 'rather inclined to think this very drama may be played again in our own day'.[7]

After this introduction Andreae began his description of the founding of Christianopolis. The city was the woman in the wilderness driven out of Jerusalem with her faithful followers.[8] Significantly, the exiled city was dedicated to education: its college was 'the innermost shrine of the city'.[9] History was an important part of the programme of studies and was listed as the first sub-department under the heading of natural science: 'History, that is, the rehearsal of the events of human tragedy, accompanies natural science. Words cannot do sufficient justice to the importance of this.'[10] The study of arithmetic had its relevance in the apprehension of the universal harmony. All forms of knowledge came together in the universal harmony to which each contributed; but heaven taught this harmony chiefly through 'prophecies

[6] Trans. and ed. Felix Emil Held, *An Ideal State of the 17th Century* (Urbana, 1914).

[7] Andreae, *Christianopolis*, ed. cit., pp. 133–4.

[8] Ibid., p. 140.   [9] Ibid., p. 173.   [10] Ibid., p. 232.

and miracles'. 'With what wonderful harmony heaven assists
the history of the earth and benefits the church in its varying
fortunes, it is hardly possible to say.'[11]

The second sub-department under natural science was
church history. 'Since the inhabitants of Christianopolis
make everything in this world second to the church, they are
concerned in its history more than any other.' The soul was
strengthened by the history of the elect in their persecutions
and victories and especially by the history of their preservation during the reign of Antichrist. The inhabitants were encouraged to keep diaries in which they might see proof of
their election. Despite Andreae's obvious belief in the
Protestant history of Antichrist, he was interested more in
individual spiritual attainment than in the Church's quarrel
with Rome. 'Meantime the inhabitants of Christianopolis
think very often not so much of the church in the larger
sense, but also of their own small one within their hearts.'[12]

Such an attitude would have tended to work against the
literal interpretation of prophecy, had it not been for the
Christianopolitans' admiration for the 'prophesying spirits'
and the training they received in a special school 'where they
might observe the harmony and truth of the prophetic
spirit'. The gift of prophecy enabled the recipient to 'adjust
all types of Scripture according to their differences', and to
'draw forth prophecies out of their most private shrines'.[13]
However all things from the spirit of prophecy to the study
of history were designed to raise the spirit of man to perfection, and although this perfection fitted into a specific pattern of history the true emphasis was upon its purely spiritual aspect. As in Tommaso Campanella's ideal city,[14] all
things conspired to remove any barriers to the spiritual life.
Christianopolis was written in a spirit at once both enthusiastic and pietistic. Andreae contributed to the influences
that would later be felt in England a utopianism supported
by the apocalyptic tradition, which was enhanced in its

---

[11] Andreae, *Christianopolis*, p. 230.
[12] Ibid., pp. 233–5.   [13] Ibid., pp. 240–4.
[14] Tommaso Campanella, *Civitas Solis* (1623). A Catholic seventeenth-century
Utopia with many similarities to Andreae's; it was especially important in the
formation of Comenius's views.

millennial character by John Henry Alsted and in its educational bias by John Amos Comenius.

Alsted was one of a number of German polyhistors and codifiers of knowledge whose intellectual heritage derived from a mixture of Ramism with the ideas of Melanchthon. These men were known as 'Mixts' or occasionally as 'Philippo-Ramists' or 'Systematics'.[15] This combination included the apocalyptic tradition in historiography. Alsted's encyclopedia (1620) contained a long section of defining and systematizing history and its study.[16] His discussion brought together the types of history discerned by Bodin, the German version of the four monarchies, and a history of Antichrist directly in agreement with non-German as well as German Protestantism. Like Bodin he listed the four types of history: universal, sacred, natural, and political.[17] As introductions to world history he recommended *Carion's Chronicle* and John Sleidan on the four monarchies.[18] Sacred history was of two sorts: either canonical, that is, contained in Scripture, or church history, which resembles political history. Church history carried on from the New Testament witness to the year 600, when it was interrupted by the history of Antichrist, in fulfilment of scriptural prophecy, until about the year 1500 when simple church history was restored and was known to him through Sleidan's *Commentaries* and the works of the martyrologists and the centuriators.[19]

The history of the Church in New Testament times fell into specific periods according to the apocalyptic tradition. There were four great periods, each subdivided into separate ages. The smaller divisions proceeded from Christ through Constantine, Gregory I, Phocas, Charlemagne, Otto I, Henry IV and Hildebrand, to Luther. 'Atque: hic incipit quarta periodus Ecclesia N.T. an. 1519: qui potest appellare tempus revelationis Antichristi, & reformationis Ecclesiae.'[20] Next he considered the history of Antichrist, who was found to have grown like one man throughout the ages. His infancy began in 597 with Gregory's announcement of his birth; his

[15] W. J. Ong, *Ramus: Method and the Decay of Dialogue*, pp. 298 et seq.
[16] John Henry Alsted, *Cursus Philosophici Encyclopaedia*, Liber XXVII (Herborn, 1620), vol. ii, Bk. XX.
[17] Ibid., col. 2812.
[18] Ibid.
[19] Ibid., cols. 2812-3.
[20] Ibid., cols. 2831-2.

adolescence endured from the time of Phocas to Charlemagne; his youth continued until Sigismund and John Huss; his 'aetas ingravescens' from 1400 to 1519; and his old age from that time forth.[21]

This interpretation of history was to form the basis of his defence of millenarianism[22] published in Frankfurt in 1627 and later quoted by George Hakewill.[23] Access to Alsted's revolutionary opinions was made easier in 1642 with the publication of an English translation[24] of this book, and Alsted too entered the lists of authorities to be popularized in pamphlet form. Alsted had a rather different interpretation of the millennium from most we have met so far. It is closest to the ideas Bale expressed in Part I of his *The Image of bothe churches*.[25] The binding of the dragon was generally believed to have occurred with Constantine and to have lasted 1,000 years, until about 1300; but Bale's first opinion in about 1540 and Alsted's in 1627 were that the binding coincided with the promised future rule of the saints and ensured their worldly felicity.

Alsted regarded the present age, dating from the early sixteenth century with the first reformation, as only a preparation for 'that great *Reformation*, which the *Epocha* or *Account* of those *thousand years* shall bring'.[26] Alsted in Calvinist Herborn, Andreae in Lutheran Germany, and Brightman in England shared a profound disappointment in the state of the reformed world. Unlike the apologists of the sixteenth-century reformation, who looked to the past to justify the present, they looked to the future to vindicate the promises the apologists had led them to expect. The

---

[21] Alsted, *Cursus Philosophici Encyclopaedia*, vol. ii, Bk. XX, cols. 2848–50, 'Historia Antichristi Qualis'.

[22] *Diatribe De Milleannis Apocalypticis, non illis Chiliastarum & Phantastarum sed BB. Danielis & Johannis* (Frankfurt, 1627).

[23] Hakewill, *An Apologie*, Bk. iv; 'a famous Professour at Herborne *Alsted* in his truely golden little work of the *thousand yeares* in the Apocalypse', quoted in *The World's proceeding Woes and Succeeding Joyes* (London, 1642) and at the end of *The Beloved City*, see below.

[24] *The Beloved City, or the Saints Reign on Earth A Thousand Years*, trans. William Burton (London, 'Printed in the Yeare of the last expectation of the Saints' 1643).

[25] See above, Chap. II, p. 43.   [26] Alsted, *Beloved City*, p. 7.

sixteenth-century reformers had managed to avoid the millenarian heresy inherent in their interpretation of the Apocalypse only by insisting that the emphasis be placed on its application to the past; but they had not built a sufficient defence
against its reintroduction, and by the seventeenth century,
when new and vocal minorities sought a justification for a
future reformation, millenarianism could claim for itself a
respectable background in the histories written in the sixteenth century, and needed only the boldness to draw conclusions already implicit in them.

Alsted's Latin title, but not the translated version, made it
clear that by millenarianism he did not mean to support the
ideas of the chiliasts, that the millennium would be an age of
perfection and eternal life and pleasure in which none of the
reprobate would remain, having been slaughtered or otherwise removed from the earth. He referred, he said, to the millenarianism of Daniel and John; by which he meant merely a
period of universal peace and harmony during, which the
reprobate would still inhabit the world with the elect. This
thousand years beginning in 1694 would not end before
2694, and even then the world would not be at an end
because after the period of universal peace followed the war
of Gog and Magog.[27] He arrived at the date of 1694 through
two computations, one based on the numbers in Daniel[28] and
the other on the seals, trumpets, and vials of Revelation.[29]
During this thousand years the remaining nations of the
world would be converted, and with them the Jews. Alsted
cited Kepler's opinion that the recent strife and competition
between Catholics and Protestants might already be said to
have begun the conversion of the American Indians. This too
would argue that the millennium was at hand.[30]

This interpretation greatly accentuated a tendency already
marked among Jesuits like Ribera and Protestants like
Broughton and Brightman to delay the completion of history
and to place in the future more and more of the prophecies
previously applied to the past. The binding of Satan, the war
of Gog and Magog, the conversion of the Jews, the universal
preaching were all expected rather than past. Nevertheless,

[27] Alsted, *Beloved City*, pp. 10-13.   [28] Ibid., pp. 49-50.
[29] Ibid., p. 13.   [30] Ibid., p. 8.

despite Alsted's removal of these from the tradition as it applied to the past, he maintained as he had in his encyclopedia the Protestant history of Antichrist and the apocalyptic sequence of seals, trumpets, and vials. The seven churches covered apostolic times, the seven seals the Church until 606, the trumpets from 606 to 1517, and three of the vials before 1625 and four to follow until 1694.

Alsted was interested in the conversion of the Jews. Broughton's commentary on Daniel was cited as an authority at one point in his encyclopedia.[31] One of the characteristics of the millennium was to be the conversion of the Jews, and to aid in this task God had promised the overthrow of Antichrist before the thousand years began. 'Therefore if the Jews should but see the wonderfull overthrow of *Antichrist*, without doubt it would afford them a great occasion of their Conversion. Upon this ground, the overthrow of Antichrist shall immediately go before, not the *last judgment*, but the *happinesse of the Church* which shall happen in this life.'[32] The influence of Broughton may also account for Alsted's defence of Antiochus Epiphanes as the Antichrist mentioned in Daniel.[33] Alsted maintained, however, that Antiochus and the story of Daniel were a type prophetic of present Europe. This drama would proceed through three stages: Protasis, Epitasis, and Catastrophe. The Protasis was past and had consisted of 'rumours from the North and East' fulfilled by the fall of Constantinople in 1453 and an invasion of Italy in 1481. The Epitasis was in progress: 'At this day *Antichrist* in the performance thereof, goes under full Sail, wanting no favour of winds.' The Catastrophe of Antichrist's fall lay in the future. The reader was referred for more information to '*Conradus Graserus* his *History of Antichrist*'.[34]

The most important channel for the opinion of Andreae

---

[31] Alsted, *Cursus Philosophici Encyclopaedia*, Bk. xx, vol. ii, col. 2855.

[32] Alsted, *Beloved City*, p. 37.

[33] Ibid., p. 47. 'How everyone of these [prophecies] severally are fulfilled in *Antiochus*, as a type of *Antichrist* it is nothing pertinent to our purpose to enquire. Neither indeed is the matter so obscure, or unknown.'

[34] Ibid., pp. 47–9. (Conradus) Francus Graserus, *Historia Antichristi* (Leyden, 1608), based his defence of the application of Daniel's prophecies to the Roman Church upon the doctrine of the four monarchies; and seems to have made the standard defence to which not only Alsted but many others referred their readers. Mede adopted a similar position.

and Alsted into England was the friendship of Samuel Hartlib with John Amos Comenius. From 1611 to 1613 Comenius had been at Herborn, where he came under the influence of Alsted. Comenius was ordained in Moravia in 1616, but any hope he had for a settled life vanished with the opening years of the Thirty Years War. After the defeat of White Mountain he was forced to flee to Brandeis and in the process he lost his wife and one of his children. In 1624 the edict against Calvinists forced him to move again. In the course of his suffering both personal and public he became involved with millenarian visionaries who sought explanation of and consolation for the defeats they had suffered. Like Andreae he combined an exalted belief in the power of knowledge and education with a form of millennialism. One cannot but agree with J. B. Neveux that 'Au fond, sa conviction que l'école peut résoudre tous les problèmes humains est seulement une forme du chiliasme, et ses traités pédagogiques sont des utopies. . . .'[35]

By 1632 Hartlib was in communication with Comenius,[36] and during the 1630s in particular campaigned for the promotion of his ideas about educational reform and saw that several of his works were published in England. Comenius, frustrated by the state of Europe, had high hopes that England might implement his programmes. In Dury and Hartlib he found allies intent upon the unification of Protestant Europe and the Protestant faith against the forces of Antichrist. All three hoped that education might remove the barriers to this universal Protestant harmony. Comenius's pansophism and utopianism had had immediate effect, but his dedication to millenarianism and the propagation of the apocalyptic tradition was not expressed in England until after she had produced her own greatest authority, Joseph Mede. When in 1650 Comenius communicated to Hartlib a commentary on the Apocalypse which most impressed him he wrote, 'I praie you communicate this to your men, if yet you have anie Joseph Medes amongest you.'[37]

Joseph Mede (1586-1638) was a man of wide interests and

[35] J. B. Neveux, *Vie spirituelle et vie sociale entre Rhin et Baltique au XVIIe siècle*, Publications de la Faculté des Lettres et Sciences Humaines de Paris-Nanterre (Paris, 1967), pp. 69-76, and Frances Yates, *The Rosicrucian Enlightenment*, pp. 197-210.

[36] Turnbull, *Hartlib, Dury and Comenius*, p. 342.

[37] For particulars see below, p. 243.

a student of philology, history, mathematics, and physics. He was an enthusiastic botanist and anatomist and was also interested in astrology. This last subject was in the seventeenth century becoming established as a legitimate science, and Mede, unlike Napier some forty years earlier, did not need to conceal his interest. Astrology was not, however, the most compelling of his interests; it was only part of the intellectual milieu in which up-to-date scholars in the universities moved. As a young man his studies in philosophy had pushed him towards pyrrhonism; but, escaping the jaws of atheism, he fled towards faith.[38] This experience left a mark upon his later thought like that it left on many others travelling the same road. Mede was convinced of the fundamental importance to faith of revelation. With a background like this it is not surprising that he became attracted to the study of those parts of Scripture laden with prophecy, nor is it surprising that he was drawn into that increasingly sophisticated study where his knowledge of philology, history, and mathematics would be of use.

Although interested in keeping abreast of current events, Joseph Mede was very much a university man. He was interested neither in the active promotion of political or ecclesiastical change nor in reaching the great mass of the English people with his ideas. He wrote in the first place for a circle of learned men, and although he complained that his correspondence kept him from completing works for publication,[39] he responded at length to even the most hopeless of correspondents such as Thomas Hayne. The task of publishing his ideas to an ever-widening circle of readers was left to his friends and admirers, of which he had many both in England and abroad in Protestant Europe. His correspondents included John Dury, Samuel Hartlib, and Sir William Boswell, ambassador in the Hague, each of whom helped to introduce his *Clavis Apocalyptica* abroad and conveyed back to Mede the admiration and ideas of some of his foreign readers. At home he corresponded with William Twisse and Dr. Meddus, with

[38] John Worthington, *The Life of the Reverend and most learned Joseph Mede, BD.* prefixed to his ed. of Mede's *Works* (1664).

[39] Mede to Thomas Hayne, 17 June 1629, Epistle VI, *The Works of Joseph Mede, BD.*, ed. Worthington (London, 1664), vol. ii, p. 902.

Samuel Ward, Master of Sidney Sussex College in his university of Cambridge, and with Archbishop Ussher.

A few words must be said about James Ussher of Armagh. The present study does not extend to the apocalyptic tradition in Ireland; but aspects of the tradition did reach there, perhaps first through the establishment of Trinity College as a Ramist academy.[40] James Ussher was very much a product of the British adaptation of Ramism in his use of Scripture and his interest in chronology. His periodic visits to England must have acquainted him with the English Hebraist involvement in the apocalyptic tradition. In one of his letters to Samuel Ward, he asked what Ward had done for Broughton's works in Cambridge.[41] However, Ussher's great achievements in chronology were more technical than interpretative,[42] and since the emphasis in this study has been upon the contribution of the apocalyptic tradition to the interpretative rather than the technical study of history and chronology, it was thought best to include a discussion of James Ussher only as he appears in relation to the tradition in Britain. The sense of this limitation can be illustrated by a comparison of the views Mede expressed to Ussher and those Ussher expressed to Mede. In this correspondence Mede always pressed for a certain validity to be granted to prophecies such as that of Elias.[43] He did this with apologies to Ussher, who expressed himself as far more sceptical of such conceits and speculations than Mede. However Ussher applauded Mede's efforts in the interpretation of scriptural prophecy such as the Apocalypse, and in a way Ussher's chronology and Mede's commentary both represent a final form of the tradition which persisted for centuries.

[40] Kearney, *Scholars and Gentlemen: Universities and Society in pre-industrial Britain 1500–1700.*

[41] *The Life of . . . James Ussher, With a collection of three hundred letters* Written between said Lord Primate . . . and most of the Eminentest Persons . . . both in England and beyond the Seas, collected by Richard Parr (London, 1686); Letter XCV, undated, p. 340: 'Remember me to Mr *Chancy*, and learn of him what he hath done for Mr. *Broughton's* Books.'

[42] The same can be said of Newton, who is also precluded from this study. See Frank E. Manuel, *Isaac Newton, Historian* (Cambridge, 1963).

[43] Mede to Meddus, undated, Epistle XXII, *Works*, ed. Worthington (1664), vol. ii, p. 950, spoke of Elias' prophecy as 'a Tradition anciently received amongst them [the Jews] whilst they were yet the Church of God'.

In 1627, the year of Alsted's *De Milleannis* and of Hake-will's *Apologie*, Joseph Mede had his *Clavis Apocalyptica* published for private circulation and sent seven copies to Ussher in Ireland. These were lost and consequently Mede sent 'three or four more'.[44] With the second lot he sent a speculation that had just occurred to him concerning the seventh millenary, 'Wherein,' he explained to Ussher, 'I had no intent or thought, nor yet have to avow the old conceit of the *Chiliasts*, That the World should as it were labour 6000 years, and in the Seventh thousand should be that glorious *Sabbath* of the Reign of Christ, (I inclined to think it much nearer).'[45] Mede may have known Ussher's opinion of the prophecy of the world-week and therefore have been anxious that Ussher should not mistake him for a chiliast. In 1615 Ussher had written[46] a response to the opinion of Mr. John Harrison, based on a rendering of the numbers involved in the world-week, that the world would end in 1630. Ussher had rejected this prophecy, calling it 'but a meer Imagination destitute of all proof from ye Word of God: and therfore generally rejected by such as have learned not to be Wise above that which is written'. Such speculation, he added, was worthy only of Jewish cabalists. In the letter accompanying his books, Mede spoke of a speculation he desired to present to Ussher for his opinion, and hoped that he would allow his curiosity, since 'the means thereof is beholding to your Grace'.[47] He had observed a way to save the idea of the 6,000 years by using Ussher's improvements in biblical chronology. The idea was simply that the final 2,000 were limited (as Elias had said) and shortened to 1,260 day-years, which, beginning with the deposition of the Roman emperor in 476, gave 1736 as the date of the start of the seventh

[44] Mede to Ussher, 22 May 1628, Epistle IV, *Works*, ed. Worthington (1664), p. 896.

[45] Ibid.

[46] 'Dr. Usher's Refutation of Mr. John Harrison his Opinion that ye World should end AD 1630 written A.1615 transcribed from his own copie', Bodleian Library, MS. Add. C301, fols. 95ʳ-97ᵛ, a reference to the John Harrison author of *The Messiah already come Written in Barbary 1610*; STC lists a second edition (Amsterdam, 1619), a work designed to convert the Jews and containing the author's conviction that the end was near, but no date is given in the above book.

[47] Mede to Ussher, 22 May 1628, Epistle IV, *Works*, ed. Worthington (1664), vol. ii, p. 896.

millenary. The curious thing was that, when Mede added the years from the Creation, given by Scaliger as 3949 B.C., to the four years discovered in the reign of Nebuchadnezzar in excess of the Jewish reckoning and the 311 Ussher had discovered missing from accounts of the Samaritans, he got the figure of 4,264, to which the addition of 1,736 gave just the 6,000 years. Although Mede said to Ussher that he thought such curiosities might be only 'a special disposition of Providence to frustrate our Curiosity', he was steadfastly curious and hoped to avoid any pitfalls. He hoped that Ussher would take more of his speculations into consideration.[48] In further correspondence, Ussher continued to praise the work on the Apocalypse but neither commented upon nor encouraged other speculations—perhaps a gentle hint that Mede's talents were best spent upon canonical Scripture.

The private circulation of Mede's *Clavis Apocalyptica*, and another issue in 1632, provoked much of his correspondence. Letters came from friends such as Dr. Meddus and Dr. Twisse asking further questions, and from some like Thomas Hayne eager to enter into controversy over several points. In many ways Mede's interpretation was not new, the bulk of it deriving from the earlier writers. He was especially noted for his discovery of patterns of synchronisms. By synchronism he meant the correspondence in time of one set of images with another. This was not an entirely new idea, but he went further than anyone else in its systematic application. Some of his synchronisms have a familiar ring. His criteria for grouping images together were two: the agreement of the quantity of time, for example the time and times and dividing of time agreed with the 1,260 days of the woman in the wilderness and with the three and a half months the witnesses lay dead; and the agreement in the description of the images, for example the seven-headed ten-horned beast agreed with the seven-hilled spiritual Babylon or Rome. Sometimes the agreement was by contrast, for example the 144,000 virgins united in time with the whore seated on the beast. Although inspired by Selden's rather different use of the word, Mede meant by his use to emphasize that in his

[48] Mede to Ussher, 22 May 1628, Epistle IV, *Works*, ed. Worthington (1664), vol. ii, p. 897.

ordering of the text he intended not so much to follow the given order as to construct an order of sets of images gathered together in accordance with historical coincidence.

Mede's originality lay in his delineation of synchronisms, and his view of the millennium, though like Alsted's, was new in Britain. Indeed, most of his correspondence dwelt exclusively upon these two aspects of his interpretation. Hayne defended a more Broughtonian separation of Daniel and the Apocalypse against Mede's synchronisms, while Twisse was ever curious for more proof or more details concerning Mede's position on the millennium. Both these aspects were couched in Mede's over-all interpretation, which on the whole may be said to resemble Napier's in method and Brightman's in spirit.

Like Napier, whose commentary he knew, Mede set out to present a systematic analysis of the text. Although he was basically a philologist, he had made a serious study of mathematics, and Henry Briggs, the receiver of some of Napier's papers,[49] was among his friends. Perhaps partly because of this, Mede's absorption of systematic analysis in the Ramist fashion was more successful than Brightman's had been. His material had more in common with Brightman's, and he had not the same drive that Napier had to reduce all to number; but nevertheless he strove for a systematic consistency and simplicity that Brightman, who had not been above naming several dates for the same event, had lacked woefully.

Like Napier, Mede began with the proposition that the Apocalypse contained a simple history which might be discovered through the application of demonstrable propositions.

The *Apocalypse* considered onely according to the naked Letter, as if it were a History and no Prophecy, hath marks and signes sufficient by the Holy Spirit, whereby the *Order, Synchronism* and *Sequele* of all the Visions therein contained, may be found out, and demonstrated, without supposall of any Interpretation whatsoever.[50]

Napier had believed that the text contained times and periods; Mede believed that it contained an order and a pattern of synchronisms as the *argumenta intrinsica*, and that therefore the patterns extracted from the text were the true founda-

[49] See above, p. 133.
[50] Mede, 'Remaines on some Passages in the Apocalyps', ed. Worthington (1664), Bk. iii, Pt. iv, vol. ii, p. 721.

tion for interpretation.[51] The first duty of the interpreter was to discover the order, and then his interpretation and examples had to fit that order. If examples were found first and then an interpretation made, other examples could in all probability be found to support a contrary interpretation.[52] A century had been time enough to prove this, and Bale's first method had certainly been to collect and order examples in order to support an interpretation. Aided by the intervening developments, Mede was able to reverse this process. This in itself would be enough to sound the death-knell of any contribution the tradition might make to historical imagination, and by the time Mede had codified and systematized the materials of the tradition it was already moribund.

Mede's interpretation lent itself to illustration; and several years after he had had it printed, Mr. Haydock, having first written to Mede[53] to suggest a design for the book sealed with seven seals different from the one Mede had described, was asked by Mede to design such an illustration. Mr. Haydock complied, and provided an illustration. Later Richard More redrew and translated it for his English edition. This version is reproduced facing p. 219. Mede believed that the Book of Daniel and the Book of Revelation were in several parts synchronistic, and that John, like Daniel, had prophesied both the affairs of the Empire and the affairs of the Church.

The large circle contains in the top half the prophecies in the Revelation that apply to the Empire, and in the bottom half those that apply to the Church. The seals, trumpets, and vials are clearly marked and shown to overlap in some instances. The first six seals were grouped together as usual to cover the time to Constantine. The opening of the seventh seal and the sounding of the first trumpet coincide. As shown, the first four trumpets are of lesser importance than the last three, which correspond to the three great woes pronounced by Gregory the Great at the sounding of the fifth trumpet. From his commentary and other remains of his interpretation it is possible to assign the dates Mede gave

[51] Mede, 'Remaines on some Passages in the Apocalyps', ed. Worthington (1664), Bk. iii, pt, iv, vol. ii, p. 721.
[52] Ibid.
[53] Worthington's discussion and the correspondence between Mede and Haydock begins, *Works*, vol. ii, p. 967.

to the opening of each seal and trumpet.[54] Constantine arrived on the scene during the sixth seal,[55] but the major change in the fortune of the Empire came with the death of Theodosius the Great (395) and the permanent division of the Empire into east and west. At that time the first trumpet sounded, and this period lasted until about 410, when the second trumpet sounded with the sacking of Rome by Alaric. The third trumpet sounded in the year 476 with the deposition of the Emperor Romulus Augustulus by Odoacer. The fourth trumpet coincided with Belisarius and the Ostrogothic wars; Mede gives the date as 542. Thus the first four trumpets tell the story of the decline of the Roman Empire. The last three tell of the wars of persecution waged by the arch-enemies of Christendom, the Saracens from 630, the Turks succeeding them (1080), and the Antichrist of Rome. With the defeat of Antichrist the seventh trumpet ushers in the millennium, represented by the final and much larger circle which unites the upper and lower halves of the diagram, illustrating the final outcome as a unification of Church and Empire. In a way, though, Mede believed the kingdom had been from the beginning with the victory of Christ,[56] and so the scheme shows the connection of that final circle with the beginning of the epoch of the Apocalypse.

The lower half of the diagram, described as the latter prophecy, begins in the text with the opening of the little book and deals with the history of the Church and religion. There are only four real divisions in this section and each corresponds to the time given in the upper half of the diagram. Thus the four cover first the time of Constantine and then in two parts to the sounding of the seventh trumpet,

[54] 'A Summary view of the Apocalyps', *Works*, ed. Worthington (1664), vol. ii, pp. 1121-9.
[55] Mede, *The Key of the Revelation*, trans. Richard More with a Preface by Twisse (London, 1643), p. 59. 'Now that chance is an admirable shaking of the heaven and the earth; whereby that wonderfull change and subversion of the State of Rome heathen by Constantine the Great and his Sucessors, the Standard-bearers of the Lamb, is figured.'
[56] Mede to Hayne, 21 Oct. 1629, Epistle X, *Works*, ed. Worthington (1664), vol. ii, p. 925. 'I know not what it is you contend for about the *Two States* of Christ's Kingdom. If you grant the Kingdom of Christ at his *Second* coming shall be of a different state from that of his *First*, you grant as much as serves my turn; and the Kingdom is neither more or less eternal, because some State thereof is not eternal.'

one from Constantine to the seventh trumpet illustrating the rise of Antichrist and the condition of the saints under his persecution, and another beginning with the destruction of the beast by the seven vials, starting under the sixth trumpet and coinciding with the Turks. The seventh vial extends into the fourth period, the millennium, and thereby shows Mede's conviction that Antichrist might linger in the world after his effective defeat,[57] an idea Broughton had expressed.

In some ways Mede designed his interpretation to maintain the old tradition that the kingdom began with Christ and that the time of the seven seals had not passed into any new revelation. The third woe, the seventh seal, trumpet, and vial all continued into the era of the millennium. He was anxious not to appear as an ancient chiliast or a Joachist. His positioning of the fight between the dragon and Michael was intentionally different from that of his predecessors. Instead of placing it in the future as an outcome of the Reformation, as many had done, he placed it in the time of the first six seals. He had a reason for this which, he explained, did not imply that he believed all his Protestant predecessors to have been chiliasts. '*Napier* would have *Michael* to be the *Holy Ghost*, which if it be admitted, then those *chief Princes* whereof *Michael* is said to be one, will be the Persons of the Trinity. May this stand? or will it help the conceit of the antient Chiliasts for *Regnum Spiritus*? But *Napier* thought not of any such matter.'[58] Mede was more sensitive than any of his predecessors to the complications involved in the interpretation of the millennium, and this sensitivity was sharpened for him and the English in general by the revival of just such a chiliasm among foreign scholars as is represented by the opinions of Alsted and his colleague at Herborn, Johann Piscator.[59]

Dr. Twisse, whose joy it was to submit the strangest of theories to Mede for criticism, was once asked to inquire of Mede how he differed from Alsted and Piscator. Mede

[57] 'A Summary view of the Apocalyps', *Works*, ed. Worthington (1664), vol. ii, pp. 1121-9.
[58] 'Remaines on some passages in the Apocalyps', ibid., vol. ii, p. 725.
[59] Johann Piscator, *In Apocalypsin Johannis Commentarius* (1621).

answered, in a letter which Twisse later quoted in his preface
to one of Mede's works:[60]

I differ therefore from *Piscator*, and agree with *Alstedius*, that the
Saints of the First Resurrection should reign on Earth during the *Millennium*, and not in Heaven.

I differ from both, in that I make this State of the Church to belong
to *Secundus Adventus Christi* or *Dies Judicii Magni*. . . . Whereas they
make it to precede the Day of Judgement and the Second coming.
Though this Notion may seem to make but little alteration of the thing
believed, yet it is of no small moment to facilitate the understanding
of Scripture. . . . But the truth is, it is neither before nor after but *ipsa
Dies Judicii, ipsum tempus Secundae apparitionis Christi.*'[61]

Twisse reported in 1644 that when the idea of the millennial
reign of the saints on earth was first proposed to him, his spirit
'was stirred up' to propose reasons against the idea; 'the improbability of it seemed very repugnant to natural reason';[62] but
he was convinced by Mede and by an anonymous book out
of Germany[63] which Mede owned and which he had copied.

Twisse's first letter to Mede on the subject of the millennium
was dated 2 November 1629.[64] In it he said that Dr. Meddus
and Mr. Briggs had lent him copies of Mede's work and that
he much admired it. However, a friend of his, 'a great student
of Mr. Brightman', had defended the usual interpretation of
the binding of Satan as the thousand years between Constantine and 1300. He had also expressed the theory that the
conversion of the Jews would be provoked by God's gift to
the Christians of some great prosperity: when the Jews saw
this they would believe the Christians to be the new elect.

In explaining his reservation of the reign of the saints for
the later period Mede expressed what must have been one of
his first dissatisfactions with the earlier tradition. Ever since
Harpsfield, English Catholics had made much of the arbitrary
way in which the Protestants had selected some martyrs and
rejected others. If the thousand years came between 300 and
1300 then many of the martyrs had supported the Roman
faith, 'And if', said Mede, 'with Mr. Brightman and others we

[60] *The Apostasy of the Latter Times, or The Gentiles Theology of Daemons*,
2nd edition (London, 1644).

[61] Ibid., pp. 1-9; Mede to Meddus, 18 Aug. 16--, Epistle XX, *Works*, ed.
Worthington (1664), vol. ii, pp. 944-5.

[62] Twisse, Preface to Mede, *The Apostasy of the Latter times*.

[63] Entitled *De die novissimo*.

[64] Epistle XIII, *Works*, ed. Worthington (1664), vol. ii, pp. 927-8.

begin the Thousand years from *Constantine*, there is no place of Scripture for a Papist to urge for *Saint-worship* like unto this.' Mede hoped to do away with arbitrariness of this sort, and had solved the problem by postponing the millennial reign. He rather thought the conversion of the Jews would be like Paul's conversion, the result of some special revelation or vision.[65]

This did not end Twisse's inquiries about the millennium, the *Regnum Christi*, New Jerusalem, or the battle between Gog and Magog, all of which Mede like Alsted had reserved for the future. In his replies, sometimes sent through Meddus, Mede defended his belief that the first resurrection coming before the day of judgement would be literally fufilled, that the day of judgement was in fact the period of the millennium (if one day equalled a thousand years, then this might apply to the judgement day). At the end of this long day would be the war of Gog and Magog and the second resurrection. During this period New Jerusalem would rule the Christian world. On the subject of New Jerusalem he came nearer to stating what Brightman had implied.

Secondly, That, for the better understanding of this *Mysterie*, we must distinguish between the State of *New Jerusalem* and State of the *Nations which shall walk in the light therof*; they shall not be both one, but much differing. Therefore what is spoken particularly of the *New Jerusalem*, must not be applied to the whole Church, which then shall be: *New Jerusalem* is not the whole Church, but the Metropolis thereof and of the New world.[66]

The New Jerusalem must be understood as one city or one nation and not generally as the reformed community or allegorically as the scattered elect. Twisse wondered whether therefore the plantations in the New World might not be the promised New Jerusalem. The discovery of the New World so late in the history of the old one seemed to imply some sort of translation.[67] Mede disagreed, saying that the New

[65] Mede to Twisse, 11 Nov. 1629, Epistle XIV, *Works*, ed. Worthington (1664), vol. ii, pp. 928-9.
[66] Mede to Meddus, 18 Aug. ?, Epistle XX, ibid., p. 944.
[67] Twisse to Mede, 2 Mar. 1634/5, Epistle XLII, ibid., p. 979. Both this idea and one that the American Indians were a lost tribe of Israel, expressed as early as 1611 by Broughton, seem to have caught on with many others. An example of interest in this can be seen in *Jewes in America, or Probabilities that the Americans are of that Race*, by Thomas Thorowgood, with a letter from John Dury prefixed (London, 1650).

World was far too inhospitable and its natives too difficult to convert.[68] Twisse occasionally asked for clarification of some point dealing with the application of prophecy to past history,[69] but most of his questions concerned the future. In this he reflected the preoccupations not only of some of his own country but also of many throughout Protestant Europe.

One of Mede's correspondents, and one with whom he became increasingly impatient, was determined to debate the interpretation of Daniel's four monarchies with him. This was Thomas Hayne,[70] and his position was that expressed by Broughton. Hayne argued that Daniel did not prophesy the fall of Rome, that the fourth beast was Antiochus Epiphanes, and that only John had received a vision of Rome's downfall and the rise of Antichrist.[71] Mede responded in defence of the earlier Protestant version, saying that what Daniel had learned generally John had later received in detail, and that Hayne's position forfeited the identification of the man of sin with the pope. Hayne repeated his argument in worse temper, and Mede, becoming exasperated, informed him that he had read Broughton and those like him and found Mr. Hayne too concerned with his own argument to listen to anyone else's. Hayne wrote twice more before Mede refused to answer. Hayne was certainly interested in the reputation of Broughton, and it is interesting that at about the time Ussher wrote to Samuel Ward asking what he had done for Broughton's works in Cambridge, Thomas Hayne wrote to Bodley's Librarian proposing the collection and binding together of Broughton's works in the library at Oxford.[72]

[68] Mede to Twisse, 23 Mar. 1634/5, Epistle XLIII, *Works*, ed. Worthington (1664), vol. ii, p. 980.

[69] Twisse to Mede, 5 Mar. 1629/30, Epistle XXIII, ibid., p. 951. He had thought the little horn among ten was Antichrist (Mede's view) but had read Conrad Grasserus who equated it with the Turk. Mede's next letter apparently converted Twisse to Mede's view.

[70] An usher at Christ's Hospital, Hayne had been educated at Lincoln College, Oxford. Anthony à Wood described him as 'a noted critic, an excellent linguist, and a solid divine, beloved of learned men, and particularly respected by Selden', *Athenae Oxoniensis*, ed. Bliss (Oxford, 1813-20), vol. iii, p. 173.

[71] This exchange begins with Hayne's letter to Mede of 5 June 1629 and continues to Mede's last letter in October. *Works*, ed. Worthington (1664), vol. ii, pp. 897-926.

[72] 'Letters to Bodley's Librarians', Bodl. MS. Add. A64, fol. 133, Thomas Hayne to Mr. Rouse, July 1638; Hayne also spoke highly of Broughton in his *The General View of the Holy Scripture* (London, 1640), A4r.

Mede dealt with Broughton's position in a manner that owed much to Brightman. He too expounded a parallel development of the Jewish church and the Christian, which with the conversion of the Jews would unite them in New Jerusalem. In the same way as he had allowed the seventh seal to encompass the trumpets and vials, he allowed the seventieth of Daniel's weeks to encompass the history of the world until the fall of the last of the Gentile monarchies.

"The Jewes shall be carried captive over all Nations, and Jerusalem trod-den down of the Gentiles, untill the times of the Gentiles should be ful-filled": That is, (as was said before) untill the Monarchies of the Gentiles should be finished. For these Times of the Gentiles are that last period of the fourth Kingdome prophecied* (*Dan 7) of a *Time, Times, and half a Time*: at the end wherof the Angel swears unto *Daniel, ca 12.7 That God should accomplish to scatter the power of the Holy People.* This is that Fulneesse of the Gentiles which being come S. Paul tels us, *"The Deliverers shall come out of Sion, and all Israel shall be saved."* And the Angel in the Apoc. 10.6 renews the same oath, to S. *John*, which he sware before to *Daniel, "That when these Times* (N.B.) *should end and be no longer, the mystery of God should be finished, as he had declared to his servants the Prophets."* Amen. [73]

The prophecy of Daniel contained two sacred calendars or almanacs; the lesser was the seventy weeks and applied espe-cially to the Jews, the greater was the prophecy of the four monarchies.

For the true account therefore of *Times* in Scripture wee must have recourse to that SACRED KALENDAR and GREAT ALMANACK of PROPHESIE, *the Four Kingdomes of Daniel* which are *A Propheticall Chronology of Times measured by the succession of Foure principall Kingdoms, from the beginning of the Captivity of* Israel *untill the Mys-terie of God should be finished*; A course of time during which the Church and Nation of the Jewes, together with those whom by occa-sion of their unbeleefe in Christ God should surrogate in their roomes, was to remaine under the bondage of the Gentiles, and oppression of Gentilisme; But these times once finished, all the *Kingdomes* of this World should become the *Kingdoms of our Lord and his Christ.* [74]

Some of the most important exchanges of letters were those between Mede and Hartlib, who often passed the letters on to Dury. Dury when contacted replied directly to Mede. The correspondence begins early in 1635 (6 March), when

[73] *Daniel's Weekes. An Interpretation of part of the Prophecy of Daniel.* (Lon-don, 1643), p. 49.

[74] *The Apostasy of the latter Times*, part I, *Works*, ed. Worthington (1664), vol. ii, p. 807.

Hartlib, returning to England, reported to Mede that his *Clavis Apocalyptica* was much sought after in Leyden, but in short supply.[75] On 11 March Dury wrote to Mede soliciting his help and advice on how best to secure ecclesiastical peace; and on 13 March added news of praise given Mede by men abroad, but confessed that he had not had the opportunity to read the work himself. On 18 March Mede sent his book to Hartlib to be forwarded to Dury, and on 9 April Dury sent his thanks.

Both Dury and Hartlib continued to try to draw Mede into their programme for ecclesiastical peace; but Mede declined, explaining

I live in the University, where we move onely *ad motum Primi mobilis*; and that discretion is expected at our hands, who are of the inferior Orbs, as not to move without our Superiors. If any one transgress this rule, and offer to meddle in ought that concerns the Publick, before the State and those in place declare themselves, he is taken notice of for Factious and a Busie-body; and if he be once thus branded, all the water of the *Thames* will not wash him clean. . . .[76]

Throughout 1635–6 he continued to correspond with them about the definition of fundamentals, but expressed doubt about the success of their plans.

In October of 1637 the correspondence took a new turn. Hartlib had been in touch with Twisse about the millennium and his curiosity had been roused: '*I pray let me reap the fruit of his confidence in the enjoying of those Papers which have passed between you on the fore-mentioned Subject.*'[77] That winter and spring Hartlib wrote with questions as Twisse had done, and his interests, like Twisse's, were centred on the millennium. One question arose after Hartlib had read a little treatise[78] on the number of the beast and wondered whether Mede had seen it.[79] He had, and it had had an interesting effect upon him.

[75] Epistle XLIV, *Works*, ed. Worthington (1664), vol. ii, p. 984.
[76] Mede to Hartlib, 9 Apr. (1635?), Epistle LXXX, ibid., p. 1062.
[77] Hartlib to Mede, 19 Oct. 1637, Epistle LXXXIX, ibid., p. 1073.
[78] Worthington describes it as by Mr. Potter, a reference to Francis Potter, *An interpretation of the number 666* (Oxford, 1642). Mede says he first saw it as *Bestia Apocalyptica* in 1626, that it was re-issued in about 1631 with a new title-page and date. The 1642 edition is the best-known and the only one listed in S.T.C.
[79] Hartlib to Mede, 24 Jan. 1637/8, Epistle XCI, *Works*, ed. Worthington (1664), vol. ii, pp. 1075–6.

I read the Book at first with as much prejudice against such *Numerical Speculations* as might be, and almost against my will, having met with so much vanity formerly in that kind; but by the time I had done, it left me as much possessed with admiration as I came to it with prejudice. He meddles with no more of the *Apocalyps* than what concerns this Number. 'Tis a Mathematical ground he builds upon, and will not be so well understood by one that hath been little versed in Arithmetick, in that part which is called *Extraction of Roots*. [80]

The arithmetical method was about to enjoy a revival. The English Hebraists and with them James Ussher had disdained such number games, and Napier's commentary had been last published in 1611. Soon it would be resurrected by John Booker the astrologer to form the basis of two apocalyptic almanacs in the early 1640s, and the whole work would be reissued in Edinburgh in 1645. It was so clearly the sort of work one would expect to find in Germany rather than England that Mede could not restrain himself from remarking to Hartlib, 'If it were in Latine, it would make some of your German Speculatives half wild.'[81] And so no doubt it would have. One small indication of influences of this sort passing between Britain and Germany can be seen in the publication in 1615 and 1627 of a German translation of Napier's commentary by Wolfgang Meyer in Frankfurt-on-Main, and in a work quoting large sections of Napier by Johannes Woltherus Rostok, called *The Gulden Arch*, published in 1623.[82]

Hartlib also sought Mede's opinion of a series of prophecies delivered by the prophet Paul Grebner which had apparently foretold the Bohemian wars. Mede said this too had occurred to him, and he had gone back to the prophecies to reconsider them after the wars had broken out, but could make nothing of them and concluded he had only imagined a connection.[83] Hartlib wrote back to say that he had not seriously considered them before Mede's judgement and was

[80] Mede to Hartlib, 29 Jan. 1637/8, Epistle XCII, *Works*, ed. Worthington (1664), vol. ii, pp. 1076-7.

[81] Ibid., p. 1077.

[82] Listed in a catalogue of Napier's works by Wm. Rae Macdonald in his translation of Napier, *The Construction of the wonderful canon of logarithms* (Edinburgh, 1889).

[83] Mede to Hartlib, 3 Apr. 1637/8, Epistle XCIII, *Works*, ed. Worthington (1664), vol. ii, pp. 1077-8.

happy to have his feelings seconded by such an authority.[84] It is a pity that Mede was not around longer to dispose of similar prophecies. He died the following autumn, and by 1641 a decade and a half fraught with popular prophets and prophecies had begun.

No authority could rival Mede, and with his death his friends took over publishing his books prefaced with their own prefaces, and Mede was transformed from scholar into prophet. He was not alone: Brightman had gone that way before him; and Napier, Alsted, and even Ussher[85] were to follow. This is not to say that a hefty body of popular literature had not been growing since about 1620. It had; but until the laws governing the censorship of books had been relaxed, following the abolition of Star Chamber in 1641, the more prophetic parts of it did not appear.[86] Before then several less important authors had written their own attacks on Bellarmine or preparations for the soul now that the end was drawing near. A few examples will serve to illustrate this. Thomas Draxe's *An Alarum to the Last Judgement* written in 1615 proved that Antichrist had already come, and since 1517 had been in retreat, a fact of which England had had special assurance in the defeat of the Spanish Armada. He mentioned Elias' prophecy and the world-week, and expected the end to come before the year 6000 of the world, or 6039 at the latest; but he thought it might well come sooner, as Elias had said, though this was 'no certaine rule, or axiome, but onely a conjecture'. Nevertheless it was certain that the sixth trumpet had already sounded and only the seventh remained. Draxe had read both Napier and Brightman, but saw more sense in Brightman's interpretation. 'Thirdly, Maister *Napier*, a learned Scot, counting the beginning of these 1335 daies (and interpreting them for years) anno Christi 360, about the year 1695; But Maister *Brightman* maketh this date the beginning of the generall conversion and

---

[84] Hartlib to Mede, 6 Apr. 1638, Epistle XCIV, *Works*, ed. Worthington (1664), vol. ii, pp. 1078–9.

[85] Ussher did not join the ranks until the 1680s when a series of prophecies were attributed to him; for example, *Strange and remarkable prophecies and predictions of . . . James Ussher* (London, 1678), one of the first.

[86] See W. W. Greg, *Some Aspects and Problems of London Printing 1550 to 1650* (Oxford, 1956).

flourishing state of the Jewes, which he holdeth shall continue divers hundred yeares afterwards.'[87] This seemed more
reasonable because recent attempts to prophesy either the
end of the world or a spectacular second coming, for 1588
and more recently 1630, were demonstrably false. (The last
was so because it seemed likely the Jews would have at least
one generation on earth after their conversion.) Although
Draxe had learned some lessons from the failure of past conjectures and felt more certain about those which left the
greater events for later centuries and promised only the most
general and vaguest of happinesses for the immediate future,
he had no doubt that 'The age wherein Christ shall come may
bee knowne because our Lord onely excepteth the day and
houre.'[88]

Another example of more popularly oriented tracts was
Thomas Thompson's *Antichrist Arraigned* (1618), a sort of
everyman s guide to the history of Antichrist. He wrote it
especially for those who had neither the time nor the money
to acquire the large volumes of the learned scholars. He used
'Master *Brightman* with other more ancient strong men of
our Israel, that I might, as neere as possibly I could, abridge
their large Volumes into a Manuell.'[89] In general this literature echoed the thoughts of the major figures already outlined. Manuals like the above, or rules of faith like Nicholas
Byfield's in 1626, included sections like his about the eight
true signs of the end. These eight covered the history of Antichrist, the general apostasy, the Reformation, the universal
preaching and conversion of the Jews, and fearful alterations
in the heavens.[90] Another group, in the guise of preparations
of the soul for death, described the kingdom of God destined
for the elect and the risen martyrs in terms which encouraged
expectation of the millennium.[91]

[87] Thomas Draxe, *An Alarum to the Last Judgement* (London, 1615), pp. 107-8.
[88] Ibid., pp. 111-12.
[89] Thomas Thompson, *Anti-Christ arraigned*; a sermon at Pauls Crosse, the
third Sunday after Epiphanie (London, 1618), A3[v].
[90] Nicholas Byfield, *The rule of faith; or an exposition of the apostles creed*
(London, 1626), pp. 512-15.
[91] e.g. Richard Sheldon, *Mans last end, the glorious vision and fruition of God*
(London, 1634); Nicholas Byfield, *The marrow of the oracles of God. Or Divers
treaties, containing directions about six of the waightiest things can concerne a
Christian in this Life* (London, 1620).

After 1641 there appeared tracts applying prophecies to
the current international and national situation. One of the
first was *A Revelation of Mr. Brightman's Revelation* (1641),
which took the form of a dialogue between a citizen of London and a visiting preacher. The title-page quoted from Amos
3: 7, 'Surely the Lord God will doe nothing, but hee reveales
his Secrets to his Servants the Prophets.' Another pamphlet
based on Brightman's commentary appeared in 1643.[92] It
was written by R. Harford, who admitted that it appeared
with 'divers materiall things added' designed to see the state
of times past, present, and future. Beginning with Brightman's interpretation of the letters to the churches, he told
how Brightman had foreseen the troubles in Germany, but
said that England should take heart, for 'this is the last Act.
For after this Theater and long Tragedy is past, there will
succeed in the room thereof happy days with abundance of
peace and all good things.' Before 1650, 'the Jews shall be
called, the whore of Romes nose shall be slit'. Harking back
to older themes, Harford added that the pope would leave
Rome for Avignon or Bologna 'or thereabout' on another
Babylonish captivity. Rome meanwhile would be burned to
the ground by a victorious emperor of Germany, it being
most proper for him to do it. Within forty-five years of this
the papacy would be utterly destroyed; and ten years after its
fall in about 1696 the Turk also would be overthrown and
Christ would reign supreme.[93]

By 14 June 1643 a new system for the censorship of books
was established. The Reader of Gresham College, at that time
John Booker, became the licenser of almanacs, prognostica-
tions, and mathematical works, bypassing ecclesiastical control altogether. He proceeded to publish the first of his
apocalyptic almanacs, *The Bloody Almanack*, based in good
part upon Napier's commentary with the added attraction of
Booker's own skill in astrology. It contained seven sections
dealing with (i) the seven seals, (ii) the trumpets, (iii) the
angels, (iv) the 'Symboll of the Sabboth', (v) the prophecy of
Elias, (vi) the prophecy of Daniel, (vii) 'Christ's owne saying'.

[92] R. Harford, *Reverend Mr. Brightmans His judgement or prophecies* . . .
(London, 1643).
[93] Ibid., 3ᵛ–4.

The bloody Almanack:

To which E N G L A N D is directed, to fore-know what shall come to passe, by that famous Astrologer, M. JOHN BOOKER.

Being a perfect Abstract of the Prophecies proved out of Scripture, By the noble NAPIER, Lord of *Marchistoun* in *Scotland*.

The guide of Astrologers.　　　The Joy of England.

The Crosse of Rome.

Astra regunt homines, sed regit astra Deus.

Rome

London

The destruction of the World.

L O N D O N,

Printed for Anthony Vincent, and are to be sold in the Old-Baily. 1643

'The guide of Astrologers.　　The Joy of England'

Title page of a popular apocalyptic almanack.

The second edition, called *A Bloody Almanack*, dispensed
with sections (i) and (ii) and got right to the heart of the
matter, the present and the future. To emphasize this it was
prefixed by a prediction of events for the coming year by
months. On the title-page of this second version Napier was
described as 'that famous Astrologer the Lord Napier'.
Prophetic almanacs continued for many years,[94] becoming
after the Revolution less and less concerned with the reformation of religion and government.

Although the study of astrology was a serious one, the
marriage between it and the historical tradition was short-
lived. Booker quickly lost interest in the past, and his successors were less interested in the mysteries hidden in the text
than in those hidden in the stars. While the marriage lasted,
the apocalyptic aspects were borrowed from others rather
than originated.[95]

In looking for the origin of the fusion of the apocalyptic
tradition with the mystical aspects of contemporary science,
one is led again to the continent and to those persons whose
thoughts and careers were studied by Miss Yates. In good
part the mystical philosophy and religious ideas of these men
may have had an English source in the later career of John
Dee. Miss Yates describes the appearance in England in the
mid-seventeenth century of this philosophy with its application of a divine arithmetic to astrology and alchemy as something of a return of Dee's influence to his native land.[96]

Among those who responded to the excitement of the
times was John Milton.[97] His background had offered ample
opportunity to encounter the apocalyptic tradition of the
millenarians: his education at Christ's College had been under
the guidance of Joseph Mede, and his travels abroad had
brought him into contact with John Diodati. There is little

[94] For their role in forming popular beliefs and their astrological content, see
K. V. Thomas, *Religion and the Decline of Magic*.

[95] An example of borrowed thoughts is *The Worlds proceeding Woes and
Suceeding Ioyes* (London, 1642) which combined opinions of Alsted and Mede
with those of Tycho Brahe.

[96] Frances Yates, *The Rosicrucian Enlightenment*, pp. 22-3, 264 et seq.,
195-6.

[97] Milton is a subject in himself. For a thorough discussion see Michael Fixler,
Milton and the Kingdoms of God (London, 1964).

evidence that during his time at Christ's College Milton became a convert to the millennial teaching of his tutor, although many of Mede's views of the future were mirrored in his early tracts some years later. In these tracts Milton did not, however, employ a series of seals, trumpets, and vials to establish his periodization. A similar view of the Apocalypse was held by John Diodati, whom Milton visited after his days at Christ's and before his tracts of 1641-2. Diodati, an eminent Genevan theologian, held that the Revelation could be divided into two sections.

It seems one may observe this distinction, that from the beginning of the fourth Chapter unto the end of the eleventh, the said state is described as it were in the ideas of Gods heavenly decrees, and in visions altogether Enigmaticall. From the twelfth to the end of the Booke, the executions and principall singularities thereof are more distinctly marked out by visions and descriptions, which are more plain and nearer matched and fitted to events.[98]

The first section of the text contained the seals, trumpets, and vials that had formed the basis of British Protestant periodization from Bale to Mede. In this view the clearly historical prophecies did not begin until the story of the Woman and the Dragon. The second section of the text supported the parallel histories of the Jewish and Gentile elect, and the history of Antichrist, and postponed the millennium of Satan's bondage until a future date.

Two of Milton's early pamphlets, *Of Reformation* (1641) and his *Animadversions* (1642), are particularly revealing of both his emotional commitment to the preparation of church and country for the approaching millennium and his knowledge of the historical tradition. There are references to periodizations used by Brightman and Mede, and to those used by Foxe.[99] Foxe would appear to have been the major source for his historical material; the importance of Wyclif, and of martyrs, and the role of wealth and ambition in the establishment of Antichrist at Rome, were all favoured themes in Foxe's book which had been somewhat obscured in more recent numerical and linguistic identifications.

[98] John Diodati, *Pious Annotations upon the Holy Bible Expounding the difficult places thereof* (London, 1643), annotations upon the Apocalypse p. 98.
[99] Milton, *Complete Prose Works of John Milton*, vol. i, ed. Don M. Wolfe (Yale, 1953), pp. 541, 524-5, 557, 602-3.

Foxe's apocalyptic history, however, offered problems as well as assistance to the Puritan cause. Repeated references to his *Acts and Monuments* by both parties in ecclesiastical controversion have raised many questions about his influence in the seventeenth century, to which some answers have been given.[1] It would be wrong to imagine that Foxe had become the private property of the Puritans.[2] He was admired perhaps equally by both parties, though for different reasons. In some ways the Puritans had more reason to find fault with Foxe than had the more conservative clergy. Foxe had revered 'prelate martyrs', and had given an important place in his scheme to Constantine. Puritan objections to 'prelate martyrs' are clear enough, but the interpretation of Constantine's reign was a more involved matter. Foxe's own position had been ambiguous; Constantine was both the ideal Christian King, establisher and protector of the Church and her bishops before the arrogance of Rome, and the chief instrument of the Church's subsequent fall, in that he gave wealth and power into the hands of a hierarchy which gradually brought about its corruption. Constantine also played an integral part in Foxe's apocalyptic scheme, for in his reign Satan was bound and persecution ceased. The newer version of the apocalyptic scheme, especially after Alsted and Mede had presented arguments for placing the binding of Satan in the future to correspond with the millennium, considered even this view of Constantine to be in error. In *Of Reformation*, where Milton speaks so highly of 'the Author of our Church History',[3] Constantine is always and only represented as the agent of corruption. The purity of the Church before Constantine was also brought into question, and Antichrist was restored to a meaning at once both spiritual and historical.

Beleeve it Sir right truly it may be said, that Antichrist is Mammons Son. The soure levin of humane Traditions mixt in one putrifi'd Masse with the poisonous dregs of hypocrisie in the hearts of Prelates that lye

---

[1] William M. Lamont in *Godly Rule, Politics and Religion 1603–60* (London, 1969) discusses the main participants in the debate over Foxe and Constantine. Despite his belief that Foxe originated a super-nationalist millenarianism, the book contains a useful discussion of the Puritan view of Foxe.

[2] Suggested by Don Wolfe, op. cit., vol. i, p. 678 n.

[3] *Complete Prose Works*, ed. cit., vol. i, p. 604.

basking in the Sunny warmth of Wealth, and Promotion, is the Serpents Egge that will hatch an Antichrist wheresoever, and ingender the same Monster as big, or little as the Lump is which breeds him. If the splendor of Gold and Silver begin to Lord it once againe in the Church of England, wee shall see Antichrist shortly wallow heere, though his chiefe Kennell be at Rome.[4]

Like many on both sides, Milton admired Foxe more than he agreed with him. The temptation to reform Foxe still further must have been great. Neither side had any desire to part company with him entirely, but perhaps another edition, newly augmented and corrected. . . . It was for fear of something of this nature that Laud refused to license a new edition in 1637.[5] Milton made a great deal of this refusal as proof of the opposition's hatred of the great Foxe beloved of all. Because of Laud the *Book of Martyrs* 'was almost come to be a prohibited *book*'.[6]

A central thesis of Foxe's argument had been that persecution, rife under the pagan emperors, had ceased with Constantine, and reappeared only after Antichrist had gained his full powers in about 1300, at the end of the millennium of Satan's binding. The time from 300 to 1300 had seen the historical rise of Antichrist, encouraged by wealth and ambition. Milton kept this part of the story, but was forced to emphasize anew the role of wealth and ambition, and blur the dates for its appearance, thus obscuring the prophetic context of these ideas. In consequence, his view of the early ages of the Church more nearly resembled that of Tyndale than that of Foxe. Significantly, there was no mention of the seven seals, which were also usually applied to the times before Constantine; and his only mention of a trumpet did not assign a number or refer to a pattern.[7]

Milton ignored both the historical millennium of Satan's binding and the pattern of the seven seals and trumpets, and this left him with only one application of the tradition to history. This was the same part of the tradition that had weathered the introduction of millennial doctrine on the continent: the history of Antichrist. Milton was convinced of a patriotic millenarianism, the sort of thing Brightman had

[4] *Complete Prose Works*, ed. cit., vol. i, p. 590.
[5] 'Animadversions', ibid., pp. 678 n.–679 n.
[6] Ibid., p. 679.   [7] 'Of Reformation', ibid., p. 525.

hinted at and Mede had reinforced by his belief that one nation would lead the others during the millennium and be the seat of Christ's empire. Milton knew that that nation would be England, and so her history was the history of election; as illustrated by the fact that Wyclif had been English, and the Spanish Armada had been so providentially scattered.[8] In the full Protestant tradition, the history of England had been subsumed under a history of Europe, and illustrated with the histories of other nations the rise of Antichrist, beginning, Bale noted, and Milton followed, with the arrival of Augustine from Rome.[9] In Foxe's version the decisive break came in about the year 1300 with the release of the dragon. Witnesses against Antichrist sprang up all over Europe, as Wyclif did in England. Foxe saw nothing special about the fact that Wyclif was English. When Brightman wrote, he left the European context with the Reformation and found each succeeding prophecy fulfilled on his home soil. Milton drew the conclusion drawn by many of his day that the prophecies of the millennium were peculiarly applicable to Britain. In *Of Reformation* he spoke of Britain's past sufferings, by invasions and at the hands of Antichrist and his ministers, as a preparation for the glory of achieving the full reformation, the beginnings of which had received God's blessing, for he had begun at the same time 'to build up this *Britannick Empire* to a glorious and enviable height'.[10]

Milton's pamphlets show that he shared the dream of the millennium and the exalted conception of Britain's place in the divine plan. He illustrated the history of Antichrist and argued that the millennium could not be identified with any period in the past. During the years when he held these opinions, he began work on a universal history;[11] but if he intended it to depict the election and preservation of Britain for a glorious destiny in fulfilment of the divine prophecies, he did not accomplish this intention in his *History of Britain* published in 1670. He had helped to destroy the periodization

---

[8] 'Of Reformation', *Complete Prose Works*, ed. cit., vol. i, p. 525.
[9] Ibid., pp. 602–3.   [10] Ibid., p. 614.
[11] Theodore Haak to Samuel Hartlib (1648), describing Milton's projects in hand, see Turnbull, op. cit., p. 40. On Milton's *History of Britain* see French R. Fogle in *Milton and Clarendon: two papers on 17th century English Historiography* (Los Angeles, 1965).

Foxe had set up; and when the new organizing principle, the principle of election, had to be abandoned as a vain conceit, nothing was left save the endless recurrence of moral judgement, the providential history of a disillusioned and disappointed man.

Not all voices after 1640 were raised in expectation of the happy millennium. One dissident was the same Thomas Hayne who had corresponded with Mede. Unlike Twisse, he had not been convinced by Mede's arguments either that the fourth beast in Daniel represented Rome or that the millennium lay in the future. Hayne opposed himself and his authorities, especially Broughton, to the ideas of that potent trio, Alsted, Brightman, and Mede: '*Dr. Alstede* was a man of vast comprehension, but he had many Irons in the fire; Mr. Brightman I leave to Dr. Coopers judgement, who says that pretending to give us a Revelation of the Revelation hee hath set forth an Obscuration thereof. Mr. Mede was my worthy and learned friend, but not to bee preferred before truth.'[12]

As he had explained to Mede, the crux of the question was the terminal date of Daniel's seventy weeks. Mede wished to extend the prophecy to the completion of the mystery with the future millennium, but Hayne held the older view that the seventieth week had expired with the death of Christ, and the millennium[13] dated from his resurrection. Except in certain specific parts, the visions of the Apocalypse were merely a representation of the trials of the soul in this world and the benefits of faith in this and the next world.[14] Those prophecies the millenarians alleged to support the millennial rule of the saints on earth, the new Heaven and new Earth, and the New Jerusalem, rather 'expresse their [the Saints] happy condition not onely in the thousand years from Christs time, but in all the dayes of the Gospel to the world's end'.[15] With almost medieval fervour he urged that the purpose of the revelation had been to prepare the soul for faith in this life and the happiness of the life to come. 'Thus a Christian may in this life by faith see, take comfort in, and rejoice most heartily in the glorious estate of the life to come, and (as wee

[12] Thomas Hayne, *Christs Kingdome on Earth*, opened according to the Scriptures [n.p.] (645), A2.
[13] Ibid., pp. 3-5.   [14] Ibid., pp. 17-27.   [15] Ibid., p. 67.

use to say) have an heaven upon earth; whence it is, that the Church on earth is called Heaven.'[16]

The single most important historical prophecy in the Apocalypse was the revelation of Antichrist's appearance and defeat. The story of the Woman and the Dragon formed the basis for the connection of Antichrist with Revelation, and raised the problem once again of the binding of Satan. The millenarians linked this with the future millennium; Hayne with the first thousand years after Christ.[17] This had been Bale's later position, but Foxe had been converted to the idea that the thousand years stretched from Constantine to 1300. Brightman had contrived to have it two ways, both as Foxe had outlined and as the millenarians insisted. Mede, however, had conclusively shown that the Scripture warranted only one such millennium, and, finding that history on closer examination did not bear out Foxe's version, he placed the millennium in the future. Hayne too used history to disprove Foxe's version[18] of the millennium, saying that Constantine had not made all that much difference to the fortunes of the early Church, and that after A.D. 1000 'Satan being loosed, did with the full height of his malice infuse into the Pope and his instruments, Pride, error, and other impieties.' From that time the pope began to take over the western world, subverting the nations and bringing about the 'grand Apostasie'. As it applied to the binding and loosing again of Satan, the millennium was literal and supported the Protestant history of Antichrist; but as it applied to the kingdom of the saints, it was founded by Christ and continued to the world's end on earth and into eternity in heaven.[19]

Many of the millenarians had ceased to look for the end of the world and instead looked for a millennial kingdom; Hayne continued to look for the end of the world, and cited for his proofs the parts of the historical tradition that had convinced the earlier reformers: the general apostasy and the appearance of Antichrist. When giving his own version of the history of the apostasy he cited Foxe, Bullinger, and even Luther.

[16] Hayne, *Christs Kingdome on Earth*, p. 70.   [17] Ibid., pp. 86–7.
[18] He attacked Brightman whose scheme was taken from Foxe. Ibid., p. 34.
[19] Ibid., pp. 16–17.

It is very probable, that the day of judgment is neer. For first there hath been (as was foretold, 2 Thess. 2) *a departure from the true religion*, and that most conspicuous and manifest about a thousand years after Christ: and the man of sin, the son of perdition, the adversary of Christ . . . and by good proof demonstrated. *Luther*, and *many other Learned Writers*, some in, many since his time have laid open to the world Antichrists wicked enterprise.[20]

The end was near because Rome had already lost the universal vicarship, and Protestant churches of Europe 'have already abandoned the Popes power and censure the Roman Church justly, as condemned by God himself in the Apocalyps'.[21]

In many ways Hayne's position was a return to the version held a century earlier; but he reached his position by pushing the method of Mede further than Mede himself had done. The Apocalypse contained not many synchronisms, but one great synchronism. However, although the distinctions were blurred, the idea remained that the prophecy dealt with time and corroborated a once again nearly self-sufficient history of Antichrist. The Apocalypse covered the whole final age of the world. Hayne was pleased to see that this interpretation avoided both the papists' triennial error about Antichrist and the problems encountered by generations of scholars.[22]

Hayne abandoned all the apocalyptic tradition as it applied to history from Christ except the history of Antichrist. This may have been partly because he no longer felt the need to prove who Antichrist was by history and prophecy. The first reformers had enlisted the fuller tradition; Hayne no longer had to. Hayne's book was published only once, and his influence was not as great as that of his opponents Alsted, Brightman, and Mede. Like Milton, he is significant, though, both of the way in which the tradition began to return to its first Protestant expression of the early sixteenth century as a revelation of Antichrist and a warning and comfort to the souls of the faithful in this world, and of the way in which this return was the natural outcome of contemporary influences upon him. Mede's method and the concentration of interest upon the future both contrived to unite the separate seals, trumpets, and vials into a single vision, and to make it the vision of Christ's kingdom. Even Mede had insisted it be

[20] Hayne, *Christs Kingdome on Earth*, pp. 88–9.
[21] Ibid., p. 89.   [23] Ibid., pp. 49–50. See above, p. 35.

recognized that in some mysterious sense the kingdom must have existed from the resurrection of Christ. Add to this a millennial utopianism, with its emphasis upon a static ideal erected by some catastrophic event, and it becomes easy to understand how interest in a historical progression from seal to seal or trumpet to trumpet became merely a matter of prerequisite knowledge learned from authority, to be covered quickly, as Booker covered it. Then the real questions could be raised: when was the millennium coming, what remained to be done before it could come, and what would it be like?

Hayne's rejection of the millennium did not cause him to abandon the belief that the end was near, nor did it exempt him from many of the same hopes and plans for the future of Britain. Although he held that the universal preaching and the conversion of the Jews had begun with the Christian era, he believed there was a special duty placed upon the men of the last days.

Concerning the Jews calling to the Gospel I have above spoken. Here onely I adde, that wee should take heed of any proud or contemptuous cariage towards them. They were broken off from the true Olive, and wee graffed in. God is able to graffe them into it again. It concerns us to use all good means to win them to Christ. If wee can trade to the *Indies* for worldly commodities, why should we not take courses for reducing some at least of that once beloved nation into Christs fold?[23]

These words appeared in his last paragraph and mark him as a man very much of his time.

Many of these pamphlets and derivative works appeared during the first years of the Long Parliament, and they helped to produce and reflected the hopes and plans of its leading members.[24] Many of the sermons given before Parliament dealt with apocalyptic themes; the thoughts of Mr. Brightman, of learned Mr. Mede, and also of Comenius, were placed in the minds of its members.[25] Hope for the new reformation spread everywhere. Hartlib encouraged Parliament to invite Comenius to England, and he came in 1641.

[23] Hayne, *Christs Kingdome on Earth*, p. 90.

[24] Many of whom are covered in Lamont, *Godly Rule*, Hill, *Antichrist in Seventeenth-century England*, and most recently in P. K. Christianson, 'From Expectation to Militance: Reformers and Babylon in the First Two Years of the Long Parliament', *J. Ecclesiastical History*, vol. xxiv, no. 3, July 1973.

[25] See H. R. Trevor-Roper, 'The Fast Sermons', in *Religion, the Reformation and Social Change*.

The intellectual atmosphere of the early 1640s was charged with a belief that great change was imminent. The crisis of the Reformation demanded the allegiance and single-minded efforts of all good men to fulfil the promises of prophecy. The trumpet had sounded.

VII

CONCLUSION

This study does not continue in any detail into the period following 1645, partly because by that time preoccupation with current events and with the nature and time of the advent of the millennium obscured the historical tradition, and partly because in those years there erupted a number of chiliastic movements whose character, although influenced by materials drawn from the historical tradition, is better approached by a specialist in the social history of the period. Fortunately there are several such specialists whose works do not underestimate the intellectual inheritance of the millenarians.[1]

In the last chapter we saw how many of the changes in the tradition after about 1620 were changes that weakened it. The postponing to some future date of prophecies hitherto applied and proved to have been fulfilled in the past had reduced the material of the historical tradition. The popularity of abstracts of the larger works, together with astrological speculations, obscured the methods of the originals, while among those whose interest had been academic the achievement and reputation of Joseph Mede met with no successful challenge. As sometimes happens, when belief was at its strongest, thought was at its weakest. The influence of millenarian doctrine, when united with a belief in the possibility of attaining a utopian society, engaged and enlivened thought about the prophecies of Scripture and directed that thought in new directions that did not contribute to the maintenance of the historical tradition.

By tracing the history of just two men's reactions to the events of the next period one can see in miniature how the historical tradition came to be abandoned by many. Both John Dury and Samuel Hartlib had been in contact with Mede, and had accepted his interpretation. They were also

[1] Most recently C. Hill, *The World Turned Upside Down* (1972); P. K. Christianson, 'From Expectation to Militance', *J. Ecclesiastical History*, vol. xxiv, no. 3 (July 1973).

agents for foreign ideas that came to be of importance in the next years. In 1641, responding to the heightened mood of expectation, Hartlib published a tiny Utopia inspired by Andreae and by Francis Bacon's *New Atlantis*.[2] Although short, the description of Macaria presents a picture not only of an ideal society but also of the millennial society of the full Reformation, for which the reader was urged to work. In an exchange between a Scholar and a Traveller, the Scholar overcomes all doubts about the imminence of the full Reformation and assures the Traveller that the meaning of Scripture on this point is to be interpreted not mystically but historically.[3] As the years passed, however, both Dury and Hartlib became less and less certain about their former beliefs, finally coming to question not only the interpretations they had formerly accepted but also the very method on which the historical tradition had been founded. As early as 1650 they reacted without enthusiasm to the presentation of yet another interpretation of the prophecies. Untouched by recent English experience, Comenius had sent the book 'concerning the periods of the Revelation-times, drawing to an end'. He asked that it be conveyed to someone of Mede's stature for comment and that it be translated into English.[4] Dury complied with the request for translation and publication, and gave it to Hartlib. The translation was dedicated by Hartlib to Oliver St. John and prefaced with a letter introducing the book sent from Dury to Hartlib. Dury confessed himself, though once drawn by such arguments, now to be both sceptical of the predictions put forward in the book and unhappy with the whole method. He feared that although the author might 'bee able demonstratively to prove the truth of the Accomplishment of all the events . . . yet he might fall

---

[2] Turnbull, *Hartlib, Davy and Comenius*, pp. 73–6; Trevor-Roper, *Religion, the Reformation and Social Change*, p. 269.

[3] Samuel Hartlib, *A Description of the Famous Kingdome of Macaria* (London, 1641), p. 13. See Charles Webster, 'Macaria, Samuel Hartlib and the Great Reformation', *Acta Comeniana* 2 (xxvi) (Prague, 1970).

[4] Comenius's letter quoted by Dury in a letter to Hartlib, 28 Nov. 1650, which became the preface to *Clavis Apocalyptica . . . by a German D.*, trans. out of *High Dutch* (London, 1651). The author has been identified as Abraham von Frankenberg. H. R. Trevor-Roper, 'Three Foreigners' in *Religion, the Reformation and Social Change*, p. 292.

short of that spiritual understanding' that gave strength to
the 'bare Historicall sense'.[5]

Since the days when he and Mede had corresponded, Dury
had altered his opinion of the importance of similar inquiries:

And truly, although I have much valued the gift and studie of those
that have set themselves, to unfold by the observation of Histories the
Mystical presignificance of events, yet I could never bring my spirit to
apply it selfe to anie such search. . . . I am cleer that they [the events]
are neither useful to us, nor necessarie to bee known, but as they are
subordinate unto this Mysterie of the Kingdom. . . . This then is the
Mysterie which I look after; viz. to finde the Manifestation of the
Spiritual Kingdom of Christ in the Nature of man, and in humane
societies so advanced that the works of the Devil are destroied therein.[6]

In this statement Dury rejected the notion that events were
the necessary means by which God revealed his will. It was
not necessary to know history but only to have a vision of
the perfectibility of man's nature and his society.

In the Book of Revelation he saw a representation of the
kingdom built in 'Regenerate souls' and 'Regenerate societies'
where faith established the 'libertie of the Sons of God'.
Dury still acknowledged Mede's authority in the study of
prophecy, especially his discovery of synchronisms, which
united the events with the 'Symbolical speeches' of Scripture; but their use was to illuminate 'the harmonie between
the great and little world' and 'the harmonical properties of
thinges visible, and invisible, wherein [are seen] the corre-
spondencie between the outward and inward man, the tem-
porarie and eternal natures of things, and the state of true
life'.[7] None of these was historical. The final blow was
delivered in Dury's enunciation of one rule which he said
must be followed and which he and Hartlib had italicized:
no prophecie is of particular interpretation.[8]

The combined prophecies of Daniel and the Apocalypse
were no longer said to pertain to the history of the Church in
this world, and even the history of Antichrist had lost its
apocalyptic significance. Dury, echoing Tyndale, cautioned
Hartlib and the readers of the book sent by Comenius to
remember that the first meaning of the beast was 'worldliness', and that the forms Satan took were many. The beast

[5] Dury to Hartlib, loc. cit., p. 14.
[6] Ibid., pp. 16–17.   [7] Ibid., pp. 17–20.   [8] Ibid., pp. 33–4.

worked not so much upon the Church as upon the bestial half of man's nature, keeping each soul from its true vocation.

As the history of the Commonwealth progressed, it became more and more vital for responsible commentators to reflect upon the spiritual sense of the text and to minimize anything that could be construed as a justification for further social or political disruption. After the Restoration it became even more difficult for the admirers of the method and interpretation of Joseph Mede to quell fears that such an interpretation led only to revolution. Nevertheless Mede had his admirers, and chief among them was his editor and biographer John Worthington.

In vain Worthington attempted to disentangle the thought of Joseph Mede from his reputation as a prophet of the Revolution. He saw these allegations as the chief detractors from Mede's deserved place as an authority, and feared that to abandon the historical interpretation of the prophecies put forward since the earliest days of the Reformation would threaten the very existence of the Protestant faith. With his contemporaries he condemned 'They of old and the late Zealots judging of things according to the lusts of Ambition and Love of the World in their Hearts.'[9] In dealing with the millennium such men had 'deprav'd and stain'd this Primitive Truth by their unspiritual Representation of it'.[10] Worthington argued that the historical interpretation could be preserved without giving rise to these errors. All agreed that chiliasm must be precluded,

But I would question whether the proper Cure for these Distempers be the turning the Sense of the Apocalypse a New Way, expounding all of it almost of the *Jewish* Church rather than the *Christian*; and of things past many Hundred Years ago; nay, and sometimes of Matters too minute and inconsiderable for the Solemnity and Majesty of the Expressions.[11]

Such a reduction in the importance of the prophecies would never, he argued, convince the fanatics and would only encourage the papists.

Another reason he saw for the eclipse of Mede's work was the cowardice of a clergy frightened of the consequences of

[9] Worthington, 'Observations concerning the *Millennium* and other Passages in the *Apocalypse*', *Miscellanies* (London, 1704), p. 20.
[10] Ibid.   [11] Ibid., p. 71.

the identification of Rome and all things Roman with the
Antichrist. The early reformers had not lacked the courage of
their convictions.

Nor were they so weak as to be affrighted, and disturbed, at every thing
which some hot Spirits did then call *Babylonish* and *Antichristian* and
there are that do so still. But surely a right Understanding and Representation of the Apocalypse is a most powerful Means to silence and
baffle those Men of Noise and Confidence, rather than Sobriety and
Judgement.[12]

One reason which he did not see, and one of the more important ones for the future of Anglican thought, was the per-
suasiveness of the scholarship associated with the New Way he
had tried so hard to ignore. The New Way was the method and
interpretation of Hugo Grotius and of his English disciple
Henry Hammond. Grotius had done what seemed impossible
to most Protestants—he had dispensed not only with the idea
that the Revelation comprehended the history of the Church
from Christ to the second coming but also with the identification of the Roman papacy with Antichrist. This struck at
the heart of the Protestant apocalyptic tradition. Grotius
limited the historical content of the Book of Revelation to
the times before Constantine; and therefore the prophecy
contained nothing of all those ages following, nothing of the
pope or of the Reformation. Only the prophecies of the millennium beginning with Constantine and stretching for an
indefinite period towards the end of the world could be said
to apply to the present, and that application was only in the
nature of a spiritual vision of the most universal aspects of
world history.

Grotius was not the first to hold these views, but both his
immediate predecessors had been Spanish Jesuits. One of
them was Ribera, Brightman's bane, the other and perhaps
the more important of the two was Alcasar. His commentary
published in 1614 established patterns that Grotius later
followed. The prophecies of the Revelation expressed the
history of the conflicts of primitive Christianity with Judaism
and paganism. The seals traced the trials of the gospel, and
the vials the victory of Christianity over pagan Rome. The
woman in the wildnerness represented the Jewish church,

_____

[12] Worthington, *Miscellanies*, p. 72.

whose child, the Messiah, represented Christianity.[13] One by one the remaining bulwarks of the Protestant apocalyptic tradition fell before the new way of interpreting the Apocalypse.

The need to see in history the fulfilment of prophecies has been an enduring and recurrent theme in western civilization. Neither proven nor entirely discredited, the theories and traditions have persisted, always awaiting a change in fashion or a time of bewilderment. The century of reformation was such a time. The concerted campaign of the early Protestants to illustrate and justify their cause in terms of a new history succeeded in giving a new expression to the old theme. This Protestant tradition survived essentially unchanged throughout the period. The tradition itself may be said to have gone through three stages in its history. First, its establishment in Britain through the work and contacts of the three Johns— Bale, Foxe, and Knox—and principally in the monumental influence exerted by Foxe's *Book of Martyrs*. A second stage occurred towards the end of the sixteenth century and is distinguished by a coming together of a variety of human arts and sciences to enlarge and elaborate the tradition, giving it the more sophisticated content thought appropriate to discoveries of such importance. The third and final stage followed upon the death of Joseph Mede but can be traced back to a new wave of continental influence from about 1620. This stage saw both the height of interest in the prophecies and the growth of dissatisfaction with the limits set upon the tradition by its earlier expositors.

The Protestant apocalyptic tradition took shape in an atmosphere of well-defined conflict. It formed itself partly out of previous traditions and agreed with certain universally received assumptions. The world of men divided into servants of the flesh and servants of the spirit, into the faithful and the apostate; and when this was seen in the aggregate the two churches on earth mirrored the two cities which transcended mere mundane history. These churches of Christ and Antichrist were at first delineated by a comparison of the

---

[13] Isbon T. Beckwith, *The Apocalypse of John; Studies in Introduction* (Michigan, 1919, reprinted 1967), pp. 330-3; R. H. Charles, *Studies in the Apocalypse*, pp. 36-42.

scriptural image of the true Church with the practices of the
Roman Church. The historical tradition began when the
history of Rome was seen and described as the fulfilment of
scriptural prophecy; the essential step in its establishment
was an identification of the papacy with the Antichrist.

This step was made as the moral and legal arguments that
Protestants had raised in debate gave way to catalogues of
tyrannies and oppressions showing the actions of the papacy
to be the actions of Antichrist, and as the study of these
instances of papal persecution discovered old prophecies of
the Hussites and Joachists that condemned the pope as Antichrist and forecast a future reformation. Beginning with
Luther's interest in the prophecies of the Franciscan John
Hilten, and continuing with the collections of Melanchthon
and Carion, of Jean Crespin and John Foxe, the first connections between Protestant history and the prophetic tradition
were made. This, however, was not enough to establish
appeal to prophecy as more than an additional condemnation
of the Roman Church: in order to maintain further that
Scripture and history were two sources of truth as certain as
the authority of the Church, the two must be made one; and
how but by revelation?

It was clear that historians could be liars; so any authority
that history might have, it had by virtue of its correspondence with the principles of Scripture, both in matters of
moral judgement and, of more importance to the apocalyptic
tradition, in so far as it illustrated the fulfilment of prophecy.
Although the prophecies of Huss, Jerome of Prague, and
others were curiosities worthy of mention and shown cred-
ible by the event, the only prophecies of true authority were
those in Scripture. From the first, scriptural prophecy was to
exert more control over the tradition among the Protestants
than anywhere else.

The development of the apocalyptic tradition among
British Protestants cannot by this criterion be said to have
begun before John Bale placed Antichrist's identification
with the papacy in a historical scheme influenced by Joachim
and based on the Book of Revelation. From then on, the two
most important characteristics of the Protestant tradition
were a history of Antichrist and a periodization based on a

succession of apocalyptic images. The correspondence between Daniel and the Apocalypse, between prophecies always
held to be literal and prophecies sometimes considered to be
spiritual representations of an eternal kingdom, strengthened
the idea that the Apocalypse was to be interpreted literally as
a description of the history of the Church from the time of
Christ. Given the necessary relationship between Scripture
and history, it was natural that the tradition should develop
simultaneously as historical commentary on Scripture and
scriptural commentary on history. Bale recognized this interdependence when he wrote:

A prophecy is the Apocalypse called, and is much more excellent than
all the other prophecies. . . . It is a full clearance to all the chronicles
and most notable histories which have been wrote since Christ's ascension, opening the true nature of their ages, times, and seasons. He that
hath store of them and shall diligently search them over, conferring the
one with the other, time with time, and age with age, shall perceive
most wonderful causes. For in the text are they only proponed in
effect, and promised to follow in their seasons, and so ratified with the
other scriptures: but in the chronicles they are evidently seen by all
ages fulfilled. Yet is the text a light to the chronicles and not the
chronicles to the text.[14]

Bale's summary of his method is a good indication of the
ideas that inspired the historiography of the Marian exiles.
In this first stage of the tradition's evolution, the historical
relevance was at its highest. Bale used the Apocalypse to
stimulate an essentially historical imagination; his desire was
to discover, by comparing one chronicle with another, the
differences between ages and times and the causes of those
differences. He was proposing a search among secondary
sources, but in this he represents only the limitation of his
time. Younger members of the international community
around the Marian exiles, Sleidan, Crespin, Foxe, and Knox,
would use newer methods, but still be guided by the principles Bale had outlined. The newer methods would not lead
immediately to new interpretations.

The same can be said of the improvements in chronology
and philology, which, though they gave new tools to the
developers of the tradition and to some extent suggested lines
of further inquiry, did not materially alter the principles of

[14] Bale, *The Image of bothe churches*, Parker Soc. ed., 'Preface', p. 252.

the prophecies' interpretation and application to history. Interest in the chronological interpretation of prophecy, in conjectures concerning the future or the possible numerical regularity in patterns of past events, had arisen among Protestants almost as early as the systematic identification of persons or places described in prophecy with historical persons and events, and it gradually produced the chronological structure of seals, trumpets, and vials. The order of the text and the order of history reinforced this sequential identification of image with event.

By the end of the sixteenth century, John Napier had set the standard in a commentary that offered demonstrative proof, consistent with Scripture and history, that the fulfilment of prophecy was a regular and observable process; and by means of those propositions thus demonstrated, he showed that future events of certain kinds could, within limits, be predicted. As God had acted in the past, so would he act in the future. Thus those periods at present shrouded in mystery, because they lay either in the future or so far in the past that untrustworthy records or none existed, could be made known by conjectures based on the principles of divine action discovered from periods of which the historian had knowledge. Napier applied his propositions to the time from Christ to the end of the world; his follower Robert Pont applied them to discover the date of the Creation by 'retrodiction' from the time of Christ.

The way was prepared for the discovery of a universal chronology and history, based on the authority of the Bible and the new advances in the art and logic of commentary and the science of chronology. The authority of universal history was tested against the moral principles of Scripture and its truth by the evident fulfilment of prophecy. Ralegh's *History of the World* made no distinction in kind between the historical and the prophetic books of Scripture but interpreted them equally. Although his work reaches no further than the zenith of pagan Rome, he expressed a belief that the prophecies of Daniel and the Revelation identified the future Antichrist, and noted as a historical conjecture the possible ancestry of the Spaniard in the tribe of Magog—indications that he had been influenced by the apocalyptic tradition in substance as well as in principle.

During the first stage of the tradition in Britain, from Bale's *The Image of bothe churches* to Foxe's *Eicasmi*, the participants were predominantly religious reformers and church historians; but by the turn of the century the major contributions were being made about equally by clergy and laymen. The tradition had broadened, to include men whose intellectual interests were more varied: mathematicians, philologists, chronologers, astrologers, controversialists, and a universal historian with universal interests. The standard of commentary on Scripture had greatly improved, and the techniques of critical chronology had been sharpened by Scaliger's methodology. Bale rarely referred to the ancient languages, Brightman constantly did. Broughton, Ralegh, and Mede showed an attention to chronological consistency that cannot be found in Bale or Foxe. All in all, the early seventeenth century fell heir to a sophisticated apocalyptic tradition in which the major historical work had already been done. After the end of the sixteenth century, few further identifications were made; and instead of searching the chronicles for patterns in the past, imagination had turned towards the discovery of clearer schemata in the prophecies already interpreted, and the projection of their fulfilment into the nearer or more remote future.

Apocalyptic history is visionary history. It is concerned as much with projection of the future as with understanding of the past. Brightman described this well when he spoke of how his age had been given the knowledge of the whole of history:

Nowe it (the Historye) is reserved for this time because there could not be a full understanding of these things before the last trumpet. The events came forth by little and little, and point by point, to the knowledge of which the world attained severally & by leasure—like, as when hangings are unfolded, but nowe when al things were at last accomplished, it was a fit time to see the whole garment displaid at once.[15]

Brightman saw his own age, the age of reformation, as a consummation and as a time for the completion of human knowledge. When the reformation was complete and the lukewarmness of Laodicea overcome, then would be the Golden Age, the millennium of the saints. Bale had sought the

---

[15] Brightman, *A revelation of the revelation*, p. 367.

pattern of the past and left the future a mystery; but when the pattern had been found, the future was a mystery no longer.

The Protestant tradition had at first discouraged projection and prediction, and under the shadow of Münster had adopted this rejection as an article of faith. The Protestant view of the future went no further, as Knox had said, than the utter destruction of Rome. Bale, Foxe, and Knox agreed that the promise of the New Jerusalem was wrapped in mystery. The predominant feeling among the early reformers was that suffering would outweigh joy in the last days. At first Foxe saw reason to hope only that persecution in this world was a preparation for joy in the next; that those brought low would be exalted in the eyes of God, and the mighty abased. Throughout, God preserved his Church among a small number of the elect scattered through the world. The reign of Elizabeth raised hope in him that, with the establishment of the Reformation, the persecution in this world might cease and the Church and nation be perfected; but he claimed no special destiny for England. No national church was the Church of God, rather, all nations were called by him. In his *Eicasmi*, Foxe explicitly denied that God had elected one church or nation above another: his Church was wherever the true faith was believed. England reformed was neither a Utopia nor a millennial kingdom, and would not be lifted above historical necessity. 'No man', he said, 'liveth in that commonwealth where nothing is amiss. But yet because God hath placed us Englishmen here in one commonwealth, also in one Church as in one ship together, let us not mangle or divide the ship, which, being divided perisheth.'[16] Bale and Foxe loved their country but neither believed it to be or presented it as the elect nation with an apocalyptic destiny.

Only after the possibility of prediction had been fully accepted could the future figure in the tradition as history. The veil that surrounded the time after the defeat of Rome and the Turk could then be penetrated. When Napier wrote, he was able to incorporate a more hopeful vision of the future: the last period of history would be characterized by

[16] Foxe, Preface 'To the true and Faithfull Congregation', *Acts and Monuments*, ed. Josiah Pratt, vol. i, p. xxiv.

universal peace and an unprecedented increase in knowledge. The latter was beginning to happen in his own day. For example, if in the past it had been wrong to search the prophecies for the history of the future, it was wrong no longer: the discovery of prophecy was one of the tasks reserved for the men of the last days. Napier's last period was not, however, a millennium of the saints' rule with God or a New Jerusalem.

The contributions to the tradition made by Broughton, Brightman, and Mede were further refinements in the schematization of the past and the construction of a pattern for the future. The changes in the periodization of the past were often made in order to free a prophecy for application to the future. A prophecy was sometimes shifted into the future because the event formerly designated as its fulfilment failed upon closer inspection to meet all the specifications. Thus, little historical battles were waged over the identification of Daniel's Antichrist with Antiochus Epiphanes, resulting in Broughton's idea that the Apocalypse was a Gentile Book of Daniel, and Brightman's belief that Daniel was a Jewish Apocalypse. The latter belief implied that the history of the Jewish church paralleled that of the Gentile, until the future completion of the reformation and conversion of the Jews.

If a prophecy had not been fulfilled in one event it would be fulfilled in another. Thus, if Foxe's opinion that the binding of Satan and the millennium had begun with Constantine and ended in about 1300 could not be supported by a more detailed study of that period, the millennium must still lie in the future. The Protestant tradition had a finite number of prophecies of absolute authority; and so the elaboration of the future had to be at the expense of the past, and often implied an unrecognized refutation of the tradition.

During the years of turmoil accompanying the Thirty Years War, Britain became a refuge of hope for many foreign Protestants. Both at home and abroad the conviction grew that Britain had a special role to play in the defence of the Protestant faith. On her soil the New Reformation might come to pass. A utopian vision nurtured abroad and set in a millenarian context found its way into Britain and there

worked upon the native apocalyptic tradition, giving it a new
life and direction.

As the tradition entered its final stage the appeal again
widened. The prophecies were no longer of interest only to
churchmen and scholars but to the nation at large. Through a
flood of pamphlets and the sermons of both itinerant and
resident preachers almost everyone could learn something
about the application of the prophecies to the national crisis.
A new era of radical thought began. Books such as Sleidan's
De Quatuor Summis Imperiis were used to support millenarian programmes for the reform of society, and others like
Foxe's *Book of Martyrs* to hearten the oppressed with the
conviction that the true Church had ever been small and
persecuted and would be so until the Reformation was complete. The tradition of exiles and scholars was seized by a
new chiliastic doctrine and from it was forged a weapon for
social revolution and civil warfare.

SELECTED BIBLIOGRAPHY

I. PRIMARY SOURCES

Abbott, Robert: *Antichristi Demonstratio, contra Fabulas Pontificias & ineptam Roberti Bellarmini de Antichristo disputationem.* London, 1603.

Acta Facultatis Artium Universitatis Sanctiandree 1413–1588, ed. Annie I. Dunlop. Edinburgh and London, 1964.

Acts and Proceedings of the General Assemblies of the Kirk of Scotland from the year MDLX, Part I, Maitland Club. Edinburgh, 1839.

Alsted, John Henry: *The Beloved City, or, the Saints Reign on Earth A Thousand Years etc.*, trans. William Burton. London, 1643.

—— *Cursus Philosophici Encyclopedia*, Liber XXVII, xx. Herborn, 1620.

—— *Diatribe De Milleannis Apocalypticis non illis Chiliastarum & Phantastarum sed BB. Danielis & Johannis.* Frankfurt, 1627.

Andreae, Johann Valentine: *Christianopolis*, trans. and ed. Felix Emil Held, 'An Ideal State of the 17th Century', Univ. of Illinois Ph.D. thesis. Urbana, 1914.

The Babylonian Talmud: tracts 'Sanhedrin' and 'Abodah Zara', trans. and ed. I. Epstein and H. Freeman. London, 1935.

Bacon, Francis: *The Advancement of Learning*, ed. William Aldiss Wright, 5th edition. Oxford, 1926.

Bale, John: *Acta Romanorum Pontificum, a dispersione discipulorum Christi usq. ad tempora Pauli quarti qui nunc in Ecclesia tyrannizat.* Basle, 1558. Trans. into English as *The Pageant of the Popes, contaynynge the lyves of all the Bishops of Rome, from the beginning of them to the yeare of grace 1555*, trans. with sundry additions by J(ohn) S(tudley). London, 1574.

—— *The actes of Englysh votaryes, comprehendynge their unchast practyses and examples by all ages.* Wesel (John Day, London?).

—— *The Dramatic Writings of John Bale, Bishop of Ossory*, ed. J. S. Farmer, Early English Drama Society. London, 1907.

—— *Index Britanniae Scriptorum Quos ex variis bibliothecis non parvo labore collegit Joannes Baleus, cum aliis*, ed. R. L. Poole and Mary Bateson. Oxford, 1902.

—— *The Laboryouse Journey and serche of Johan Leylande for Englandes Antiquitees, geven of hym as a newe yeares gyfte to Kynge Henry the VIII in the xxxvii yeare of his Reygne, with declaracyons enlarged by J. Bale.* London, 1549.

—— *A mysterie of inyquyte contained within the heretycall Genealogye of Ponce Pantolabus, is here both dysclosed and confuted* (1542). Geneva, 1545.

—— *The second part or contynuacyon of the English votaries*, etc. London, 1551.

Bale, John: *Select Works of Bishop Bale*, Parker Society. Cambridge, 1849.
—— *The vocacyon of Johan Bale to the bishoprick of Ossorie in Irelande his persecucions in ye same, and finall delyueraunce* 'Imprinted in Rome, before the castel of S. Angell. . . .' (London: Hugh
Singleton, 1553?).
—— *Yet a course at the Romyshe foxe: A dysclosynge or openynge of
the Manne of synne*. Zürich, 10 Dec. 1543.
Barnes, Robert: *Vitae Romanorum Pontificum, quòs Papas vocamus
summa diligentia ac fide collectae*. Basle, 1535.
—— *The Whole Works of W. Tindall, John Frith, & Doct. Barnes three
worthy martyrs, etc. collected and compiled in one tome together*,
ed. John Foxe. London, 1573.
Baronius, Caesar, S.J.: *Annales ecclesiastica cum critica historico-
chronologica*, vol. i. Lucae, 1738.
Beard, Thomas: *The Theatre of God's Judgements, revised and augmen-
ted*. London, 1631.
Bellarmine, Robert, S.J.: *De Translatione Imperii Romani a Graecis ad
Francos*. Antwerp, 1589.
Beroaldus, Matthaus: *Chronicum, Scripturae sacrae Autoritate Consti-
tutum*. (n.p.) 1575.
—— *A short view of the Persian monarchie, and of Daniels weekes;
beeing a peece of Beroaldus workes, with a censure in some points
by Hugh Broughton*. London, 1590.
Bodin, Jean: *Method for the Easy Comprehension of History*, trans.
Beatrice Reynolds. Records of Civilization: Sources and studies, gen.
ed. A. P. Evans. New York, 1945.
Booker, John: *The Bloody Almanack*. London, 1643.
—— *A Bloody Almanack*. London, 1647.
Brightman redivivus . . . in foure sermons. (Anon.) London, 1647.
Brightman, Thomas: 'Against Bellarmine touching Antichrist', in *A
revelation of the revelation*. Amsterdam, 1615.
—— *A commentary on the Canticles or the Song of Solomon*. Amster-
dam, 1644.
—— *A most comfortable exposition of the prophecies of Daniel.*
. Amsterdam, 1635. Another edition London 1644.
—— *A revelation of the revelation . . . opened clearly with a logicall
resolution and exposition etc.* Amsterdam, 1615.
Brocardus, Jacobus: *Libri duo; alter ad Christianos de prophetia; alter
ad Hebraeos de primo et secundo Domini adventus*. Leyden, 1581.
—— *The Revelation of S. John reveled*, trans. James Sanford. London,
1582.
Broughton, Hugh: *A concent of scripture* [n.p.d.] and another edition.
London, 1590.
—— *Daniel his Chaldie visions and his Ebrew*. London, 1596.
—— *A defence of the booke entitled A concent of Scripture*. Middle-
burg, 1609.
—— *Letters to the Vice chancellor & others in the Univ. of Oxford in
defence of A concent of scripture*. (London, 1591?).

Broughton, Hugh: *Letters to Queen Elizabeth, Abp. Whitgift, Bp. J. Aylmer touching the Vice-chancellor of Oxford etc.* (London, 1591?)

—— *Master Broughton's letters esp. his last pamphlet to a. ag. the Abp. of Canterbury about Sheol a. Hades answered.* (n.p.)

—— *Principall positions for groundes of the holy bible.* (n.p.) 1609.

—— *A require of agreement to the groundes of divinitie studie.* (Middleburg) 1611.

—— *A revelation of the holy apocalypse.* (Amsterdam?) 1610.

—— *A seder olam, that is, order of the worlde; or yeares from the fall to the restoring.* (London?) 1594.

—— *Sundry workes for B. Simson, and W. White.* [London, 1591?]

—— *Textes of scripture chayning the holy chronicle untyll the sunne lost his lyght.* (Init. H. B.) for G. Simson and W. White. London, 1591.

—— *Two epistles unto great men of Britaine in 1599, printed now the second time.* (Amsterdam?) 1606.

Bullinger, Heinrich: *A hundred sermons upon the Apocalyps.* Newly set forth London: Day, 1561; another edition 1573.

Byfield, Nicholas: *The marrow of the oracles of God. Or Divers treaties containing Directions about six of the waightiest things can concerne a Christian in this life.* 2nd edition. London, 1620.

—— *The rule of faith, or, An exposition of the apostles creed etc.* London, 1626.

Calvin, John: 'Acts of the Council of Trent with the Antidote' (1547), in *Calvin's Tracts and Treatises*, vol. iii, trans. Henry Beveridge, ed. T. F. Torrance. London and Edinburgh, 1958.

—— 'Advertissement contre L'astrologie qu'on appelle Judiciaire et autres curiositez qui regnent auiourd'Huy au Monde' (Geneva, 1549), in *Corpus Reformatorum, Calvini Opera*, vol. vii.

—— 'Brieve Instruction pour armer tous bons Fideles contre les erreurs de la secte commune des Anabaptistes' (Geneva, 1544), in *Corpus Reformatorum, Calvini Opera*, vol. viii.

—— '*Commentaries on the Book of the Prophet Daniel*', trans. and ed. Thomas Myers, Calvin Translation Society, 2 vols. Edinburgh, 1852.

—— 'De Aeterna Dei Praedestinatione, qua in salutem alios ex Hominibus elegit, alios suo exitio reliquit etc.' (Geneva, 1552), in *Corpus Reformatorum, Calvini Opera*, vol. viii.

—— 'The Epistles of Paul the Apostle to the Romans and to the Thessalonians', trans. Ross Mackenzie, vol. 4 in *Calvin's Commentaries*, ed. D. W. Torrance and T. F. Torrance, 12 vols. London and Edinburgh, 1959–72.

—— 'Epistolae ad annos 1528–1539 Pertinentes', Thesauri Epistolici Calviniani, in *Corpus Reformatorum, Calvini Opera*, vol. x.

—— 'The First Epistle of John', trans. T. H. L. Parker, vol. 3 (1961) in *Calvin's Commentaries*, ed. Torrance and Torrance. London and Edinburgh, 1959–72.

—— 'The First Epistle of Paul the Apostle to the Corinthians', trans.

J. W. Fraser, vol. 2 (1960), in *Calvin's Commentaries*, ed. Torrance and Torrance, London and Edinburgh, 1959–72.

Calvin, John: *Institutes of the Christian Religion*, trans. Henry Beveridge, 2 vols. Edinburgh, 1863.

—— 'The Necessity for Reforming the Church', in *Calvin's Tracts and Treatises*, vol. i, trans. Henry Beveridge, ed. T. F. Torrance. Edinburgh and London, 1958.

—— 'Sermons sur les huit derniers chapitres du livre de Daniel', in *Corpus Reformatorum, Calvini Opera*, vols. xli, xlii.

Carion, John: *Chronicon Carionis expositum et auctum a P. Melanthone et C. Peucero. Adiecta est narratio historica de electione & coronatione Caroli V imperatoris*. Wittenberg, 1580.

—— *The Thre Bokes of cronicles &c gathered wyth great diligence of the beste authours; whereunto is added an appendix by John Funcke.* London: Gwalter Lynne, 1550.

Comenius, John Amos: *Historia revelationum Christophe. Kotteri, Christina Ponitovice, Nic. Drabicii.* (n.p.) 1659.

—— *The Labyrinth of the World and the Paradise of the Heart*, trans. and ed. Count Lutzow. London, 1905.

—— *A Patterne of Universall Knowledge*, trans. Jeremy Collier M.A. London, 1651.

The Complaynt of Scotlande (1549), ed. James A. H. Murray, Early English Text Society. London, 1872.

Crespin, Jean: *Actes des Martyrs deduits en sept livres depuis le temps de Wiclef & de Hus, jusques a present.* Geneva, 1565.

Diggs, Leonard: *A Prognostication of Right Good Effect etc.* London, 1555.

Diodati, John: *Pious Annotations upon the Holy Bible Expounding the difficult places thereof.* London, 1643, annotation upon the Apocalypse.

Draxe, Thomas: *An Alarum to the Last Judgement or An exact discourse of the second comming of Christ, and of the generall and remarkable Signes and Fore-runners of it, past, present, and to come; soundly and soberly handled and wholesomely applied.* London, 1615.

—— *The Worldes Resurrection or The generall calling of the Jewes.* London, 1608.

Dury, John: *Israel's call to march out of Babylon unto Jerusalem: a fast sermon on Isa. Iii. 11.* London, 1646.

—— 'An epistolicall discourse to Mr. Thoroughgood concerning his conjecture that the Americans are descended from the Israelites . . .' prefixed to Thomas Thorowgood's *Jewes in America*. London, 1650.

—— 'An epistolical discours to Mr. Sam. Hartlib', prefixed to Hartlib's trans. from the German of *Clavis Apocalyptica*. London, 1651.

—— Letters to Joseph Mede, in *The Works of Joseph Mede, B.D.*, ed. John Worthington. London, 1664.

Early Records of the University of St. Andrews, ed. J. M. Anderson, Scottish History Society, 3rd series, vol. 8. Edinburgh, 1926.

Egnati, John (Giovanni Battista Cipelli): *De Origine Turcarum*. Basle, 1533.

Faucigny-Lucinge, René de: *The Beginning, continuance and Decay of estates*, trans. J(ohn) F(inet). London, 1606.

Forbes, Patrick: *An exquisite commentarie upon the Revelation of St. John*. London, 1613.

—— *An learned commentarie upon the Revelation of St. John*. Middleburg, 1614.

Foxe, John: *Acts and Monuments of these latter and perilous days etc.* London, 1563. Another edition *Acts and Monuments of John Foxe* (1583), 4th edition, revised and corrected by The Rev. Josiah Pratt, 8 vols. The Religious Tract Society, London, 1877.

—— *Christus Triumphans et De Christo Triumphante eiusdem autoris Panegyricon*. Basle, 1556.

—— *Commentarii rerum in ecclesia gestarum, maximarumque per totum Europam Persecutionum, a Wiclevi temporibus ad hanc usque aetatem descriptio*. Frankfurt, 1554.

—— *Eicasmi seu meditationes in sacram Apocalypsin*. London?, 1587.

—— *A Sermon preached at the Christening of a certaine Jew, at London conteining an exposition of the xi Chapter of S. Paul to the Romans*, trans. James Bell. London, 1578.

Franck, Sebastian: 'A letter to John Campanus', Strassburg (1531?), trans. and ed. G. H. Williams, in *Spiritual and Anabaptist Writers*, Library of Christian Classics, vol. xxv. London, 1957.

Frankenberg, Abraham von: *Clavis Apocalyptica . . . by a German D.* trans. out of High Dutch In two treatises, by Samuel Hartlib. London, 1651.

Frith, John (pseud. Richard Brightwell): 'A pistle to the Christen reader', and 'Antithesis', in his translation of Martin Luther, *De Antichristo, The Revelation of Antichrist*. Antwerp, 1529.

Fulke, William: *Praelections upon the Sacred and holy Revelation of S. John*, trans. George Gyffard. London, 1573.

Geneva Bible: two editions (1) London: Christopher Barker, 1576, and (2) Edinburgh: Alexander Arbuthnet, 1579.

Goodman, Christopher: *How superior powers ought to be obeyed etc.* Geneva: Crespin, 1558.

Graserus, (Conradus) Francus: *Historia Antichristi illius magni, Exercitationibus in alteram partem Cap. XI Prophetiae DANIELIS, quae decem posterioribus versibus capitis continetur*. Leyden, 1608.

Hakewill, George: *An Apologie of the Power and Providence of God in the Government of the World or An Examination and Censure of the common errour touching Natures Perpetuall and Universall Decay*. Oxford, 1627.

Harford, R(aphael): *Reverend Mr. Brightman His judgment or prophesies what shall befall Germany, Scotland, Holland, and the churches adhering to them; likewise what shall befall England and the hierarchy therein; collected out of his Exposition on the Revelation*. London, 1643.

Harpsfield, Nicolas: *Dialogi Sex contra Summi Pontificatus, Monasticae vitae, Sanctorum, Sacrarum Imaginum Oppugnatores, et Pseudo-martyres.* Antwerp, 1566.

Harrison, John: *The Messiah already come, Written in Barbarie in the year 1610.* 2nd edition, Amsterdam, 1619.

Hartlib, Samuel: 'Preface' *Clavis Apocalyptica . . . by a German D. trans. out of High Dutch In two treatises,* by Samuel Hartlib. London, 1651.

—— *A Description of the Famous Kingdome of Macaria.* London, 1641.

—— Letters to Joseph Mede, in *The Works of Joseph Mede, B.D.,* ed. John Worthington. London, 1664.

Harvey, Gabriel: *Letterbook of Gabriel Harvey,* ed. E. J. L. Scott, Camden Society, new series 33. Westminster, 1884.

Harvey, John: *A discoursive probleme concerning prophesies.* London, 1588.

Hayne, Thomas: *Christs Kingdome on Earth, opened according to the Scriptures.* 'Herein is examined: What Mr. Th. Brightman, Dr. J. Alstede, Mr. J. Mede, Mr. H. Archer, *The Glympse of Sions Glory* and such as concurre in opinion with them'. (n.p.) 1645.

—— *The General View of the Holy Scriptures or The Times, Places, and Persons of the Holy Scriptures,* 2nd edition revised and enlarged. London, 1640.

—— Letters to Joseph Mede, in *The Works of Joseph Mede, B.D.,* ed. John Worthington. London, 1664.

Holland, Henry: *The Historie of Adam or the foure-fold state of Man, well formed in his Creation, Deformed in his Corruption, Reformed in GRACE, and Perfected in Glory.* London, 1606.

Hooker, Richard: *The Works of Mr. Richard Hooker.* Oxford, 1850.

James I, King of England: *His Apothegems or Table Talk.* London, 1643.

—— 'A Fruitfull Meditation containing A Plaine and easie exposition, or laying open of the VII, VIII, IX, X Verses of the 20 Chapter of the REVELATION in forme and matter of a Sermon', in the *Works of the most High and Mighty Prince James.* London, 1616.

Joye, George: *An Apology to W. Tindale* (1535), ed. Edward Arber, The English Scholar's Library. Birmingham, 1882.

—— *The exposicion of Daniel the Prophete, gathered oute of Philip Melanchton, Johan Ecolampadius, Chonrade Pellicane, & out of John Draconite &c.* Geneva, 1545.

—— *The unite and scisme of the olde chirche.* (Antwerp) 1543.

Kirchmeyer, Thomas: *The Popish Kingdome, or reigne of Antichrist,* writen in latin by Thomas Naogeorgus, trans. Barnabe Googe. London, 1570.

Knox, John: *An Answer to a Great number of blasphemous cavillations written by an Anabaptist.* Geneva: Crespin, 1560.

—— *An answer to a letter of a Jesuit named Tyrie.* St. Andrews, 1572.

—— 'A Comfortable Epistle to Christ's Church' (1556), in *The Works of John Knox,* collected and edited by David Laing. Woodrow Society, Edinburgh, 1848–64.

Knox, John: *The First Blast of the Trumpet against the monstrous regiment of women.* Geneva: Crespin, 1558.

—— *The History of the Reformation in Scotland*, in *Works*, ed. David Laing. Edinburgh, 1848-64.

—— *A Sermon Preached by John Knox, 19 August 1565.* Edinburgh, 1566.

—— 'To Christ's Afflicted Church' (1556), in *Works*, ed. David Laing. Edinburgh, 1848-64.

Lambert, Francis: *Exegeseos in Sanctam divi Joanis Apocalypsim.* Basle, 1539.

La Popelinère, H. Lancelot voisin de: *L'histoire des histoires avec l'idée de l'histoire accomplie . . . et . . . la refutation de la descente des fugatifs de troie aux Paulus Maeotides.* Paris, 1599.

Lilly, William: *Merlini Anglici Ephemeris or Astrological Judgments for the year 1666.* London, 1666.

Lindsay, David: 'The Monarche' and 'Ane Satyre on the thre estates', in *The Works of Sir David Lindsay of the Mount 1490-1555*, ed. Douglas Hamer, Scottish Text Society, vols. i and iii. Edinburgh, 1934.

Lively, Edward: *True Chronologie of the times of the Persian Monarchie, and after to the destruction of Jerusalem by the Romanes . . .* 'with a declaration of the Angel Gabriels message to Daniel in the end of his 9. Chap. against the frivolous conceits of Mathew Beroald'. London, 1597.

Luther, Martin: 'An Appeal to the Ruling Class of German Nationality as to the Amelioration of the State of Christendom' (1520), ed. John Dillemberger, in *Martin Luther selections from his writings.* New York, 1961.

—— prefaces to the Apocalypse, in *Die Deutche Bibel*, vol. vii *D. Martin Luthers Werke.* Weimar, 1931.

—— 'The Freedom of a Christian' (1520) in *Martin Luther selections from his writings*, ed. Dillenberg. New York, 1961.

—— *The Revelation of Antichrist*, trans. John Frith. Antwerp, 1529.

Marshall, Stephen: *A Sacred Record to be made of God's Mercies to Zion, a thanksgiving sermon before parliament 19 June 1645.* London, 1645.

Mede, Joseph: *The Apostasy of the Latter Times, or The Gentiles Theology of Daemons, ie inferior powers supposed to be mediators betweene God & Man.* 2nd edition corrected,London, 1644.

—— 'Clavis Apocalyptica', in *Works*, ed. Worthington. London, 1664.

—— *Daniels Weekes An Interpretation of part of the Prophecy of Daniel.* London, 1643.

—— *The Key of the Revelation searched and demonstrated out of the Naturall and proper Charecters of the Visions*, trans. Richard More. London, 1643.

—— *A Paraphrase and Exposition of the Prophesie of Saint Peter Concerning the day of Christ's second coming.* 2nd edition, London, 1649.

—— 'Remaines on some Passages in the Apocalyps', in *The Works of Joseph Mede, BD.*, ed. John Worthington. London, 1664.

Mede, Joseph: 'A Summary view of the Apocalyps', in *Works*, ed. Worthington. London, 1664.

—— Letters of Joseph Mede, in *Works*, ed. Worthington. London, 1664.

Melville, Andrew: *Commentarius in divinam Pauli epistolam ad Romanos*, ed. William Lindsay. Edinburgh, 1850.

Melville, James: *The Autobiography and Diary of Mr. James Melville*, ed. Robert Pitcairn, Woodrow Society. Edinburgh, 1842.

Meyer, Sebastianus: *In Apocalypsim Johannis apostoli commentarius.* Tiguir [n.d.].

Milton, John: 'Animadversions' in *Complete Prose Works of John Milton*, vol. i, ed. Don Wolfe. New Haven: Yale, 1953.

—— 'Commonplace Book (1630?-1665?)', trans. Ruth Mohl, *Complete Prose Works*, vol. i.

—— 'Milton's Correspondence' in *Complete Prose Works*, vols. i–iv.

—— 'The History of Britain', *The Works of John Milton*, gen. ed. F.A. Patterson, vol. x. New York, 1932.

—— 'Prolusions (1628-32)', trans. Phyllis B. Tilly and in *Complete Prose Works*, vol. i.

—— 'Reason of Church Government', in *Complete Prose Works*, vol. i.

—— 'Of Reformation (May 1641)', *Complete Prose Works*, vol. i.

Morton, Thomas: *A Catholike Appeale for Protestants.* London, 1610.

—— *Ezekiel's Wheels: A Treatise concerning Divine Providence: very seasonable for all Ages.* London, 1653.

Mylaeus, Christophorus: *De Scribenda Universitatis Rerum Historia Libri Quinque.* Basle, 1551.

The Mysterie of Iniquity Yet working In the Kingdomes of England, Scotland and Ireland, for the destruction of Religion truly Protestant. London, 1643.

Napier, John: *A Plaine Discovery of the whole Revelation of Saint John: set downe in two treatises: The one searching and proving the true interpretation thereof: The other applying the same paraphrastically and Historically to the text.* Edinburgh, 1593; another edition, London, 1611.

Nicolaus of Lyra: *Expositas in decologum, cum compendio vitae Antichristi.* [n.p.d.] The life of Antichrist.

—— *Liber apocalipsis Sancti Johanis cum glosis.* [Rome: Ulr. Han?; n.d.]

—— *Postillae in Bibliam (cum additionibus Pauli episcopi Burgensis, ac replicis Matthiae Dorinck).* Venice, Fr. Renner de Hailbrun, 1482. Section on the Apocalypse.

Original Letters, 1537-1558, ed. Hastings Robinson, Parker Society, Cambridge, 1846.

Osiander, Andreas: *The conjectures of the ende of the worlde*, trans. George Joye. (Antwerp) 1548.

Otto of Freising: *The Two Cities*, trans. and ed. Charles Mierow. New York, 1928.

Pareus, David: *A Commentary upon the Divine Revelation of the*

Apostle and Evangelist John, trans. Elias Arnold. Amsterdam, 1644.

Parker, Matthew: *De Antiquitate Britannicae Ecclesiae & Privilegiis Ecclesiae Cantuariensis cum Archiepiscopis eiusdem*. London, 1572.

—— *The Correspondence of Matthew Parker*, ed. John Bruce and Thomas Thomson, Parker Society. Cambridge, 1853.

Parsons, Robert, S.J.: *Commentariorum in Danielem prophetam*. Lyons, 1591.

—— *A Treatise of Three Conversions of England from Paganism to Christian Religion*. St. Omes, 1603.

Pont, Robert: *A newe treatise of the right reckoning of the yeares, and ages of the world, and mens lives and of the estate of the last decaying age thereof this 1600 year of Christ etc*. Edinburgh, 1599.

Postel, Guillaume: *De la Republique des turcs . . . des meurs & loys de tous Muhamidistes*. 3 Parts, Poitiers (1565?)

Ralegh, Walter: 'A Discourse of War in General', in *The Works of Sir Walter Ralegh, Kt.*, vol. viii: Miscellaneous Works. Oxford, 1829.

—— *The History of the World*, in *The Works of Sir Walter Ralegh, Kt.*, vols. ii–vii. Oxford, 1829.

—— 'Of the Voyage for Guiana', appendix to the Hakluyt Society edition of *The Discovery of the Large, Rich, and Beautiful Empire of Guiana*, ed. Robert Schomburgh. London, 1848.

Reformed Confessions of the Sixteenth Century, collected and edited by Arthur C. Cochrane. London, 1966.

A Revelation of Mr.' Brightman's Revelation. London, 1641.

Reverend Mr. Brightman's Judgement on Prophecies. London, 1643.

Ribera, Francis, S.J.: *In Sacram Beati Joannis Apostoli & Evangelistae Apocalypsin Commentarii*. Antwerp, 1603.

Rogers, Thomas: *Of the ende of this world, and seconde commyng of Christ, a comfortable and necessary Discourse for these miserable and daungerous dayes*. London, 1577.

Ross, Alexander: *The history of the world; the second part .in six books; being a continuation of the famous history of Sir Walter Raleigh*. London, 1652.

Scaliger, Joseph Justus: *Autobiography of Joseph Scaliger*, ed. George W. Robinson. Cambridge, Mass., 1927.

—— *de Emendatione Temporum*. Paris, 1583.

—— *Lettres françaises inédites de Joseph Scaliger*, ed. Philippe Tamizey de Larroque. Paris, 1879.

—— *Scaligerana, ou Bons mots, Rencontres Agréables et Remarques Judicieuses & Sçavantes de J. Scaliger*. Cologne, 1695.

Selden, John: *The History of Tithes*, in *opera omnia tam edita quam inedita Collegit ac recens D. Wilkins*. London, 1726.

—— 'Of the Revelation', in *opera omnia*, ed. D. Wilkins. London, 1726.

Sheldon, Richard: *Man's last end, The glorious vision and fruition of God*. London, 1634.

Sleidan, John: *A briefe Chronicle of the foure principall Empyres etc.*, trans. Stephan Wythers. London, 1563.

—— *De Quatuor Summis Imperiis Babylonico, Persico, Graeco, & Romano.* London, 1584.

Sleidan, John: *De Statu Religionis et Reipublicae Carolo Quinto, Caesare, Commentarii.* Strasburg, 1555.

—— *A Famouse Cronicle of oure time, called Sleidanes Commentaries,* trans. John Daus. London, 1560.

Strange and remarkable prophecies and predictions of . . . James Ussher. London, 1678.

Sutcliffe, Matthew: *The Subversion of Robert Parsons his confused and worthless work, entitled A treatise of three conversions of England.* London, 1606.

The Worlds proceeding Woes and Succeeding Joyes: The Triple Pressage of Henry Alsted. London, 1642.

Thompson, Thomas: *Anti-Christ arraigned*; a Sermon at Pauls Crosse, the third Sunday after Epiphanie. London, 1618.

Thorowgood, Thomas: *Jewes in America, or Probabilities that the Americans are of that Race.* Epistle preface by John Dury. London, 1650.

Tyndale, William: *The New Testament* (1534), ed. with variants of edition of 1525 by N. Hardy Wallis. Cambridge, 1938.

—— *Doctrinal Treatises of William Tyndale,* ed. Henry Walter, Parker Society. Cambridge, 1848.

—— *Exposition and Notes on Sundry Portions of the Holy Scriptures,* ed. Henry Walter, Parker Society. Cambridge, 1849.

Ussher, James: 'Collection of Three Hundred Letters between the said Lord Primate and most of the Eminentest Persons . . . in his time etc.', added to *The Life of the most Reverend Father in God, James Usher, Late Lord Arch-Bishop of Armagh, Primate and Metropolitan of all Ireland,* written and ed. by Richard Parr. London, 1686.

Vinet, Élie: *Schola Aquitanica Programme d'Études du Collège de Guyenne au XVIe siècle* (1583), ed. Louis Massebieau. Paris, 1886.

Worthington, John: 'A Collection of Epistles written to Mr. Hartlib of Pious Memory', in *Miscellanies.* London, 1704.

—— 'Observations concerning the *Millennium* and other Passages in the *Apocalypse*' in *Miscellanies.* London, 1704.

Wyclif, John: *The Holy Bible. . . by John Wyclif and his followers,* ed. Josiah Forshall and Frederic Madden. Oxford, 1850.

—— 'De Papa', in *Select English Writings of John Wyclif,* ed. Herbert E. Winn. Oxford, 1929.

Zürich Letters, 1558-79, ed. Hastings Robinson, Parker Society. Cambridge, 1842, and second series, *1558-1602,* Cambridge, 1845.

II. REFERENCE WORKS, CATALOGUES, AND LIBRARY LISTS

Dictionary of National Biography, ed. L. Stephen and S. Lee. Oxford and London (1917-).

Fuller, Thomas: *The History of the Worthies of England,* new edition by John Nichols, 2 vols. London, Edinburgh, and Perth, 1811.

SELECTED BIBLIOGRAPHY   265

Haag, Eugène, and Émile Haag: *La France Protestante*. 2nd edition, gen. ed. Henri Bordier. Paris, 1877–88.
The Jewish Encyclopedia, ed. Isidore Singer. London, 1906.
The Library of James VI, ed. G. F. Warner, Scottish History Society, vol. xv, Misc., vol. 1. Edinburgh, 1893.
Michaud, M.: *Biographie universelle*. Paris, 1856.
A Short Title Catalogue of Books Printed in England, Scotland, and Ireland and of English Books Printed Abroad 1475-1640, ed. A. W. Pollard and G. R. Redgrave. New York and London, 1906.
Second edition revised and enlarged, begun by W. A. Jackson and F. S. Ferguson, completed by Katharine F. Pantzer, 2nd vol. The Bibliographical Society. London, 1976.
—— *1641-1700*, ed. Donald Wing. New York, 1948.
'Sir Walter Ralegh's Library', ed. Walter Oakeshott, *The Library*, 5th series, vol. xxiii. Dec. 1968.
Williams, Franklin B.: *Index of Dedications and Commendatory verses in English Books before 1641*. London, 1962.
Wood, Anthony à: *Athenae Oxonienses*, ed. Philip Bliss. Oxford, 1813–20.

III. BOOKS AND ARTICLES

Bauckham, Richard: *Tudor Apocalypse*, Courtenay Library of Reformation Classics (8), series ed. G. E. Duffield. Appleford, 1978.
Bietenholz, Peter G.: *History and Biography in the Work of Erasmus of Rotterdam*, Libraire Droz. Geneva, 1966.
Blatt, Thora Balslev: *The Plays of John Bale*. Copenhagen, 1968.
Boissonnade, Prosper Benjamin: *Histoire de l'Université de Poitiers 1432-1932*. Poitiers, 1932.
Bouwsma, William J.: *Concordia Mundi: The career and thought of Guillaume Postel, 1510-1581*. Cambridge, Mass., 1957.
Burch, V.: *Anthropology and the Apocalypse*. London, 1939.
Burke, Peter: 'A Survey of the Popularity of Ancient Historians, 1450-1700', *History and Theory*, vol. v. Middleton, Conn., 1966.
Campbell, W. E.: *Erasmus, Tyndale and More*. London, 1949.
Capp, B. S.: *The fifth monarchy men, a study in 17th century millenarianism*. London, 1972.
Charles, R. H.: *Lectures on the Apocalypse*, The Schweich Lectures, 1919. London, 1922.
—— *Studies in the Apocalypse*. Edinburgh, 1913.
Christianson, P. K.: 'From Expectation to Militance. Reformers and Babylon in the First Two Years of the Long Parliament', *Journal of Ecclesiastical History*, vol. xxiv, no. 3, July 1973.
Clebsch, William A.: *England's Earliest Protestants*. New Haven and London, 1964.
Clouse, Robert: 'The Apocalyptic Interpretation of Thomas Brightman and Joseph Mede', *Bulletin of the Evangelical Theological Society*. Fall 1968.
Cohn, Norman: *The Pursuit of the Millennium*. London, 1957.

Collingwood, R. G.: *The Idea of History*. Oxford, 1946.

Curtis, M. H.: *Oxford and Cambridge in Transition 1558-1642*. Oxford, 1959.

Dean, Leonard F.: 'Bodin's *Methodus* in England before 1625', *Studies in Philology*, no. 39, 1942.

Durkan, John and Anthony Ross: *Early Scottish Libraries*. Glasgow, 1961.

Firth, Sir Charles: 'Sir Walter Ralegh's *History of the World*', *Proceedings of the British Academy*. London, 1918.

Fixler, Michael: *Milton and the Kingdoms of God*. London, 1964.

Fogle, French R. and H. R. Trevor-Roper: *Milton and Clarendon: two papers on 17th century English Historiography*. Los Angeles, 1965.

Fraenkel, Peter: *Testimonia Patrum: The Function of the Patristic Argument in the Theology of Philip Melanchthon*, Travaux d'Humanisme et Renaissance xlvi. Geneva, 1961.

Franklin, Julian H.: *Jean Bodin and the sixteenth century revolution in the methodology of law and history*. New York and London, 1963.

Friedlaender, Marc: 'Growth in the Resources for Studies in Earlier English History 1534-1625'. Chicago, 1938.

Fristedt, Sven L.: *The Wycliffe Bible*, Stockholm Studies in English. Stockholm, 1953.

Fueter, Eduard: *Geschichte der neueren Historiographie*. Berlin, 1936.

Fussner, F. Smith: *The Historical Revolution*. London, 1962.

Garrett, Christina H.: *The Marian Exiles: A study in the Origins of Elizabethan Puritanism*. Cambridge, 1938.

Gaullieur, Ernest: *Histoire de Collège de Guyenne*. Paris, 1874.

Greg, W. W.: *Some Aspects and Problems of London Printing 1550 to 1650*. Oxford, 1956.

Haller, William: 'John Foxe and the Puritan Revolution', *The Seventeenth Century*, ed. R. F. Jones. Stanford, Calif., 1951.

—— *Foxe's Book of Martyrs and the Elect Nation*. London, 1963.

Harris, Jesse W.: *John Bale: A Study in the Minor Literature of the Reformation*, Illinois Studies in Language and Literature, vol. xxv, no. 4. Urbana, 1940.

Headly, John M.: *Luther's View of Church History*. New Haven and London, 1963.

Hill, Christopher: *Antichrist in Seventeenth-century England*. Oxford, 1971.

—— *Intellectual Origins of the English Revolution*. Oxford, 1965.

—— *The World Turned Upside Down*. London, 1972.

Hirsch, Rudolph: *Printing, Selling and Reading 1450-1550*. Wiesbaden, 1967.

Janton, Pierre: *John Knox (ca. 1513-1572) L'Homme et l'œuvre*, Études Anglaises. Paris, 1967.

Johnson, James William: 'Chronological Writing: its Concepts and Development', *History and Theory*, vol. ii. Middleton, Conn., 1962.

Josten, C. H.: *Elias Ashmole*. Oxford, 1966.

Jourdain, Charles: *Histoire de l'Université de Paris au XVIIe et au XVIIIe siècle*, 2 vols. Paris, 1888.

Kearney, Hugh: *Scholars and Gentlemen: Universities and society in pre-industrial Britain 1500-1700.* London, 1970.

Kelley, Donald R.: *Foundations of Modern Historical Scholarship, Language, Law and History in the French Renaissance.* New York and London, 1970.

Knappen, Marshall Mason: *Tudor Puritanism, a Chapter in the History of Idealism.* Chicago and London, 1939.

Lamont, William M.: *Godly Rule: Politics and Religion 1603-60.* London, 1969.

LeFranc, Pierre: *Sir Walter Ralegh écrivain: l'œuvre et les idées*, Libraire Armand Colin. Paris, 1968.

Levy, F. J.: *Tudor Historical Thought.* San Marino, Calif., 1967.

McCrie, Thomas: *Life of Andrew Melville.* Edinburgh, 1819.

—— *Life of John Knox*, 2nd edition. Edinburgh, 1861.

McCusker, Honor: *John Bale: Dramatist and Antiquary.* Bryn Mawr, Pa., 1942.

Manuel, Frank E.: *Isaac Newton, Historian.* Cambridge, Mass., 1963.

Mattingly, Garrett: *The Defeat of the Spanish Armada.* London, 1959.

Mozley, J. F.: *John Foxe and his Book.* London and New York, 1940.

Napier, Mark: *Memoirs of John Napier of Merchiston, His Lineage, Life and Times with a History of the Invention of Logarithms.* Edinburgh and London, 1834.

Neveux, J. B.: *Vie spirituelle et vie sociale entre Rhin et Baltique au XVIIe siècle de J. Arndt à P. J. Spener*, Publications de la Faculté des Lettres et Sciences Humaines de Paris-Nanterre. Paris, 1967.

Ong, Walter J.: *Ramus: Method, and the Decay of Dialogue.* Cambridge, Mass., 1958.

Oyer, John S.: *Lutheran Reformers against Anabaptists: Luther, Melanchthon, and Menius and the Anabaptists of central Germany.* The Hague, 1964.

Patrides, C. A.: 'Renaissance Estimates of the Year of Creation', *Huntington Library Quarterly*, no. 26, 1963.

—— 'Renaissance and Modern Thought on the Last Things: A Study of Changing Conceptions', *Harvard Theological Review*, vol. 51, July 1958.

Pattison, Mark: *Essays by the late Mark Pattison*, collected by Henry Nettleship. 2 vols. Oxford, 1889.

Pineas, Rainer: 'William Tyndale's use of history as a Weapon of Religious Controversy', *Harvard Theological Review*, vol. 55, Apr. 1962.

Popkin, Richard H.: *The History of Scepticism from Erasmus to Descartes.* N. V. Assen, Netherlands, 1960.

Quistrop, Heinrich: *Calvin's Doctrine of the Last Things*, trans. H. Knight. London, 1955.

Reeves, Marjorie: *The Influence of Prophecy in the Later Middle Ages: A Study in Joachimism.* Oxford, 1969.

Ridley, Jasper: *John Knox.* Oxford, 1968.

Rogers, Charles: *Life of George Wishart*. London, 1876.

Ryan, E. A.: *The Historical Scholarship of Saint Bellarmine* [sic]. Louvain, 1936.

Secret, F.: 'Guillaume Postel et les courants prophétiques de la Renaissance', *Studie francesi*, vol. i, 1957.

Secret, F.: *Les Kabbalistes chrétiens de la Renaissance*. Paris, 1964.

Snow, E. G. Sinclair: *The Times, Life and Thought of Patrick Forbes, Bishop of Aberdeen, 1618-1635*. London, 1952.

Southern, A. C.: *Elizabethan Recusant Prose 1559-1582*. London, 1950.

Steele, Robert: 'Notes on English Books Printed Abroad, 1525-1548', *Transactions of the Bibliographical Society*, vol. xi, 1919-21.

Thomas, K. V., *Religion and the Decline of Magic*. London, 1971.

Thompson, James W.: *A History of Historical Writing*. New York, 1942.

Trevor-Roper, H. R.: *Religion, the Reformation, and Social Change and other Essays*. London, 1967.

Turnbull, G. H.: *Hartlib, Dury, and Comenius: gleanings from Hartlib's papers*. London, 1947.

—— *Samuel Hartlib, A sketch of his Life and his Relations to J. A. Comenius*. Oxford, 1920.

Tuveson, Ernest Lee: *Millennium and Utopia: A Study in the Background of the Idea of Progress*. New York, 1964.

Walker, D. P.: *Spiritual and Demonic Magic from Ficino to Campanella*, The Warburg Institute. London, 1958.

Watt, Hugh: *John Knox in Controversy*. London, 1950.

Webster, Charles: 'Macaria, Samuel Hartlib and the Great Reformation', *Acta Comeniana* 2 (xxvi). Prague, 1970.

Weiss, Robert: *Humanism in England during the 15th Century*. Oxford, 1967.

Williams, Arnold: *The Common Expositor: an account of the Commentaries on Genesis 1527-1633*. Richmond, Va., 1948.

Williams, G. H.: *The Radical Reformation*. London, 1962.

Williams, Glanmore: 'Some Protestant views of Early British Church History', *History*, new series, vol. xxxviii, Oct. 1953.

Wright, Louis B.: *Middle Class culture in Elizabethan England*. Ithaca, N.Y., 1958.

Yates, Frances A.: *The French Academies of the sixteenth century*, The Warburg Institute, vol. 15. London, 1947.

—— *Giordano Bruno and the Hermetic tradition*. London, 1964.

—— *The Rosicrucian Enlightenment*, Paladin edition. St. Albans, 1975.

I. INDEX OF IMAGES

Some of the more important images are here placed in context and arranged in biblical text order. Quotations are from the Authorized (King James) Version.

OLD TESTAMENT

NEW TESTAMENT

Matthew
Chap. 24   'For there shall arise false Christs, and false prophets, and shall show great signs and wonders, insomuch that, if it were possible, they shall deceive the very elect.'
false prophets, Calvin, 37; *see below Revelation* 6 & 20

2 Thessalonians
Chap. 2   'Let no man deceive you by any means: for that day shall not come (of Christ's return) except there come a falling away first, and that man of sin be revealed, the son of perdition,'
Man of sin, Bale, 47; Calvin, 34; Foxe, 102-3; Hayne, 239; Knox, 115-6; Mede, 224; Osiander, 65

'For the mystery of iniquity doth already work . . .'
mystery of iniquity, Bale, 49-50, 52, 54, 87; Calvin, 35; Hakewill, 201

1 Timothy
Chap. 4   'Now the Spirit speaketh expressly, that in the latter times some shall depart from the faith giving heed to seducing spirits . . . Forbidding to marry . . .'
Apostasy of the latter times (with 2 Thess. 2, & 2 Peter 2) Abbot, 177; Calvin, 33, 37; Geneva Bible, 123; Hayne, 238; Thompson, 229

1 John (also *2 John*)
Chap. 4   'many false prophets are gone out into the world . . . . And every spirit that confesseth not that Jesus Christ is come in the flesh is not of God: and this is that spirit of antichrist, whereof ye have heard that it should come; and even now already is it in the world.'
Antichrist; the history of, 78-80, 156, 168-9, 182, 200, 208, 209-12, 229, 233, 235-6, 239, 244-5, 248; identification of, 6-7, 12, 18-9, 25, 34-5, 50, 52-3, 67, 85, 99-101, 102, 104, 123, 132, 134, 177, 185, 246, 248; Legend of, 6-7, 171-2; the revelation of, 27, 29, 37, 68, 77, 82-4, 87, 103, 123, 195, 199, 209, 238

Revelation
Chap. 1-3   Letters to the seven churches: Ephesus, Smyrna, Pergamum, Thyratira, Sardis, Philadelphia, Laodicea
Letters to the seven churches, Brightman, 166; Forbes, 176; Foxe, 92; Harford, 230

Laodicea 'thou art lukewarm', Brightman sees as a type of the Church of England, 167-8, 204, 251

Chap. 4-5   John is taken up into heaven and the vision begins. One sits upon a throne and in his hands there is 'a book written within and on the backside sealed with seven seals'
seven seals, Alcasar, 246-7; Alsted, 211; Bale, 42-4; 58; 120; Booker, 230-1; Brightman, 166-71, 175; Bullinger, 81; Diodati, 233; Forbes, 177; Foxe, 92-4; Geneva Bible, 122; Harvey, 151; Hayne, 239-40; Joachim of Fiore, 4; Luther, 12; Mede, 219-21, 225; Milton, 235; Napier, 143-5; Pont, 192-3; Ribera, 172

Chap. 6   The first four seals when opened send out the four horsemen.

Four horsemen, Bale, 42, 79; Brightman, 168; Foxe, 93

The fifth seal reveals the souls under the altar, and the sixth seal is accompanied by an earthquake. The sun turns black, the moon as blood and stars fall.
Souls under the altar, Crespin, 77-8, Foxe, 93

Chap. 7   Four angels appear 'standing on the four corners of the earth, holding the four winds of the earth'. They are restrained from hurting the earth until the 144,000 faithful souls are sealed.
Four angels at the four corners, Bale, 42-3; Luther, 12; Wimbeldon, 86
144,000 faithful souls, Foxe, 77-8

Chap. 8   The seventh seal opens and there is silence for half an hour. Seven angels prepare to sound seven trumpets
seven angels and trumpets, Alsted, 211; Bale, 44-6; Brightman, 166-71, Broughton, 161; Bullinger, 80-1; Draxe, 228; Foxe, 93-5; Hayne, 239; Mede, 219-21; Napier, 143-4

Three trumpets bring destruction. The fourth angel sounds his trumpet and another angel appears 'flying through the midst of heaven' crying 'Woe, woe, woe, to the inhabiters of the earth'.
Angel in the midst of heaven, Bale, 44, 48-9; Brightman, 169; Mede, 219-21 *see also* Gregory I, pope

Chap. 9   The fifth angel sounds and a star falls to earth and opens the bottomless pit from which issue locusts and scorpions to torment men for five months. The sixth angel sounds loosing the angels bound in the Euphrates.
locusts and scorpions, Bale, 44, 51; Brightman, 169; Broughton, 158; Foxe, 95-6, 100; Geneva Bible, 123; Jesuits, 162; Mede, 220-1; Napier, 143; Ralegh, 188

Chap. 10   John sees 'another mighty angel . . . and he had in his hand a little book open'.
little book, Bale, 46; Mede, 220

Chap. 11   John measures the temple and hears of the two witnesses who shall prophesy in the city for 1260 days, 42 months, be slain and lie dead for 3½ days and then rise again.
two witnesses, Bale, 46, 50-1; Foxe, 103; Mede, 217; Napier, 144-5

'And the seventh angel sounded; and there were great voices in heaven, saying, The kingdoms of this world are become the kingdoms of our Lord, and of his Christ; and he shall reign for ever and ever.'
seventh angel, Brightman, 170, 175; Mede, 220

Chap. 12   There appears a woman 'clothed with the sun and the moon under her feet . . . being with child' and the dragon 'having seven heads and ten horns' waits to devour the child. But after the child is born the woman flees into the wilderness and remains there 1260 days, for a time and times and half a time.
Woman in the wilderness, Alcasar, 246; Andreae, 207; Bale, 50-2; Brightman, 169; Diodati, 233; Foxe, 105; Hayne, 238; Mede, 217; Napier, 144

'And there was war in heaven.' Michael defeats the dragon called

the Devil and Satan and he is cast from heaven. On earth he perse-
cutes the woman.
Archangel Michael, Brightman, 174; Mede on Napier, 221

Chap. 13 The first beast arises 'out of the sea, having seven heads and ten
horns' each head crowned. It is 'like unto a leopard' with 'the feet
of a bear' and 'the mouth of a lion'. One head is wounded but heals
again. He has power 42 months to make war with the saints.
First beast, 7, Brightman, 169; Calvin, 34-5; Foxe, 89-90; Mede,
217; Napier, 145; Osiander, 64-5; Ralegh, 186 *see also* Roman
Empire

The second beast arises 'out of the earth' with 'two horns like a
lamb'. He has the power of the first beast, performs great wonders
and deceives men. His number is 666.
Second beast, 7, Bale, 52; Brightman, 169; Calvin, 34-5; Foxe, 96-
100, 105; Geneva Bible, 123; Napier, 145, Ralegh, 186 *see also*
Roman church, Antichrist

number of the beast, 666; Bale, 52; Foxe, 96, 98; Geneva Bible,
123; Hartlib to Mede, 226-7; Napier, 145; Osiander, 65; Selden and
James I, 178

Chap. 14 Another angel is seen flying in the midst of heaven preaching the
gospel. He is followed by two more, one announcing the fall of
Babylon and another denouncing the followers of the beast. The
Son of man appears seated on a cloud and begins the harvest and
vintage 'and the winepress was trodden . . . and blood came out of
the winepress, even unto the horse bridles'.
Harvest and Vintage, Brightman, 170; Geneva Bible, 123; Napier,
144

Chap. 15-
16
Seven angels with seven last plagues receive seven golden vials. Four
fall upon the earth. The fifth falls upon the seat of the beast and
the sixth upon the 'great river Euphrates' drying the waters preparing 'the way of the kings of the east'. The seventh completes
the series.
seven vials, Alcasar, 246; Alsted, 211; Brightman, 170-1; Forbes,
177; Joachim of Fiore, 4; Mede, 221; Napier, 143
Kings of the east, Brightman 172-3; Foxe, 95-6

Chap. 17 'Judgment of the great whore' seated on a scarlet beast with seven
heads and ten horns. On her forehead is written 'MYSTERY,
BABYLON THE GREAT, THE MOTHER OF HARLOTS, AND
ABOMINATIONS OF THE EARTH.' The angel explains the seven
heads and ten horns.
Whore of Babylon, Foxe, 99; Knox, 116, 120, 130; Mede, 217;
Ridley, 72

Chap. 18-
19
The angel announces the final fall of Babylon and there is rejoicing.
Heaven opens and a rider on a white horse whose name is The Word
of God goes with his army to make war against the beast and his
army, and against the false prophet.
False prophet, Ralegh, 188

Chap. 20 The dragon is bound a thousand years and cast into the bottomless
pit, but after that 'he must be loosed a little season'. The faithful

are to live and reign with Christ for the thousand years. The first
resurrection releases those slain by the beast.
Binding and loosing again of Satan, Alsted, 210–11; Bale, 43, 51–2,
54–6; Diodati, 233; Foxe, 82, 92, 102, 253; Hayne, 238; Milton,
234; Napier, 145; Otto of Freising, 3–4; Twisse to Mede, 222–3
First and second resurrections, Bale, 54–5; Mede, 222–3

Upon his release the dragon shall gather Gog and Magog to battle.
Gog and Magog, Alsted, 211; Bale, 55; *Carion's Chronicle*, 18; Foxe,
96, 100; James VI, 132; Luther, 11, 12; Mede, 223; Napier, 145;
Ralegh, 186–7, 250

Chap. 21–
    22

'And I saw a new heaven and a new earth. . . . And I John saw the
holy city, new Jerusalem.'
new heaven and new earth, Bale, 38–9, 54, 56; Hakewill, 201;
Hayne, 237; Lindsay, 119–20; Ralegh, 181 *see also rennovatio
mundi*
New Jerusalem, Andreae, 207, Brightman, 164, 168, 172–4; Funck,
66; Hayne, 237; Mede, 223, 225

II. GENERAL INDEX